The Culmination of Capital

Also by Martha Campbell

NEW INVESTIGATIONS OF MARX'S METHOD (*editor, with Fred Moseley*)

Also by Geert Reuten

VALUE-FORM AND THE STATE: The Tendencies of Accumulation and the Determination of Economic Policy in Capitalist Society (*with Michael Williams*)

THE CIRCULATION OF CAPITAL: Essays on Volume II of Marx's 'Capital' (*editor, with Christopher Arthur*)

The Culmination of Capital

Essays on Volume III of Marx's *Capital*

Edited by

Martha Campbell
College at Potsdam, Department of Economics
State University of New York

and

Geert Reuten
University of Amsterdam, Department of Economics

palgrave

First published 2002 by
PALGRAVE
Houndmills, Basingstoke, Hampshire RG21 6XS and
175 Fifth Avenue, New York, N.Y. 10010
Companies and representatives throughout the world

PALGRAVE is the new global academic imprint of
St Martin's Press LLC Scholarly and Reference Division and
Palgrave Publishers Ltd (formerly Macmillan Press Ltd).

ISBN 0–333–96493–4 hardback

This book is printed on paper suitable for recycling and made from fully managed and sustained forest sources.

A catalogue record for this book is available from the British Library.

Library of Congress Cataloging-in-Publication Data
The culmination of capital : essays on volume three of Marx's capital / edited by Martha Campbell and Geert Reuten.
p. cm.
Includes bibliographical references and indexes.
ISBN 0–333–96493–4
1. Marx, Karl, 1818–1883. Kapital. 2. Marxian economics.
I. Campbell, Martha, 1946– II. Reuten, G. A.

HB501 .C89 2001
335.4'11—dc21 2001036884

10 9 8 7 6 5 4 3 2 1
11 10 09 08 07 06 05 04 03 02

Printed and bound in Great Britain by
Antony Rowe Ltd, Chippenham, Wiltshire

Contents

List of Figures

Preface

In this collection, four philosophers and four economists consider the third volume of Marx's *Capital*. Taking into account the most recent scholarship, the essays deal with each of Marx's themes in Volume III and seek to explain why these conclude the argument that begins in Volume I. The collection is meant both for specialists in the field of Marxian theory and for students of the history of economic thought and methodology.

For all the authors, both the concept of social form and methodology are central to Marx's work. The authors are participants in the annual International Symposium on Marxian Theory (ISMT), a week-long working conference held annually since 1991. These meetings have been a fruitful source of many individual papers. They have also been the origin of three previous collections by the group as a whole: *Marx's Method in 'Capital'*, edited by Fred Moseley, Humanities Press 1993; *New Investigations of Marx's Method*, edited by Fred Moseley and Martha Campbell, Humanities Press 1997; *The Circulation of Capital: Essays on Volume II of Marx's 'Capital'*, edited by Christopher Arthur and Geert Reuten, Macmillan Press 1998.

Initial versions of the papers collected in the current volume were discussed in depth at the July 2000 ISMT meeting at the University of Amsterdam. This and the further cross refereeing of the revised versions should insure the quality and coherence of the collection.

The ISMT Amsterdam meeting was sponsored by the Social Sciences Research Council of the Netherlands Organization for Scientific Research (NWO – MAGW) to whom we should like to express our gratitude. We also thank Nicola Viinikka of Palgrave for her support of the project as well as two anonymous referees for their stimulating comments.

May 2001

Martha Campbell
Geert Reuten

Notes on Contributors

Christopher J. Arthur studied at the universities of Nottingham and Oxford and taught philosophy for 25 years at the University of Sussex. He has published in numerous journals and books on the dialectics of Hegel and Marx. He is the author of *Dialectics of Labour: Marx and his relation to Hegel* (1986). He edited and introduced: Marx and Engels, *The German Ideology* (1970); *Marx's Capital: A Student Edition* (1992); *Friedrich Engels: A Centenary Appreciation* (1996); and (with Geert Reuten) *The Circulation of Capital: Essays on Volume II of Marx's 'Capital'* (1998).

Riccardo Bellofiore is Professor of Economics at the University of Bergamo, Italy. He wrote a book on the Italian Marxist scholar Claudio Napoleoni (1991), and edited a collection on Piero Sraffa (1986) – both in Italian. He acted as guest editor of a special issue of the *International Journal of Political Economy* on 'Marxian Theory: The Italian Debate' (Summer 1997). He also edited: *Marxian Economics: A Reappraisal* (1998); *Global Money, Capital Restructuring and the Changing Patterns of Labour* (1999); (with Mario Baldassarri) 'Classical and Marxian Political Economy: A Debate on Claudio Napoleoni's Views', special issue of the *Rivista di Politica Economica* (1999/4–5); and (with Piero Ferri) two volumes on Hyman Minsky's economics – *Financial Keynesianism and Market Instability* and *Financial Fragility and Investment in the Capitalist Economy* (2001).

Martha Campbell is Assistant Professor of Economics at Potsdam College, State University of New York. She received her PhD in Economics from the New School for Social Research in 1991. She is a member of the International Symposium on Marxian Theory and has contributed to the group's three previous collections, editing (with Fred Moseley) *New Investigations of Marx's Method* (1997).

Paul Mattick, Professor of Philosophy at Adelphi University (New York), is the author of *Social Knowledge; An Essay on the Nature and Limits of Social Science* (1986), edited *Eighteenth-Century Aesthetics and the Reconstruction of Art* (1993) and is editor of the *International Journal of Political Economy*. He is completing a book of essays on Marx's *Capital*.

Comments and criticisms on the chapter included here are welcome at pm16@nyu.edu.

Fred Moseley is Professor of Economics at Mount Holyoke College (Massachusetts). He received a BS in Mathematics from Stanford University in 1968 and a PhD in Economics from the University of Massachusetts in 1980. He was the Book Review Editor of the *Review of Radical Political Economics* from 1986 to 1995. He organized the ISMT in 1991, and edited its first two books, *Marx's Method in 'Capital': A Reexamination* (1993) and (with Martha Campbell) *New Investigations of Marx's Method* (1997). His other books include the monograph *The Falling Rate of Profit in the Postwar United States Economy* (1991).

Patrick Murray is Professor of Philosophy at Creighton University, Omaha, Nebraska. He received his PhD in Philosophy of Science from St Louis University in 1979. He is the author of *Marx's Theory of Scientific Knowledge* (1988) and editor of *Reflections on Commercial Life: An Anthology of Classic Texts from Plato to the Present* (1997). He is a member of the ISMT and has contributed to the group's three previous books. His writings on Marx, Hegel, critical theory, modern philosophy and the philosophy of social science have appeared in numerous scholarly books and journals.

Geert Reuten is Associate Professor of Economics at the University of Amsterdam. He studied at Erasmus University Rotterdam and the University of London (Birkbeck College), and holds a PhD in Economics from the University of Amsterdam. With Michael Williams he wrote *Value-Form and the State; the tendencies of accumulation and the determination of economic policy in capitalist society* (1989). Edited works include (with Christopher Arthur) *The Circulation of Capital: Essays on Volume II of Marx's 'Capital'* (1998).

Tony Smith is Professor of Philosophy and Political Science at Iowa State University. He received his PhD from the State University of New York at Stony Brook after graduate studies at the universities of Tubingen and Munich. He is the author of four books: *The Logic of Marx's 'Capital': Replies to Hegelian Criticisms* (1990); *The Role of Ethics in Social Theory* (1991); *Dialectical Social Theory and its Critics: From Hegel to Analytical Marxism and Postmodernism* (1993); and *Technology and Capital in the Age of Lean Production: A Marxian Critique of the 'New Economy'* (2000).

1
Marx's *Capital III*, the Culmination of Capital
General introduction

Geert Reuten

This introductory chapter starts with a brief discussion of why writing about Marx's *Capital III* is not only interpretative – this is true for any work – but is also bound to be reconstructive. The next section outlines a general overview of *Capital III*'s seven Parts in the light of the earlier two volumes. Finally, the essays in this book are introduced.

1. 'The Shapes of the Whole Process': interpretation and reconstruction

The first volume of Karl Marx's life work *Das Kapital* was published in 1867. When Marx died in 1883 at the age of 64 he left Volumes II and III as unfinished manuscripts, which range anywhere from mere notes or outlines to text all but ready for publication. The manuscript for Volume III is a single draft, and, relative to the other volumes, an early one, having been written between the summer of 1864 and December 1865. It was not until 30 years later, in 1894, that the third volume was published in German; like the second (1885), it was edited by Friedrich Engels. One year after the 1894 publication Engels himself died at the age 75.[1]

1. Regarding the current German and English editions of the book, a transcription of the Volume III manuscripts, from which Engels did his editorial work, was published in 1992 in the *Marx–Engels Gesamtausgabe* (Marx 1894M). The widely used German text identical to Engels's edition of 1894 is published

These few biblio-biographical facts are relevant to the interpretation of *Capital* since, for Marx, architectonic and *Darstellung* (presentation) are an essential stage of scientific work. Almost certainly, if Marx had lived long enough to publish Volumes II and III himself, they would have been quite different from the works we now have.[2] Most likely also their difference would have led, in turn, to another revision of Volume I (which Marx had already changed between the first edition and the second of 1873).[3]

The reading of any text, complete or incomplete, of course involves interpretation – behind the author's back so to speak. There are, however, three particular reasons to be extra cautious in the case of Marx's works. First, as Engels says of his editing in his Preface to *Capital III*:

> I confined this simply to what was most necessary, and wherever clarity permitted I retained the character of the original draft, not even deleting certain repetitions where these grasped the subject-matter *from a different angle or expressed it in another way, as was Marx's custom.*
>
> Engels 1894F: 93, emphasis added

Such repetitions appear not only in Volume III of *Capital* but in the earlier volumes as well. Apart from those related to the draft character of the text, they are due to aspects of Marx's method. In particular, he emphasizes throughout the double character of entities in capitalism (material shape and capitalist value-form) and the related differentiation between 'general' (transhistorical) and 'determinate' (capitalist) categories.[4] Further, as

---

in the *Marx–Engels Werke* (Marx 1894G). The first English translation, by Ernest Untermann, appeared in 1909; a current edition based on it is published by Lawrence & Wishart/Progress Publishers (Marx 1894U). It is also available on disc (Marx 1894D) with full search possibilities, although with different page numbers. A second English translation, by David Fernbach, was published in 1981 (Marx 1894F). It is currently more widely used than the former, which does not imply that the translation is always superior – translation necessarily implies interpretation.

2. That is, if he had lived long enough, and also had enough energy. Marx's last work on *Capital*, which is a draft for the third part of Volume II, probably dates from 1878 (see Oakley 1983: 101–3). After that time his faculties for creative scientific work gradually faded away.
3. Engels remarks in his Preface to the third edition that Marx indeed intended 'to rewrite a great part of the text of the first volume'.
4. See Murray (1988) on general versus determinate categories; see also his Chapter 11 in the current volume. Mészáros (1970: 79) calls these first order versus second order mediations (cf. Arthur 1986: 11–12).

Marx's presentation proceeds, it discloses new features of the entities under consideration, so that these are continually reconceptualized (and 'redefined' so to say). Apart from such aspects of method, however, Marx often obviously struggles with the material at hand, either to *find* the most appropriate way of presenting it, *or* indeed to present it from different angles because there *is* more than one appropriate aspect.

Second – and related to the first point – in the view of all the contributors to this book at least, Marx makes a fundamental break with the political economy and philosophy of his time.[5] Without implying that all my co-authors share this view, I also hold that the initiator of a break can never realize it completely. Because initiators are brought up in the tradition from which they break, their work is shaped by the central concerns of that tradition, and they must, to a considerable extent, speak in its language. Especially in the case of *Capital III*, these central concerns arise, in large part, from Ricardo's theory.[6] It is left to the heirs, setting out from different questions, to unfold all that the break entails – or retreat from it. Hence 'interpreting' the work of the initiator of a break is bound to be an unfolding or a retreating reconstruction. It follows also that there may not be full consistency in the initiator's work. As regards 'interpretation' then, it is generally easier to see a particular interpretation confirmed by the texts than to see it not falsified.

In view of the foregoing, the contributors to this book adopt different stances towards the interpretation of Marx. At one end, Tony Smith (Chapter 7) holds that any interpretation of Marx's texts is always a reconstruction. At the other, in Fred Moseley's view (Chapter 4), Marx's aims are clear enough to allow for an interpretation close to the intention of the author. Others see a need for reconstruction for several reasons: because of defects in, or of, acknowledged, concurrent theoretical lines in Marx's writing (the presence of different lines is not by itself a problem) and because certain abstract treatments by Marx require further mediation and concretion.

The third reason to be extra cautious in the interpretation of Marx's work, particularly *Capital III*, is more straightforward: the text is clearly influenced by Engels's editing. This should not be read as a criticism of

5. 'Break' in the fundamental sense of epistemological rupture (*césure*).
6. This necessary double-mindedness can be detected in both the most heatedly discussed parts of the book, especially the value to price transformation and the tendency of the rate of profit to fall, and those that have attracted less attention, e.g. on rent. See also, concerning especially Marx's theory of value, Reuten 1993; 2001.

Engels; it is only because of his dedication that Volumes II and III were published at all. As already noted, *Capital III* was published in 1894, eleven years after Marx's death and nine years after the publication of Volume II. In its Preface Engels explains why there was such a delay: political activities, other theoretical work, his health; but the main reason appears to have been the state of Marx's draft for Volume III.[7] Given the state of the manuscript, Engels could never have been successful in all respects. For example, one might complain that he should have taken out repetitious parts (which would have implied a choice of emphasis), that he should not have included chapters that obviously were just notes (which might have concealed the intended architectonic) or that he should have been more specific in indicating his own alterations and interpolations (which might have marred the continuity of the text). In any case, it must be recognized that Engels left his mark on the text.[8] In his Preface Engels writes: 'Wherever my alterations or additions are not simply editorial in character ... I have put the entire passage in pointed brackets and indicated it with my initials' (Engels 1894F: 93).[9] We may grant that this was Engels's intention but dispute his claim to have observed the limits he set.[10]

By way of illustration, attention is drawn here just to one point: the sub-title of Volume III. It is notorious that for the English edition of Volume I, Engels changed Marx's sub-title from *The Production Process of Capital* to *The Process of Capitalist Production*. These are of course quite different issues.[11] In line with his revision of the sub-title of Volume I, Engels imposed on Volume III the sub-title *The Process of Capitalist Production as a Whole* (*Der Gesammtprozeß der Kapitalistischen Produktion*).

7. Deciphering Marx's handwriting, apparently, was only a minor problem, although, Engels tells us, before he could work on it he first had to dictate the entire manuscript – note that the book in its final shape contains some 900 printed pages.
8. For a fuller discussion see Vollgraf and Jungnickel (1944), Vygodskij (1995) and Heinrich (1996). See also Arthur (1996) as well as Oakley 1983: 125–6.
9. Fernbach, in his English translation for the Pelican edition, adds here the misleading footnote (which does not appear in the German edition or the Untermann translation): 'In the present edition, all Engels's substantial interpolations in the main body of the text are placed simply in parentheses and followed by initials' (93). 'All' creates the impression of an extra check, which obviously is not the case.
10. See, for example, the discussion of the text of Part Three in Chapter 8 of this book.
11. It should be noted, however, that this alteration is given some justification by the French edition of 1872, which Marx authorized.

Marx's own title in his draft of Volume III is different; it is 'The Shapes of the Whole Process' ('Die Gestaltungen des Gesammtprozeß'). Marx says in his introduction that this meant the 'unity' of the first two books.[12] Engels gives credence to his sub-title by inserting (unmarked) the first three sentences of the opening chapter of Volume III.[13]

This collection of studies is based on Marx's *Capital III* as edited by Engels. The authors do not take the view that the 'real' text (whatever real may mean in this context) is that of Marx's manuscripts. The manuscript of 1864–65, for example, is a work on its own (as are those of e.g. 1857–58 and 1861–63) and they should be the subject of a study of their own. Nevertheless, although the *Capital III* text is our platform, some of us, from that platform, further develop Marxian theory in reference to later, e.g. twentieth century, works, while others for their purposes refer back to earlier work of Marx, including the published manuscripts just mentioned.

2. *Capital III* in light of the first two volumes[14]

2.1 Levels of abstraction

Descriptions of the interconnection of the three volumes of *Capital* and relatedly of Marx's general method are bound to be reconstructive as well as controversial. Among the authors of this book, at least, there is agreement about three interdependent aspects of Marx's method. First, the dialectic is not unnecessary jargon that could be dispensed with, but key to the understanding of *Capital*. Nevertheless views differ as to differences between the (systematic) dialectics of Hegel and Marx.[15]

12. This formulation, in fact, goes back to the 1861–63 draft (MECW 33: 69). At that time the main title was still to be 'Capital and Profit'.
13. More accurately the first three-and-a-half sentences of the chapter (i.e., down to 'production process' in the fourth sentence). Cf. *Collected Works* (MECW) Vol. 37: 3, 30 and Marx–Engels *Gesamtausgabe (*MEGA*)* Vol II. 4.2: 7. (Thanks to Chris Arthur for pointing this out.)
14. In this section I provide a brief overview of *Capital III* in relation to Volumes I and II. Although I try not to impose too forcefully my own opinions about the work as a whole, this account reflects my own views and not those of all my co-authors.
15. These differences and systematic dialectics itself are not spelled out much in the current book. See the essays by the same authors in Moseley (ed. 1993) and Moseley and Campbell (eds 1997) and Bellofiore and Finelli (1998). Earlier works are Arthur (1986), Murray (1988), Reuten and Williams (1989) and Smith (1990; 1993). See also the more recent Arthur (1998; 2000), Murray (2001a; 2001b), Reuten (1998; 2001) and Smith (1999). Note that in Paul Mattick's view Marx's break with Hegel is such that the term 'systematic dialectic' is not appropriate (see Mattick 1986; 1993).

Second, all authors agree that the movement in *Capital* is from abstract and simple categories to concrete and complex ones, and is marked by conceptual levels of abstraction/concretion. Nevertheless there are different views about what this implies, especially about whether and how the later more concrete levels modify the earlier and more abstract ones.[16] Third, all agree that these levels are marked by the Parts within each of the volumes of *Capital*, many of which are also conceptual conversions or transformations.[17] Nevertheless views may differ as to whether these can be 'defined' into each other (as in a linear or formal logic) allowing perhaps also for quantitative 'translations' between levels.[18]

In addition, all the authors emphasize – although with different accentuations – that the monetary value-form is key to the understanding of *Capital*. These general agreements, it should be noted, differentiate the current work from what may be considered its complement: the collection of papers edited by Bellofiore (1998a; 1998b).[19]

2.2 From Capital I *and* II *to* Capital III

Marx's *Capital* is an exposition of the logic of capital – its production and reproduction. The work describes the object of enquiry from within, developing the object's own standards and processes to its logical conclusions, and thus assessing the object internally. In *Capital I*, after having established the capitalist social form – the value-form, and its expression in money and capital itself – capital's *need* for labour for the production of value and surplus-value is developed in extenso. Capital's need can be fulfilled because of its social *dominance* over labour – dominance, since capital is also the social materialization of property in the means of production. For this reason, capital can impose its form on society. Therefore also we have the social production of capital. The German subtitle of Volume I brings out this double meaning very well:

16. Engels says in his Preface to the English edition of 1886, that *Capital I* is 'in a great measure a whole in itself'. If 'in itself' is, dialectically, meant as 'implicitly' this is fine. As such, however, it is insufficient. When we still lack essential determinations (such as the rate of profit at the level of *Capital I*) because they have not yet been shown to exist, we lack essential understanding of the whole. In the end the comprehension of the concrete, when that state has been reached, informs the abstract.
17. The last Part of *Capital I*, in particular, seems to be an exception – it is pretty clearly a digression from the systematic ordering (see Smith 1990 on the explanation for this exception).
18. In this book Moseley (Chapter 4) argues that this can be done.
19. An earlier collection on Volume III is edited by Eberle (1973) – its main focus is 'the' transformation problem.

Der Produktionsprozeß des Kapitals, where *des* means both the process of production 'of' and 'by' capital, i.e., need and dominance.

Having established this in Volume I, capital can move on, so to say, to its own workings in Volume II and III (in jargon: its own business). Labour moves to the background. It literally scarcely makes an appearance, except for a few instances such as in the circuit of capital, where labour occurs as only a formal element (Vol. II, Part One), or the social reproduction of capital where labour appears merely in its function of buying part of the consumer goods produced (Vol. II, Part Three).[20]

Consequently, whenever Marx discusses aspects of crisis and the cycle of production in *Capital II* and *III,* it is no longer in terms of a shortage or abundance of labour as in Volume I.[21] Rather it is from the standpoint of the dominance of *capital*: in terms of *its movement* from slack to over-production – predicated on the movement of production of surplus-value in relation to capital investment (Vol. II, Part Three; Vol. III, Part Three); or even more sublimated, in terms of the *shortage or abundance of money capital* – seemingly disconnected from production (Vol. III, Part Five).

2.3 The seven Parts of Capital III

The first three Parts of *Capital III,* fifteen chapters in all, are on aspects of the rate of profit of 'capital in general'.[22] From the concepts of surplus-value and the rate of surplus-value – treated at length in the first volume – Marx develops in Part One the core concepts of profit and the rate of profit. They are effects or results of the whole process at any point in time – and as such the concentration of many determinants – but simultaneously they are decisive or causative for the reproduction of capital; they are capital's continuity measures. 'The rate of profit is the motive power of capitalist production, and nothing is produced save what can be produced at a profit.'[23]

Part Two shows one side of the dynamics of this continuity, that is, how the competition between capitals for the highest rate of profit, results in an averaging out of the rate of profit. The flow of capital from

20. See the papers in Arthur and Reuten (eds 1998).
21. say *aspects* of crisis and the cycle of production because for Marx a *systematic* treatment of these goes beyond the three volumes (see e.g., 1894U: 358).
22. This concept of 'capital in general' is expanded upon in Chapter 3 by Chris Arthur. In an alternative usage of the term, we leave 'capital in general' behind – and go to the level of 'many capitals' – as soon as we take into account differences among sectors in organic composition and turnover times of capital.
23. Marx 1894M: 333; 1894U: 259; 1894F: 368 (translation amended).

branches producing at a relatively lower profit rate, to branches producing at a higher, thus results tendentially in the establishment of a *general* rate of profit, which, as before, is both effect and cause. Along the way it is shown how the concept of price, as developed in Volume I, gets modified.

Thus we see, first, how the oneness of the capitalist social form, that is the oneness, or one-dimensionality, of the value-form as expressed in prices (established in Volume I), brings forth a common measure, or scale, for capitalist success: the rate of profit, which is money over money. Next we see how this measure – generalizing prices into prices of production, that is prices formed in terms of the rate of profit – tendentially brings forth a common quantity on this scale.

Whereas Part Two sets out, so to speak, the synchronic dynamics of capitalist continuity – although this is a synchronic process in time – Part Three presents the diachronic dynamics of continuity, that is the development of the general rate of profit itself. Thus within the synchronic tendency to the formation of a general rate of profit, that rate itself changes diachronically – and again we have a further determining moment of the production of surplus-value.

This diachronic dynamics is the culmination of Marx's architectonic of 'capital in general'. Its basis is the profit-enforced introduction of cost-reducing techniques of production, which are reflected in a rising organic composition of capital, and which generate rate of profit increases to the *initiating* capital but simultaneously operate as a drain on the *average* rate of profit. With this capital goes through treadmill-like cyclical movements in which valorization of capital gets expressed in devalorization, and accumulation of capital in devaluation.

Up to this point capital was presented as an organic unity: (1) of capitals in synchronic concurrence (competition) for profit (Part One);[24] (2) synchronically establishing their general rate of profit (Part Two).[25] This has been based on (reading backwards through *Capital*) the presentation of capital (3) as synchronically connected in its material constituents, that is, the means of production and means of consumption both in their material character and as values (Vol. II, Part Three); (4) as synchronizing its diachronic movement so as to trim the time that capital is tied up in the phases of its circuit (Vol. II, Part Two); (5) diachronically moving through the stages by which it is posited and reposited as capital, from the money form of capital (M), to its commodity form (C), to its

24. 'Competition' and 'concurrence' meaning a joint operation, which is the etymological root of both.
25. Again, these synchronies are dynamic synchronical processes in time. Synchronics and diachronics are thus a matter of emphasis.

valorizing productive form (P), to an ideally valorized new-commodity form (C') and back to the *valorized* money form (M'), that is, in

M–C ... P ... C'–M'

or from any other point of departure, constituting the circuit of capital (Vol. II, Part One). (6) Nevertheless, capital is an organic unity that has only apparent self-subsistence. To be more than a formal 'organic' unity it needs the other of and for itself, that is the subsumption of labour as its valorizing foundation so as to exist and generate fruit (Vol. I).[26]

At the level of capital in general all this culminates in the forces raising the value productivity of labour by revolutionizing the 'technical' constituents of the labour process. The concomitant accelerating valorization for the revolutionizing 'echelons' of capital goes along with devalorization and devaluation of capital as a whole, giving rise to crises and cycles in accumulation (Part Three).

Even if capitals are invested in different branches of production, and competing, they are all alike up to this point in Marx's presentation in that they go through the same process of valorization and its cycle. In Parts Four to Six this unity seems to fall apart: capital in general separates into functionally different factions of capital. In Part Four capital divides into Industrial Capital, Commercial Capital and Money-dealing Capital. Though functionally different they are still alike in that they all equally share, tendentially, in the one for all general rate of profit. Note also that in hindsight this division is implicit in the 'synchronizing diachronic' of the second part of *Capital II*.

The rigorous split seems to occur in Part Five when Marx, via a number of intermediate steps, develops what now is called Finance Capital. This he initially counterposes to the management of functioning capital. At this stage of the analysis these factions are in conflict and it is their relative power (as well as the stage of the cycle) that decides their shares in the general rate of profit. With Marx's 'presentation' of share capital, however, the counterposition seems to supersede into the dominance of Finance Capital.[27] Thus we see capital 'actually' developed into $(M) \rightarrow (M + \Delta M)$,

26. On the concept of subsumption in *Capital*, see Murray 1998 and 2001b.
27. This description is, I believe, fair to Marx but a very idealized one. First it requires a regrouping of the order of the chapters; second the state of the manuscript at times does not even reach the status of an analysis, let alone the systematic required for dialectical presentation. (See further Chapters 8 and 9.)

as money breeding money, into this 'irrational form' as Marx calls it, which is anticipated early in Volume I. In interest-bearing capital, which is capital in its most fetishistic form, we see another culmination of capital and of *Capital*. It is reinforced by another culmination that is unfolded along with it, the development of money into credit money, which also hints back to the starting point of *Capital*. Capital develops into itself (but see the previous note).

One might wonder what, qua presentation equally underdeveloped, Part Six on land and ground rent should add to this. From one point of view Marx 'merely' treats an important phenomenal shape of his time. There are, however, two other reasons – not particularly emphasized by Marx – why this part deserves to be placed at the very end. The first reason is in line with the general argument of *Capital*: 'even' nature must take on the form of value, and in so far as it can be appropriated it can be capitalized. (The 'even' needs qualification of course as, already, even labour-power and its labour have taken on the form of value.) The second reason apparently tempers the 'conclusion' of the previous part, of capital developing into itself: capital can mould nature – and labour – but it is ultimately limited by them. Capital cannot reproduce land or nature. Marx does not emphasize this particular point explicitly, but uses it to develop the category of monopoly and monopoly profits generally. The category of monopoly may be seen as positing capital's mirror for the capital-form of the monopoly over the means of production generally.

The last part, Part Seven, consists of five relatively short and diverse chapters that cap off Volume III's presentation of the shapes of capital and of its valorization (interest, profit of enterprise, and rent). In addition, they emphasize Marx's fundamental point that capitalism is a historically specific and mutable mode of production that conceals its class structure. These chapters might be considered as outlines for setting out the concrete manifestations of the whole.

3. Introduction to the essays

The next chapter, written by Paul Mattick, takes as its starting point *Capital III*'s incomplete final Chapter 52 on Classes. He reviews the development of the argument over the course of the three volumes, arguing that *Capital* abstracts from occupational groupings and income levels to focus attention on the distinction between the producers and appropriators of surplus-value. This distinction takes on central social importance in periods of economic crisis, when the insufficiency of surplus-value extracted from the working class disrupts the normal functioning of the social system. At such times, Marx thought, capitalism itself might be called into question. *Capital*, Mattick argues, is ultimately a study of the conditions of this possibility; its theory of class points to the eventual abolition of class distinctions.

From a very different perspective Chapter 3, by Christopher Arthur, also covers the three volumes of *Capital* as a whole. Basing himself on Marx's 1857–58 outline for *Capital*, the *Grundrisse*, he sets out an entirely new view of the overall structure of the work. Contrasting 'capital in general' with 'capital in its particularity' and 'capital in its singularity' he shows how that schema – as a three by three matrix – maps both within and across the three volumes. Along with this he also provides a novel conceptualization of the apparently heterogeneous contents of Volume III.

In Chapter 4 Fred Moseley argues that the main subject of *Capital III* is the distribution of surplus-value. Going through all the Parts of the work he indicates that via the equalization of rates of profit across branches, surplus-value is divided into industrial profit, commercial profit, interest and rent. Moseley argues further that the production of surplus-value is unaffected by the distributive processes set out in Volume III. Thus, these processes are based on the premise that the total amount of surplus-value has been fully determined at the level of analysis of Volume I. This means that the individual parts of surplus-value being explained in Volume III are 'necessary forms of appearance' of the common substance, surplus labour.

Riccardo Bellofiore's Chapter 5 deals with the transformation problem in Part Two of *Capital III*. He offers an alternative to the 'new interpretation' of Duménil and Foley, shifting the focus to the labour theory of value as an explanation of the origin of the capitalist surplus instead of an explanation of money prices. The problems of Marx's original presentation, Bellofiore maintains, arise from his theory of commodity money. He argues for a reconstruction of Marx's theory along the lines of a monetary theory of production, involving a credit theory of money (where money enters circulation as banks' initial finance) and a credit theory of exploitation (where money capital gives firms command over the whole of abstract labour and over the division of the social working day in production).

In Chapter 6 Christopher Arthur takes on the same Part Two and its chapter on the formation of a general rate of profit. In it, two discourses are in play; one which takes this rate to be determined systemically, and one which takes it as a reference point for capital migration. Their reconciliation is achieved by arguing that capital is a totality, and yet necessarily composed of many capitals subject to forces of 'repulsion and attraction', as Marx terms them. The transformation problem arises because the general concept of capital is particularized both formally and materially. While this results in 'particular real capitals', the 'general form' also has separate 'real existence' in banking. There arises a general rate of profit attributable to capital considered as an individual totality.

As we have indicated, the development of Marx's theory in *Capital* consists of a systematic ordering from relatively simple and abstract categories to determinations that are progressively more complex and concrete. In Chapter 7 Tony Smith argues that for much of the three volumes this ordering proceeds simultaneously along two dimensions, one devoted to the reproduction of total social capital in any given period, the other to the dynamism of capital from one period to the next. These two dimensions come together in Volume III in a manner that requires us to introduce a distinct theoretical level in Marx's theory, 'surplus profits due to innovation'. From a logical standpoint this level falls prior to the Parts of Volume III investigating overaccumulation crises and financial crises.

Parts Three through Five of *Capital III* are discussed in Geert Reuten's Chapter 8. On the basis of the texts of Marx's manuscript, he argues that Part Three presents a theory of the rate of profit 'cycle'. Its name, the 'tendency for the rate of profit to fall' is, therefore, rather misleading. In a review of Parts Four and Five, it is argued that Marx finally arrives at the view that Finance Capital is dominant. It is shown that this view neglects the independent role of Managerial Capital. A potential conflict between Managerial and Finance Capital modifies the way the profit rate cycle gets expressed, namely, in the devaluation and revaluation of capital and, consequently, the course of the cycle.

Chapter 9, by Martha Campbell, deals with another aspect of Part Five, the credit system. With it, Marx introduces credit money, presenting it as the form of money capital creates (hence as money's modern and adequate form). By contrast, precious metal money, to which Marx appeals in Volume I, is the form of money that capital encounters on its historical emergence. The turn from the one to the other is an intentional revision, typical of Marx's method. Questions arise, however, because of Marx's insistence that credit money retains its linkage to gold. This suggests that, having developed the credit system, Marx collapses money back into its primitive form. Rejecting this interpretation, it is argued that Marx refers to gold to make the point that institutional design of the credit system does not subjugate capital to intentional social control.

Marx's theory of rent, Part Six of *Capital III*, is considered in Chapter 10 by Martha Campbell. Opposing Ricardo, Marx argues that rent is determined by the interaction between capitalist production and the private ownership of an element of production that capital cannot produce. In support of this thesis, Marx identifies the conflicts inherent in the lease relationship. Further, he redefines fertility as the relation between production techniques and the characteristics of land and extends his theory of technological innovation to agriculture. Although the quantitative dimension of the theory of absolute rent is flawed, it is argued that this can be detached from Marx's main point, which is that ownership necessarily confers economic power.

The last chapter, Chapter 11, by Patrick Murray, takes us back to the Seventh and final Part of Marx's work, especially its chapter on the Trinity Formula. Key to *Capital* is the idea that there is no production, no wealth, no need *in general*; they always have a definite *social form* involving specific social purposes. The idea that there can be 'production in general' is what Murray terms 'the illusion of the economic'. He argues that *Capital* is made up of two movements of thought. The first centres on the fetishism of the product; the second on the fetishism of the factors involved in the labour process in capitalism. The Trinity chapter concludes this second movement. It dispels the illusion of treating the capitalist mode of production as if it were 'production in general' – lacking a specific social form and purpose – and as if its specific social forms (wages, interest, rent) were general natural 'forms'. Consequently it concludes Marx's theory of value, so also revealing its profound distance from the classical labour theory of value as well as from any notion of isolating the 'wealth added' by this or that factor for the simple reason that there is no common measure of use value.

Bibliography

Superscripts indicate first and other relevant editions; unless otherwise indicated the last mentioned year in the bibliography is the edition cited.

Arthur, Christopher J. (1986), *Dialectics of Labour: Marx and his relation to Hegel* (Oxford/New York: Basil Blackwell).

— (1996), Engels as interpreter of Marx's economics, in C.J. Arthur (ed.), *Engels Today: A Centenary Appreciation* (Basingstoke: Macmillan now Palgrave).

— (1998), Systematic Dialectic, *Science & Society*, 62/3: 447–59.

— (2000), From the Critique of Hegel to the Critique of Capital, in T. Burns and I. Fraser (eds), *The Hegel–Marx Connection* (Basingstoke: Macmillan now Palgrave) 105–30.

— (2001), The spectral ontology of value, *Radical Philosophy*, 107: 32–42; reprinted in Andrew Brown, Steve Fleetwood and John Roberts (eds), *Critical Realism and Marxism* (London/New York: Routledge).

Arthur, Christopher J. and Reuten, Geert (eds) (1998), *The Circulation of Capital: Essays on Volume II of Marx's 'Capital'* (Basingstoke: Macmillan now Palgrave).

Bellofiore, Riccardo (ed.) (1998a), *Marxian Economics: A Reappraisal (Volume 1)* (London/New York: Macmillan/St Martin's Press).
— (ed.) (1998b), *Marxian Economics: A Reappraisal (Volume 2)* (London/New York: Macmillan/St Martin's Press).
Bellofiore, Riccardo and Finelli, Roberto (1998), Capital, labour and time: the Marxian monetary labour theory of value as a theory of exploitation, in R. Bellofiore (ed. 1998a): 48–74.
Eberle, Friedrich (ed.) (1973), *Aspekte der Marxschen Theorie I; Zur methodischen Bedeutung des 3. Bandes des 'Kapital'* (Frankfurt am Main: Suhrkamp).
Engels, Frederick (1894F), Preface to *Capital III* (see Marx 1894F).
Heinrich, Michael (1996), Engels' edition of the Third Volume of Capital and Marx's original manuscript, *Science & Society*, 60/4: 452–66.
Marx, Karl (1867[1]; 1890[4]), *Das Kapital, Kritik der Politischen Ökonomie, Band I, Der Produktionsprozeß des Kapitals* (MEW 23), English trans. (S. Moore and E. Aveling, 1886[1]), Ben Fowkes, *Capital, A Critique of Political Economy, Volume I*, (Harmondsworth: Penguin, 1976).
— (1885[1],1893[2]), ed. F. Engels, *Das Kapital, Kritik der Politischen Ökonomie, Band II, Der Zirkulationsprozeß des Kapitals* (MEW 24), English trans. (Ernest Untermann 1907[1]), David Fernbach, *Capital, A Critique of Political Economy, Volume II*, Harmondsworth: Penguin, 1978).
— (1894G), ed. F. Engels, *Das Kapital, Kritik der Politischen Ökonomie, Band III, Der Gesamtprozeß der kapitalistischen Produktion* (MEW 25) (Berlin: Dietz Verlag, 1972).
— (1894U), *Capital, A Critique of Political Economy, Volume III, The Process of Capitalist Production as a Whole*, trans. of 1894G (Ernest Untermann, 1909[1]) (London, Lawrence & Wishart, 1974).
— (1894F), *Capital, A Critique of Political Economy, Volume III*, trans. of 1894G (David Fernbach, 1981[1]) (Harmondsworth: Penguin, 1981).
— (1894M), *Ökonomische Manuscripte 1863–1867* [Transcription of manuscript for *Das Kapital III*, 1894G], eds M. Müller, J. Jungnickel, B. Lietz, C. Sander and A. Schnickmann, MEGA, Vol. II. 4.2 (1992).
— (1894D), *Capital III* [Disc version of 1894U], K. Marx and F. Engels, Classics in Politics (London: The Electronic Book Company [ElecBook]).
Marx, Karl and Engels, Frederick *Collected Works* (MECW) (London/New York/Moscow: Lawrence & Wishart/International Publishers/Progress Publishers).
— *Marx–Engels Gesamtausgabe* (MEGA) (Berlin/Amsterdam: Dietz Verlag/ Internationales Institut für Sozialgeschichte Amsterdam).
— *Werke* (MEW) (Berlin: Dietz Verlag).
Mattick, Paul, Jr (1986), *Social Knowledge; An Essay on the Nature and Limits of Social Science* (London/Armonk, NY: Hutchinson/M.E. Sharpe).
— (1993), Marx's Dialectic, in F. Moseley (ed. 1993): 115–34.
Mészáros, István (1970), *Marx's Theory of Alienation* (London: Merlin).
Moseley, Fred (ed.) (1993), *Marx's Method in 'Capital'; A Reexamination* (Atlantic Highlands, NJ: Humanities Press).
Moseley, Fred and Campbell, Martha (eds) (1997), *New Investigations of Marx's Method* (Atlantic Highlands, NJ: Humanities Press).
Murray, Patrick (1988), *Marx's Theory of Scientific Knowledge* (Atlantic Highlands, NJ: Humanities Press, 1990).

— (1998), Beyond the 'commerce and industry' picture of capital, in C.J. Arthur and G. Reuten (eds 1998): 33–66.
— (2001a), Marx's 'truly social' labor theory of value: abstract labor in Marxian value theory, Part I, *Historical Materialism*, 6 (Summer 2000): 27–65.
— (2001b), Marx's 'truly social' labor theory of value: abstract labor in Marxian value theory, Part II, *Historical Materialism*, 7 (Winter 2000): 99–136.
Oakley, Allen (1983), *The Making of Marx's Critical Theory; A Bibliograhical Analysis* (London: Routledge & Kegan Paul).
Reuten, Geert (1993), The difficult labour of a theory of social value; metaphors and systematic dialectics at the beginning of Marx's 'Capital', in F. Moseley (ed. 1993): 89–113.
— (1998), Marx's method, in J. Davis, W. Hands and U. Mäki (eds), *The Handbook of Economic Methodology* (Cheltenham/Northampton: Edward Elgar): 283–7.
— (2001), The interconnection of Systematic Dialectics and Historical Materialism, *Historical Materialism*, 7 (Winter 2000): 137–65.
Reuten, Geert and Williams, Michael (1989), *Value-Form and the State; the tendencies of accumulation and the determination of economic policy in capitalist society* (London/New York: Routledge).
Smith, Tony (1990), *The Logic of Marx's Capital: Replies to Hegelian Criticisms* (Albany, NY: State University of New York Press).
— (1993), *Dialectical Social Theory and its Critics: from Hegel to Analytical Marxism and Postmodernism* (Albany, NY: State University of New York Press).
— (1999), The Relevance of Systematic Dialectics to Marxian Thought: A Reply to Rosenthal, *Historical Materialism*, 4: 215–40.
Vollgraf, Carl-Erich and Jungnickel, Jürgen (1994), 'Marx in Marx's Worten?' – Zu Engels' Edition des Hauptmanuskripts zum dritten Buch des *Kapital, MEGA-Studien*, 1994/2: 3–55.
Vygodskij, Vitalij (1995), Was hat Engels in den Jahren 1885 und 1894 eigentlich veröffentlicht? – Zu dem Artikel von Carl-Erich Vollgraf und Jürgen Jungnickel 'Marx in Marx's Worten?', *MEGA-Studien*, 1995/1: 117–20.

2
Class, Capital and Crisis

Paul Mattick

'The concept of class has never remained a harmless concept for very long.'

Ralf Dahrendorf[1]

1. Last and first

Dahrendorf states a common view when he writes, 'Marx postponed the systematic presentation of his theory of class until death took the pen from his hand. The irony has often been noted that the last (52nd) chapter of the last (third) volume of *Capital,* which bears the title "The Classes", has remained unfinished. After a little more than one page the text ends with the lapidary remark of its editor, Engels: "Here the manuscript breaks off." '[2] Unfortunately, the colourful picture this suggests, of the pen dropping from the hand of the dying Marx just as he was on the point of completing his masterwork, isn't ours to keep: the draft containing this chapter was completed in 1867, before Marx turned to the preparation of Volume I for publication. Nevertheless, some have taken Marx's delay in returning to the chapter – until it was too late – as an admission *in actu* of failure, attesting to a basic flaw in his theory. Engels's explanation is less dramatic: Marx liked to leave conclusions 'for the final editing, shortly before printing, when the latest historical events would supply him, with unfailing regularity, with

1. Ralf Dahrendorf, *Class and Class Conflict in Modern Society* (Stanford: Stanford University Press, 1959): 3.
2. *Ibid.*: 8.

illustrations of his theoretical arguments, as topical as anyone could desire'.[3] Reopening the question of the relation of Marx's final page and a half to the rest of *Capital*, I wish to explore what Marx's willingness to leave the matter in so sketchy a state might indicate about the nature, or even the existence, of a Marxian theory of class.

The matter is of importance, since Marx's critique of political economy stands from the start under the sign of the category of class. The preface to *Zur Kritik*, the publication that began the examination of 'the system of bourgeois economy', promises an analysis of 'the economic conditions of existence of the three great classes into which modern bourgeois society is divided'. This was to be carried out in the first three of the six books which Marx proposed to write, those on capital, landed property and wage labour.[4] In this plan Marx echoed Ricardo's identification of 'the principle problem in Political Economy' as to 'determine the laws which regulate' the distribution of 'the produce of the earth' among 'three classes of the community', the proprietors of land, the owners of the capital employed in cultivating it and the labourers who work it.[5] The nature of Marx's critique of political economy may be indicated elliptically by pointing to the replacement of 'distribution' by 'conditions of existence' as analytical focal point. The former conceptualization takes the existence of the 'three great classes' for granted as a feature of society, asking only how the social product is shared out between them. Marx, in contrast, is interested in the historically specific conditions under which society can be characterized in terms of these three groupings.

Marx's early studies of the dismal science reflected his discovery of the centrality of economic categories to the ideological terms in which bourgeois society represents itself. His serious reengagement with economic theory after the 1848 revolutions was more directly provoked by his perception of a relation between the rise and fall of radical mass

3. Karl Marx, *Capital*, Vol. III, trans. David Fernbach (Harmondsworth: Penguin, 1981): 97.
4. Karl Marx, *Contribution to the Critique of Political Economy*, in Karl Marx and Frederick Engels, *Collected Works* [henceforward MECW], Vol. 29 (New York: International Publishers, 1987): 261. Marx adds, with respect to the three books to come, that 'the interconnection between the other three headings [the state, foreign trade and world market] is self-evident'. In the event, Book One, on capital, expanded to three (or four, if we include *Theories of Surplus-Value*) volumes, of which Marx himself finally published only one.
5. David Ricardo, *On the Principles of Political Economy and Taxation*, Piero Sraffa (ed.), *Works and Correspondence*, Vol. 1 (Cambridge: Cambridge University Press, 1966): 5.

movements on the Continent and the (inverse) movements of the economy. In the 'Review' of events he wrote with Engels, from exile in London, for the *Neue Rheinischen Zeitung*, Marx discussed in detail the correlation of crisis and revolt, arguing that the prosperity sure to return to Germany and France in response to renewed expansion in England would rule out any rapid revival of the movement.

> With this general prosperity, in which the productive forces of bourgeois society develop as fully as this is in general possible within bourgeois [social] relations, there can be no question of a real revolution. Such a revolution is only possible in those periods in which *both* of these *factors, the modern forces of production* and the *bourgeois forms of production,* come into *contradiction* with each other. ... *A new revolution is only possible as a consequence of a new crisis. But it is also as certain as this.*[6]

At the time these words were written, Marx was essentially a follower of Ricardo in economics; a particular motive for a return to his economic studies was the incompatibility with Ricardian theory of the course of events of the late 1840s.[7] These studies, which eventually led to the writing of *Capital*, would involve a fundamental break with Ricardian theory, and in fact with classical political economy as a whole. Nonetheless, the statement quoted above can stand as a summary of the central underlying idea of the work which was to occupy Marx for the 30-odd years that followed its writing. Its basic elements reappear, for instance, in the summary of 'the guiding principle of my studies', reached by 1845, with which Marx introduced the first installment of his study of capital in 1859. Here Marx describes human social existence as a matter of 'relations of production appropriate to a given stage in the development of their material forces of production'. While 'no social formation is ever destroyed before all the productive forces for which it is sufficient have been developed', that development produces a conflict between 'the material productive forces of society' and 'the existing relations of production' which have turned 'into their fetters. Then begins an era of social revolution.'[8] In such an era, as Marx envisioned it, what he described with the theoretical abstractions of 'forces' and

6. Karl Marx and Friedrich Engels, 'Revue, Mai bis Oktober 1850', in Karl Marx and Friedrich Engels, *Werke*, Vol. 7 (Berlin: Dietz, 1964): 440.
7. See the discussion in Fred E. Schrader, *Restauration und Revolution* (Hildesheim: Gerstenberg, 1980): 15–23.
8. Marx, *Contribution*: 262–3.

'relations' would take practical form in the struggle between classes which he had identified in the *Communist Manifesto* as the central drama of history. Again, in a letter to Engels of 1868, Marx discussed the theoretical advances at the heart of the third volume of *Capital* as a matter of relations between economic entities: the distribution of surplus-value, the differentiation of forms of capital, the equalization of profit rates and the tendency of the rate of profit to fall. Yet he promises that, at the end of it all, he will show that economic theory constitutes only a set of appearances of a reality to be analysed, ultimately, in terms of 'the *class struggle*, into which the movement and the smash-up of the whole greasy mess resolves itself'.[9]

But if *Capital*, with all its three (or four) volumes, was intended only as the first book of a study of the 'three great classes', why does the chapter on classes appear at its conclusion? Roman Rosdolsky suggested one answer in his study of the development of Marx's theory. Rosdolsky argued that while writing his magnum opus Marx found that the intended books on landed property and wage labour 'had to be incorporated into' the study of capital because the latter 'would have been inconceivable without a treatment of the questions which they deal with'.[10] This seems a mistake, however.[11] For one thing, the treatment of rent in *Capital* should be distinguished, as Marx himself put it, from 'the analysis of landed property in its various historical forms', which 'lies outside the scope' of *Capital*.[12] As we know, Marx occupied himself to a great extent during his last years in collecting information for such an analysis (even learning

9. Letter of 30 April 1868, K. Marx and F. Engels, *Selected Correspondence* (Moscow: Foreign Languages Publishing House, n.d.): 250 (translation amended).
10. Roman Rosdolsky, *The Making of Marx's 'Capital'*, trans. Pete Burgess (London: Pluto Press, 1977): 23.
11. I leave undiscussed Rosdolsky's contention that Marx integrated into Capital not just the books on private property and wage labour but also the sections of his study of capital devoted to competition, the credit system, and the stock market, originally planned for separate books following the analysis of 'capital in general', the features shared by all capitalist entities. In this I take advantage of Winfried Schwartz's essay, 'Das "Kapital in algemeinen" und die "Konkurrenz" im ökonomischen Werk von Karl Marx', in *Gesellschaft. Beiträge zur Marxschen Theorie*, 1 (Frankfurt: Suhrkamp, 1974): 222–47. Schwartz argues that, contrary to Rosdolsky's interpretation, the treatment of 'capital in general' concludes with Part One of the third volume, the rest of which contains material for the remaining sections of the analysis of capital.
12. Marx, *Capital*, Vol. III: 751. For a discussion of Marx's unwritten book on landed property, see Felton C. Shortall, *The Incomplete Marx* (Aldershot: Avebury, 1994): 170 ff.

Russian to read documents relevant to the history of landed property in Russia). In *Capital*, however, he studied, under the heading of rent, not a form of property but a form of revenue – a claim to income rather than a social relation mediated by claims to ownership of natural resources; he was concerned with the former 'only in so far as a portion of the surplus-value that capital produces falls to the share of the landowner'.[13]

Second, the discussion (in the first volume of *Capital*) of wages, the market-representation of the value of labour-power, is similarly to be distinguished from an analysis of wage labour as a social institution – that is, of the waged working class, with a variety of characteristics in different periods and locations, and internally differentiated at any time and place by the distinction between employment and unemployment, by job status and wage differentials, and by gender, age, and racial inequalities. It is true that Volume I contains a great deal of historical and analytical material bearing on the historical conditions of appearance and the development of waged labour, notably in Chapter 10, 'The Working Day'; Chapter 15, 'Machinery and Large-Scale Industry'; Chapter 25, on the effects of capital accumulation on the working class in the form of unemployment and immiseration; and Part Eight, which discusses the creation of the preconditions for capitalist production by separating producers from land and other means of production. But all this material considers the working and living conditions of wage-earners primarily as presupposition and function of the accumulation of capital. Marx is concerned above all to destroy (as he put it in the unfinished 'Sixth Chapter' of *Capital*) 'the last vestiges of the illusion ... that ... in the market-place, two equally matched *commodity owners* confront each other, and that they, like all other commodity owners, are distinguished only by the material content of their goods ...'. He wishes to demonstrate as well that wage labour is 'one of the *essential* mediating forms of capitalist relations of production, and one constantly reproduced by those relations themselves'.[14]

The existence of wage labour is in fact a socio-historical requirement for the production of surplus-value and so for the existence of capital. To explain this, however, is not to provide an analysis of wage labour as a distinct category of social relations. Marx observes in a brief chapter (22) on national wage differentials that to compare wages in different parts of the world we must 'take into account all the factors that determine

13. *Ibid.*
14. K. Marx, 'Results of the Immediate Process of Production', in *Capital*, Vol. I, trans. Ben Fowkes (Harmondsworth: Penguin, 1976): 1062, 1064.

changes in the amount of the value of labour-power: the price and the extent of the prime necessities of life in their natural and historical development, the cost of training the workers, the part played by the labour of women and children, the productivity of labour, and its extensive and intensive magnitude';[15] some fragmentary remarks on trade unionism in the 'Sixth Chapter' suggest the topic of workers' oppositional activity as a determining factor of the value of labour-power.[16] Such matters, considered at once historically and analytically, would no doubt have provided the content of the third book of Marx's critique of political economy.

If *Capital* was not meant to absorb the unwritten books on the labouring and landowning classes, it is all the more remarkable that Marx's chapter on classes concludes it. For the chapter begins in Ricardian fashion with the listing of 'the owners of mere labour-power, the owners of capital and the landowners' as 'the three great classes of modern society based on the capitalist mode of production'.[17] Why then did Marx embark on a theory of class structure before the books to be devoted to the other two class categories, wage labour and landed property? The answer is to be found in the context: Part Seven, the concluding section of Volume III, deals with 'The Revenues and Their Sources', that is, with 'the estranged and irrational forms' in which the capitalist production process appears to those who live by its laws.[18] To explain how this section and the chapter on classes fit into Marx's argument requires a brief survey of that argument, the critique of political economy, as a whole.[19]

2. Economic appearances and social reality

Capital begins, as it ends, with appearances: the appearance that wealth in 'societies in which the capitalist mode of production prevails' is an 'immense collection of commodities'.[20] Wealth seems to crystallize in the market place, as the accumulation of commodities. But, as Marx quickly demonstrates, wealth in modern society is specifically the accumulation of *capital*, of money invested in the means of production and labour-power required to produce goods saleable for a larger sum of money. Capital

15. Marx, *Capital*, Vol. I: 701.
16. *Ibid.*: 1069–70.
17. Marx, *Capital*, Vol. III: 1025.
18. *Ibid.*: 969.
19. For a more extended account, see my 'Theory as Critique: On the Argument in Capital', in Fred Moseley and Martha Campbell (eds), *New Investigations of Marx's Method* (New Jersey: Humanities Press, 1997): 66–88.
20. Marx, *Capital*, Vol. I: 125.

thus requires the existence on the market of the commodity labour-power, owned by people unable to employ it themselves because of their lack of access to means of production. Indeed, it is only when such people exist that the commodity becomes the general form of wealth, since only then must the producers purchase a portion of their product, made for the owners of the means of production, with the wages paid for their ability to work.

If Marx thereby shows that wealth consists in the control of other people's labouring, he emphasizes that control is exercised in a particular way in this particular society: 'The specific economic form in which unpaid surplus labour is pumped out of the direct producers determines the relationship of domination and servitude' in different types of society.[21] In capitalism, surplus labour, work performed in addition to that which provides for the consumption of the producers, is appropriated as surplus-value, through the medium of market exchanges between employers and employees, in which first the latter and then the former appear as sellers of commodities to each other. Since the social relation of domination between them is represented in a roundabout way by the circulation process, the exploitative relationship is hidden behind the equality of market partners. Hence it is that wealth appears to be a matter of commodity ownership, or the possession of money, a means to ownership, rather than a relationship between people *manifested* in differential access to goods.

In so far as capital takes the form of produced goods and means for producing them, it is wealth whose use yields an income. The owner of capital, as just observed, is in a position to appropriate that part of the product made with it – translated into money terms – that exceeds the reproduction requirements of the producers. 'Capital thereby becomes a very mystical being, since all the productive forces of social labour appear attributable to it and not to labour as such.'[22] Alternatively expressed, each capitalist ascribes to the productive virtue of his individual capital the amount he manages to obtain from the surplus labour of employed workers. This appearance is all the more convincing because the amount of profit extracted by each capital does not in fact depend on the surplus production of the workers it employs but is drawn in a complex way from the surplus labour performed for the totality of capitalist employers.

It is only in the process of circulation – the totality of market exchanges that mediate, on the one hand, the relation between productive labour

21. Marx, *Capital*, Vol. III: 927.
22. *Ibid.*: 966.

and producers' consumption, and, on the other, the relation between capital investment and the extraction of surplus-value – that surplus labour is crystallized in a form (money) utilizable for future investment. Surplus labour in capitalism (unlike noncapitalist forms of society) is therefore a phenomenon definable only in relation to total social labour, and not firm by firm. Just as the labour engaged in at an individual workplace only counts as a part of social labour in so far as its product takes the form of a commodity sold on the market, so the surplus labour performed at that workplace exists as surplus-value – in a form (money) utilizable for capital accumulation – only as market exchange makes it a portion of the social surplus produced under the dominance of the totality of capital.[23] This is why that totality (what Marx calls 'social capital') is not just a mental aggregate of individual firms, but a fundamental unit in the functioning of the social system.[24]

We will return to this aspect of the economic system below, because it is the society-wide character of exploitation that, in Marx's view, provides the basis for class as the peculiarly modern mode of social stratification. From the capitalist's viewpoint, however, the ratio of the total surplus-value produced to the amount of value required for the worker's consumption – the socially specific measure of work done for employers relative to that done for the producers themselves – is unimportant. What counts is the rate of profit, the ratio of surplus-value appropriated by the individual firm to capital investment in means of

23. This point is discussed in Fred Moseley's contribution to this volume, in the form of the theoretically prior determination of social surplus-value before its division among capitalist revenues.
24. It is also why the so-called problem of the transformation of values into prices that seemed so insuperable from the point of view of Ricardian theory does not arise for Marx. See my 'Some Aspects of the Value-Price Problem' (1981), in *International Journal of Political Economy*, 21:4: 9–66, and 'The Value-Price Problem: Marx's Solution to a Ricardian Conundrum', unpublished ms.,1999. In brief, the theory of value describes social production as organized through commodity exchange in a capitalist society, that is, one in which goods typically must be sold at a profit. Indeed, commodity exchange is fundamentally a means for the extraction of surplus labour from workers by the owners of capital. Hence values (social labour-time contents) are not defined for commodities except as the latter are exchanged for prices differing from those values. By the same token, while the theoretically conceivable labour values of commodities, playing no role in actual exchange relations, where value is (mis)represented by the exchange of goods against money, are unknown, social value relations – the rates of exploitation and profit – make themselves felt as constraints on individual pricing and production decisions ('competition').

production and labour-power. Of course, as Marx restates a point demonstrated (in other terms) in the fifth chapter of Volume I, 'the capital value advanced cannot form surplus-value simply by means of its having been used up and forming therefore the cost price of the commodity' produced.[25] But the ability of a capitalist's investment to bear fruit seems to depend just on the willingness of the market to buy his product at a sufficiently high price. His investment counts for him as an individual gamble, rather than as a contribution to the social production process, the product of which includes the social surplus that is distributed among individual firms. A sufficient demand for his goods allows him to collect a sum causally linked to his investment, since it represents money in excess of that needed to pay for labour-power: 'surplus-value itself does not appear as having been produced by the appropriation of labour-time but as the excess of the sale price of commodities over their cost price ...'.[26] The latter 'appears to each capitalist as a given quantity',[27] the price he must pay for the inputs consumed in his production process, so that the relation between surplus-value and the labour-power set in motion as labour disappears from view. Surplus-value is therefore conceptualized as profit, a 'return to capital'.

In Part Two of *Capital*, Vol. III, Marx traces the further obscuring of the relation between profit and surplus labour as a result of competition between the individual firms that constitute social capital. The attempt by firms to maximize profits through various manners of adjustment between quantities of product and prices involves a shifting of claims on the social surplus-value among firms that conceals any relation between profits earned by firms and surplus labour performed by their workers. This effect is redoubled by the fact that some capital is invested in economic activities – such as commerce and banking – that are themselves unproductive of surplus-value but that claim a share of the social surplus. A special category is that of rent, a share of surplus-value demanded by the owners of natural resources for the use of their property. The process that obscures of the source of profits, interest and rent is basic to the operation of the system; the redistribution of surplus-value effected by price competition is an aspect of the mechanism that effectively socializes the labour performed for various employers. It is because of this socialization of their labour by way of its uniform representation by money in the marketplace that, despite the fact that workers are hired

25. Marx, *Capital*, Vol. III: 126.
26. *Ibid.*: 135.
27. *Ibid.*: 1010.

by individual firms, they may be more properly said to be exploited as a group by capitalists as a group.

The last part of Volume III examines forms in which the social organization of surplus-value extraction appears 'on the surface of society ... in the everyday consciousness of the agents of production themselves'.[28] This 'everyday consciousness' provides the material for what Marx calls 'vulgar economics', the direct ancestor of the dominant economic theorizing of the last hundred years, which 'actually does nothing more than interpret, systematize and turn into apologetics the notions of agents trapped within bourgeois relations of production'.[29] The annual social product seems to arise through the cooperation of three factors of production, the trinity of land, labour and capital. Stand-ins for natural resources, human activity and products of previous human activity, these are historically specific forms of the universal constituents of the labour process[30] masquerading as transcultural universals. Their historically specific character appears in the asserted link between them as forms of property and the corresponding forms of revenue – rent, wages and interest – sums of value from which seem to arise the prices of commodities.

> Capital-profit (or better still capital-interest), land-ground-rent, labour-wages, this economic trinity as the connection between the components of value and wealth in general and its sources, completes the mystification of the capitalist mode of production, the reification of social relations, and the immediate coalescence of the material relations of production with their historical and social specificity: the bewitched, distorted, and upside-down world haunted by Monsieur le Capital and Madame la Terre, who are at the same time social characters and mere things.[31]

But if the social character of the production process is invisible in the marketplace, where relations between individuals are on view, it makes itself felt not only in the despotic domain of the workplace but in the impersonal economic dynamics of the social system as a whole. Throughout the history of capitalism, as Marx explains at the start of his study, value 'magnitudes vary constantly, independently of the will,

28. *Ibid.*:117.
29. *Ibid.*: 956.
30. See the discussion in *Capital,* Vol. I, Chapter 9.
31. Marx, *Capital,* Vol. III: 968–9.

knowledge, and actions of the exchangers'.[32] The social rate of surplus-value and the general rate of profit determine the possibilities for capital accumulation; experienced by capitalist entities in the form of interfirm competition, the constraints set on the activities of individuals by social relationships unknown to them are represented as the workings of 'the economy', as if this were a structure or mechanism independent of human action. The 'law of value' that Marx claims to have discovered regulating modern society only makes itself known in daily life 'the same way that the law of gravity asserts itself when a person's house collapses on top of him'.[33]

This conflict between the social character of production and the individual character of property 'impresses itself most strikingly on the practical bourgeois in the changes of the periodic cycle through which modern industry passes, the summit of which is the general crisis'.[34] At a time of economic crisis, the relation of value – the representation of the social character of labour by the exchangeability of all capitalist products against money – to labour as actual human activity manifests itself in the form of the existence of unsaleable products. Produced for sale at a profit, capitalist commodities cannot be consumed (at least within the framework of the market-exchange system) if this condition cannot be met; the abstract social labour-time they contain is revealed to be equal to zero. It is then the (historically specific) social nature of the labour involved in commodity production that renders its products unusable by society, a paradox that exposes the limits capitalism sets to people's ability to use their ability to work to meet their needs. Such moments clarify the choice that exists as soon as capitalism has reached a relatively high stage of development, between the preservation of the existing society and its transformation into one more adequate to people's needs.

It is for this reason that Marx devotes much of the argument in Volume III to demonstrating that the accumulation of capital, the form of exploitation mediated by commodity exchange, leads to a tendential fall in the rate of profit, which limits accumulation and, by way of economic crisis, increases the potential for social upheaval. Economic crisis brings to light the fact that 'it is the appropriation of unpaid labour, and the proportion between this unpaid labour and the objectified [previous] labour [owned as capital] ... that determines the expansion or contraction of production, instead of the proportion between production and social

32. Marx, *Capital*, Vol. I: 167.
33. *Ibid.*: 168.
34. *Ibid.*: 103.

needs ...'.[35] It points towards a generalized social crisis because it is, according to Marx, 'the direct relationship of the owners of the conditions of production to the immediate producers ... in which we find the innermost secret, the hidden basis of the entire social edifice, and hence also the political form of the relationship of sovereignty and dependence', the state.[36]

3. Economic class and social structure

Just as the value of commodities is the representation in money terms of social labour in capitalism, the rate of profit is the money representation of 'the proportion between unpaid labour and objectified labour'. As such it represents in an economic quantity the relationship between the interests of the producers and those of their employers, for 'unpaid labour' is the work the producers must perform in addition to that necessary for their own reproduction. Groups defined by such a relationship are what Marx, using the terminology that developed gradually during the late eighteenth and early nineteenth centuries, called classes.[37]

According to Marx, the 'historical tendency of capitalist accumulation' includes 'the dissolution of private property based on the labour of its owner', such as that of the peasant, artisan and small shopkeeper who emerged out of feudal society, and the transformation of the majority of people into sellers of labour-power to capitalist employers.[38] Capitalist social structure is experienced both as a complex system of social differences and as involving a trend towards social equality. The salience of equality derives from the fact that, in contrast to precapitalist society, 'the domination of the exploiters loses the form of a power relationship and makes an indirect appearance, on the basis of the equality of commodity exchange, which mystifies the capitalist exploitation relation in an economic form, but also thereby legitimates it'.[39] The apparent

35. *Ibid.*: 927.
36. Marx, *Capital*, Vol. III: 367.
37. For a brief history of the concept 'class', see Raymond Williams, *Keywords* (New York: Oxford University Press, 1983): 60 ff.
38. Marx, *Capital*, Vol. I: 927. This view – basic to Marx's critique of the Classical economists' labour theory of value – should not be confused with a mythical doctrine, often ascribed to Marx, of the disappearance of the middle classes in capitalism. See the discussion in Hal Draper, *Karl Marx's Theory of Revolution*, Vol. II, 'The Politics of Social Classes' (New York: Monthly Review Press, 1978): 613 ff.
39. Michael Mauke, *Die Klassentheorie von Marx und Engels* (Frankfurt: Europaïsche Verlagsanstalt, 1970): 22. Mauke's book remains the best introduction to the subject of Marx's conception of class.

homogenization of social personality was clearly stated by Adam Smith, despite his acute recognition of the persistence of social hierarchy: 'every man ... lives by exchanging, or becomes in some measure a merchant ...'.[40] Because the social character of production is only indirectly acknowledged, by the exchange of commodities for money, the relations between commodity exchangers – capitalists and workers alike – are represented in the form of contracts (explicit and implicit) between legal equals.

This kind of equality, understood as legal equivalence or the abstract uniformity of civil or human rights, is compatible with the existence of myriad forms of inequality, both those defined in noneconomic terms, such as gender and race, and those defined in terms of level of wealth, the particular good or service brought to market, or position in the complex hierarchy of production. The resulting conceptual (and even practical) conflict is typically resolved by locating the origins of inequality outside social relations proper. For example, the concept of race, which emerged in Europe in the eighteenth century to become a durable peculiarity of modern thought, serves to explain social inferiority as a function of biological difference, as do explanations of social success as due to personal characteristics like 'talent' or 'drive'. Specifically economic inequality is seen as the result of differential access to goods rather than as a product of the functioning of the market-exchange system,[41] and in any case the economy is imagined as an autonomous dynamic structure regulating society. The ability to buy others' labour-power appears due to the possession of money, rather than to the existence of a form of society in which social labour is represented by money.

40. Adam Smith, *An Inquiry into the Nature and Causes of the Wealth of Nations*, ed. R.H. Campbell, A.S. Skinner and W.B. Todd, Volume I (Oxford: Clarendon Press, 1979): 37. It is this homogenization, in contrast to the premodern essentialization of status differences, to which Smith gives expression in his theory of the 'impartial spectator', the 'man within' each person who adjudicates conflicts of interest between individuals conceived of as fundamentally equal. See A. Smith, *The Theory of Moral Sentiments*, ed. D.D. Raphael and A.C. Macfie (Oxford: Clarendon Press, 1976): 135 ff.
41. Indeed, a central argument of classical economics was that the operation of 'commercial society' had the effect of redistributing wealth; thus, in his *Theory of Moral Sentiments*, Smith asserted that in satisfying their taste for luxury the rich 'are led by an invisible hand to make nearly the same distribution of the necessaries of life, which would have been made, had the earth been divided into equal portions among all its inhabitants ...' (iv, i.10). For a discussion of this theme in classical political economy, see Donald Winch, *Riches and Poverty. An Intellectual History of Political Economy in Britain, 1750–1834* (Cambridge: Cambridge University Press, 1996), Chapter 2 and *passim*.

Thus, Marx says in the fragment on classes that closes Volume III, the question 'what makes wage-labourers, capitalists and landowners the formative elements of the three great classes?' seems 'at first sight' to find an answer – where John Stuart Mill, most famously in the early nineteenth century, found it – in 'the identity of revenues and revenue sources'.[42] The classes are defined by the commodities they own, whose economic utilization yields a particular form of income. The even more 'vulgar' conception of class as income level – probably, in combination with a conception of class as social status, the dominant folk and social-scientific concept of class in the United States at the present time – abstracts from type of resource brought to market to simply compare revenues, the differences between which can then be explained as a function of kinds and amounts of property owned.

As this example suggests, while Marx's analysis is primarily focused on the 'classical' and 'vulgar' economics of the nineteenth century, it remains applicable to current conceptions of class. A striking case in point is what is probably the best-known recent attempt to produce a Marxist theory of class, that of Eric Olin Wright. Highly elaborated in the form of a sociological research programme as well as an abstract economic argument, Wright's position is only a recent example of a longstanding tendency within Marxism to distinguish 'class analysis' from 'economic theory'.[43] Wright defines class in terms of exploitation, itself defined following the 'analytic Marxist economics' of John Roemer, who abandoned Marxian value theory in favour of a combination of Neo-Ricardian economics and game theory.[44] In this analysis, one class is said to exploit another when, *ceteris paribus*, consumption would increase and toil decrease for the

42. Marx, *Capital*, Vol. III: 1026.
43. In the strictly economic literature we may note Joseph Schumpeter's division, in his *History of Economic Analysis* (New York: Oxford University Press, 1954), of 'the pieces' into which Marx's theoretical structure decomposes: 'two groups, one sociological and one economic', with no essential connection between them (389); Schumpeter's pupil, Paul Sweezy, argued that Marx's value theory, while unnecessary (given the development of neoclassical equilibrium economics) for the derivation of his economic results, is worth saving because in its qualitative dimension it spotlights capitalist class structure (see *Theory of Capitalist Development* (New York: Oxford University Press, 1942): 129). Thirty years later, Mario Cogoy, responsible earlier for a devastating critique of Sweezy's work, came to roughly the same conclusions on the similar but then more fashionable grounds of Neo-Ricardian theory (see 'Das Dilemma der neoricardianischen Theorie', in H.G. Backhaus *et al.* (eds), *Gesellschaft. Beiträge zur Marxschen Theorie* 2 [Frankfurt: Suhrkamp, 1974]: 204–63).
44. See John Roemer, *A General Theory of Exploitation and Class* (Cambridge: Harvard University Press, 1982).

latter if the former did not exist. That is, class exploitation consists in the taking of the surplus produced by the exploited class. Although this seems close to Marx's analysis, it conceptualizes exploitation (in terms curiously reminiscent of the position of J.S. Mill) as the appropriation of a produced surplus through the process of distribution. In Marx's understanding of capitalism, as in reality, the surplus – by definition – belongs to capital as soon as it has been produced; successful capitalist production *is* the production of surplus-value. For Wright, in contrast, exploitation is 'market based'.[45]

According to Roemer and Wright, 'there is complete symmetry in the structure of exploitation in a system in which capital hires wage labourers and in a [hypothetical] system in which workers rent capital ...' and thereby exploit capital owners.[46] Labour and capital are, that is, here conceived of as two types of 'asset', and classes are defined 'by the productive assets which [they] control'.[47] The kinship of this conception with the vulgar economics Marx criticizes in *Capital* is evident in the ahistorical understanding of 'labour' and 'capital' as 'factors of production', common to all social systems. This is why Wright can imagine that feudal exploitation can be analysed in the same theoretical terms as the extraction of surplus-value in capitalism, despite the earlier nonexistence of the system of generalized commodity production that alone makes the concepts of value, labour-power, surplus-value and capital significant.[48]

As in this case, so generally in bourgeois thought, the reality of class is hidden behind economic categories; or rather, it appears only in the form of economic interest groups, classes of agents defined by their relation to sources (or quantities) of revenue rather than by their relations to each other in the performance of social labour and surplus labour. Seen in this way, as a collection of interest groups (or of income levels), a population can be classified into an indefinite number of classes and subclasses, in a rather arbitrary manner. [49] Asking, 'What makes a class?'

45. Eric Olin Wright, 'A General Framework for the Analysis of Class Structure', in E.O. Wright *et al.*, *The Debate on Classes* (London: Verso, 1989): 10.
46. *Ibid.*
47. E.O. Wright, *Classes* (London: Verso, 1985): 73.
48. For a thorough criticism of Wright's argument, see Guglielmo Carchedi, 'Classes and Class Analysis', in Wright *et al.*, *Debate*: 105–25; for another, showing the drawbacks of Wright's approach from a sociological point of view, see John Clarke, *New Times and Old Enemies. Essays on Cultural Studies and America* (London: HarperCollins, 1991): 44 ff.
49. For an interesting study of the way in which differing conceptions of class structure produce different categories of statistical information in use by social scientists, see Michael Donnelly, 'Statistical Classification and the Salience

Marx observes at the very end of Volume III of *Capital* that the answer at first sight seems to be the 'identity of revenues and revenue sources'. For these seem indeed to identify the 'three great classes' of Ricardian theory. But '[T]he same would hold true for the infinite fragmentation of interests and positions into which the division of social labour splits not only workers but also capitalists and landowners – the latter, for instance, into vineyard-owners, field-owners, mine-owners, fishery-owners, etc.'[50]

'At this point the manuscript breaks off', Engels noted. This is because the essential theoretical point had already been made: that class structure, in the sense of interest to Marx, cannot be adequately theorized from the standpoint of political economy – or, more generally, from that of bourgeois ideology in which economic thinking has such a central place. The category of class was produced by bourgeois society as a means of stating its distinction from the earlier European system of social stratification conceptualized in terms of 'ranks' and 'orders'. Unlike precapitalist hierarchies, class is not a permanent attribute of individuals but is carried by money, whose possession signifies control over social labour. Class itself thus appears as social power abstracted from relations between people, incarnated in the symbol of value, something individuals can acquire and lose, like the commodities with which it is often equated. 'Class' is an unavoidable category in a culture pervaded by the inequality whose systemic centre is the relation between worker and capitalist defined by the extraction of surplus-value. But since this relation is represented ideologically by the generalization of commodity relations, as one of market exchange between legal equals who may have differing assets, class is (so to speak) dispersed throughout the social system rather than localized at the point of exploitation.

This dispersal of class can be seen in its most sophisticated form in the thinking of Pierre Bourdieu, whose book *Distinction* offers perhaps the most valuable contemporary analysis of class difference.[51] Bourdieu locates a chief failing of what he calls the Marxist theory of class – the dominant political framework among his fellow French intellectuals, whose tradition has been shaped over the past half-century by a range of relationships to the Communist Party – in its inability to explain 'all those oppositions

of Class', in John R. Hall (ed.), *Reworking Class* (Ithaca: Cornell University Press, 1997): 107–31.

50. Marx, *Capital*, Vol. III: 1026.
51. Pierre Bourdieu, *Distinction. A Social Critique of the Judgement of Taste*, trans. Richard Nice (Cambridge: Harvard University Press, 1984).

which structure the social field and which are not reducible to the opposition between owners and non-owners of the means of economic production', such as the ambiguous class position of intellectuals and other cultural producers.[52] In contrast to the two-class system imagined by Marxists, 'the social space is a multi-dimensional space, an open set of relatively autonomous fields', such as the field of culture, within which we might distinguish the academic field, the artistic field, etc., 'fields which are more or less strongly and directly subordinate, in their functioning and their transformations, to the field of economic production'.[53] Social class position is therefore multidimensional, as individuals occupy locations in more than one such field; in each a person's position can be defined in terms of a relation to a type of social power, which Bourdieu calls a mode of capital on the model of the dominant form of social power. For instance, university professors possess 'cultural capital', in the form of degrees, institutional connections, mastery of certain jargons, etc., which allow them to dominate others, both in their particular field of action, the university, and outside it, say as experts on television or advisors to trade unions or governments. Successful exercise of this power yields 'cultural profits' in the form of increased prestige, higher positions, etc.; and cultural capital can be converted into economic capital, yielding above-average salaries and other privileges. This model explains why cultural capitalists, who share power and therefore interests with the monied upper class but base their social advantages on a competing social principle, both serve the bourgeoisie in various ways and have traditionally seen themselves as to some degree at odds with the latter, and even, on occasion, behaved accordingly.

As this example shows, Bourdieu's theory stays within the explanatory logic of modern understandings of social class as 'sets of agents who occupy similar positions and who, being placed in similar conditions and submitted to similar types of conditioning, have every chance of having similar dispositions and interests, and thus of producing similar practices and adopting similar stances'.[54] In contrast, 'class' in Marx's use is not a set of sociological descriptions but, like his value theory, an attempt to expose a dynamic structure hidden by the complexity of 'economic' and 'sociological' phenomena. This structure, he believed, emerges to view

52. Pierre Bourdieu, 'Social Space and the Genesis of "Classes" ', in *Language and Symbolic Power*, trans. Gino Raymond and Matthew Adamson (Cambridge: Harvard University Press, 1991): 244.
53. Bourdieu, 'Social Space': 245.
54. *Ibid.*: 231.

at moments of extreme social crisis, but is normally obscured by more immediate interests.

Under normal conditions, the bourgeois discourse of class is the dominant one, because it corresponds to the immediate problems faced by all sectors of society. As Marx and Engels wrote already in *The German Ideology*, 'separate individuals form a class only insofar as they have to carry on a common battle against another class; in other respects they are on hostile terms with each other as competitors'.[55] Workers organize their mutual competition by means of ethnic, gender, national and other groupings – as well as on a purely individual basis – groupings that effectively obscure the commonalities in which Marx was interested. Similarly, although the shared class interest of capital is expressed in a general insistence on the basic rightness and even necessity of the existing social order, capitalists compete with each other by all convenient means, forming interest-group coalitions where this is helpful. Class struggle, as the mutual competition for the stakes defined by capitalist property relations, is a normal feature of bourgeois society, which in itself does not call that society's conceptions of property into question.[56] This is why, as Engels suggested in his editorial note, Marx would have been able to illustrate his conclusion to *Capital*, in which the application of economic categories points to their systematic inadequacy, from reports in any week's newspapers.

The correctness of Marx's understanding of the ideological structure here in play is demonstrated by the history of social politics since his time, in which right and left alike have tended to couch their programmes by reference to a general (classless) social interest and at the same time to conceive of the organizational basis of politics in terms of interest-group formations. The bourgeois discourse of class has thus moved historically between economic apologetics, which discover in the operation of the market the principle of fair rewards for each of the factors of production (and, as in such different frameworks as Smith's political economy and modern general equilibrium economics, the optimization of social welfare), and leftwing demands for a fairer (re)distribution of social

55. Karl Marx and Frederick Engels, *The German Ideology*, in MECW, Vol. 5 (New York: International Publishers, 1976): 77.
56. It may be remembered that by his own account Marx first became aware of the centrality of economic categories to modern politics when, as a journalist in the early 1840s, he covered disputes in the Rhineland over 'thefts of wood and the division of landed property': see Marx, *Contribution*: 262.

wealth. Revolutionary movements, in contrast, represent not the definition of a group interest but the calling into question of a form of society.

It is to illuminate not the existence of conflicting social interests, which are indeed legion, but the question of fundamental social transformation that Marx's analysis abstracts from the myriad occupational groupings and income levels to focus attention on the distinction between the producers and appropriators of surplus-value. With respect to these groups – employees and owners of industrial capital, enterprises producing capitalist commodities – 'the class relation between capitalist and wage-labourer is ... already present, already presupposed, the moment the two confront each other' in the employment contract, for 'although in the act [of exchanging money for labour] the possessor of money and the possessor of labour-power relate to each other only as buyer and seller, ... the buyer appears right from the start as the possessor of the means of production which form the objective conditions for the productive expenditure of labour-power by its possessor'.[57]

The power of this approach is visible in its ability to assimilate social groupings outside the definitions basic to the theory of surplus-value. Surplus-value is appropriated not only by the industrial capitalists in whose enterprises it is produced but also by commercial and financial capitalists and owners of natural resources. Commerce and finance are, Marx explains, necessary aspects of capitalist activity, involving as it does the sale of commodities and the handling of money; just as 'money capital, commodity capital, and productive capital ... do not denote independent varieties of capital' but 'simply particular functional forms of industrial capital, which takes all three forms in turn',[58] the specialization of these functions in specific enterprises does not create a new social class, but further divisions (in addition to those due to industrial competition) within the class of exploiters. Similarly, workers in these non-surplus-value-producing forms of capital encounter the structure of exploitation, since they are wage earners, participating, along with their employers, in reproducing industrial capital.[59] While they create no surplus value, 'their unpaid labour ... does create [their employer's] ability to appropriate surplus-value, which, as far as this capital is concerned, gives exactly the same result; i.e. it is its source of profit'.[60]

57. Karl Marx, *Capital*, Vol. II, trans. David Fernbach (Harmondsworth: Penguin, 1978): 114–15.
58. *Ibid.*:133.
59. See Marx, *Capital*, Vol. II: 210–11.
60. Marx, *Capital*, Vol. III: 407. Marx's prescience here is quite striking: 'The commercial worker belongs to the better-paid class of wage-labourer; he is

In other words, Marx's analysis of surplus-value production as an operation carried out on the level of society as a whole, rather than firm by firm, appears again in the understanding of class as the social relation of wage-labourers to capitalists. This is clear from the way the concept of 'labour-power' is introduced in Volume I of *Capital* as embodied not in the actual employees of any moment, but in their families, from which both the individual and his or her eventual replacement must come.[61] Necessary labour, the value of labour-power, is represented by the money required to buy consumption necessities for the worker's family as a whole (and by extension, even for the currently unemployed, in so far as money is advanced to keep them alive). Similar considerations apply to the economics of the state, a topic not treated in *Capital* but reserved for the last of Marx's intended six books. It is easy to see how his analysis could be extended, on the one hand, to the members of the capital-owning elite who take on state functions, or who enter the ruling class by way of governmental careers, performing tasks necessary for capital and rewarded with a share of surplus-value;[62] and, on the other, to state employees, also paid out of surplus but with wages and working conditions appropriate to those paid for their labour-power.

---

one of those whose labour is skilled labour, above-average labour. His wage, however, has a tendency to fall, as the capitalist mode of production advances, even in relation to average labour. Firstly, because the division of labour within the commercial office means that only a one-sided development of ability need be produced ... Secondly, because basic skills, knowledge of commerce and languages, etc., are reproduced ever more quickly, easily, generally, and cheaply, the more the capitalist mode of production adapts teaching methods, etc. to practical purposes' (*ibid*.: 414–15).

61. 'Hence the sum of means of subsistence necessary for the production of labour-power' – whose price determines the price of labour-power – 'must include the means necessary for the worker's replacements, i.e. his children, in order that this race of peculiar commodity-owners may perpetuate its presence on the market', Marx, *Capital*, Vol. I: 275.
62. Similarly, Pierre Bourdieu's description of the academic and cultural intelligentsia as 'the dominated fraction of the dominating class' may be justified in Marxian terms by reference to its activity as a sort of class-wide household servitors of the bourgeoisie. The homology between their position and that of bourgeois housewives might be taken to explain their traditional gendering as feminine by comparison to the masculinity of business and financial managers. It also goes far to explain the relation of cultural to economic capital: it is not their incomes, high in relation to those of most wage earners but mostly not based on capital-ownership, that set cultural producers in the dominant class; it is their class function that is signalled by the award of relatively high income or, when this is not convenient (as with an increasing majority of academics) of status.

We can now understand Marx's placement of the critique of class discourse at the end of his treatment of capital, before the projected books on landed property and wage labour. While from the point of view of 'everyday life' – or its theoretical representative, vulgar economics – three factors, each rewarded by its own form of revenue, cooperate equally in production, according to Marx capital has theoretical, because practical, primacy over landed property and wage labour. Labour-power takes the form of a commodity because both the means of labour and the product of past labour confront the worker in the form of capital. And 'the transformation of these conditions of labour into capital also involves the expropriation of the immediate producers from the land, and hence a specific form of landed property'.[63]

This specific form is theoretically secondary to capital in that its revenue is a portion of the surplus-value extracted from the labour force by the social capital; the burden of Marx's theory of rent is just to demonstrate that this is the reality measured by the appearance of rent as a 'return' to land employed in production. Here the distinction of classes, in part a residue of the central economic importance of land-ownership in precapitalist society and in part a mode of inter-capitalist competition, hides the unitary origin of rent and profit (and interest) alike in surplus-value.

As this in itself suggests, things are somewhat different with respect to the relation between capital and wage labour. As Marx explains in Chapter 26 of the first volume of *Capital* ('The Secret of Primitive Accumulation'), 'in themselves, money and commodities are no more capital than the means of production and subsistence are. They need to be transformed into capital.' For this to happen, there must be

> the confrontation of ... two very different kinds of commodity owners; on the one hand, the owners of money, means of production, means of subsistence, who are eager to valorize the sum of values they have appropriated by buying the labour-power of others, and therefore the sellers of labour. ... [W]ith the polarization of the commodity-market into these two classes, the fundamental conditions of capitalist production are present.

Even though it is one process 'which operates two transformations, whereby the social means of subsistence and production are turned into capital, and the immediate producers are turned into wage-labourers', Marx

63. Marx, *Capital*, Vol. III: 1018.

specifies the resulting social relation as the 'capital-relation'.[64] Labour is 'the universal condition for the metabolic interaction between people and nature, ... and it is therefore ... common to all forms of society in which human beings live'. Specifically, 'the general character of the labour process' – the transformation of elements of the environment into forms assimilable by human beings – 'is evidently not changed by the fact that the worker works for the capitalist instead of for himself ...'.[65] What is changed is that the means of production and subsistence confront the worker as capital, the property of an employer. It is this that forces him or her to become an employee, and the labour performed to become wage labour.

In everyday parlance it is the capitalist who is the producer of a product; from the capitalist point of view, as Marx says, 'the labour process is a process between things the capitalist has purchased, things which belong to him', as therefore the product will also belong to him.[66] *Capital* is a study of the production system as seen from this viewpoint, that of political economy (and economics), because this is the dominant viewpoint in a society in which capital is the dominating social category. Accordingly, the category of class arises at the conclusion of Marx's study – as in historical reality – as an attribute of society dominated by capital, and so as it is conceptualized in everyday life and its social-scientific theorizations, defined by source of revenue. The division of the social product among the three forms of income both reflects and reproduces the distribution of property (and propertylessness) that in reality defines the 'three great classes'. 'The so-called relations of distribution' that Ricardo identified as 'the principle problem in political economy' thus 'correspond to and arise from historically particular and specific forms of the production process'.[67] This is what Marx had substituted for Ricardo's problem: that of the 'conditions of existence' of the modern classes, whose solution is the analysis of the capital relation.

4. Class and crisis

A deeper – more abstract – understanding of class than that embodied in the Trinity Formula is required only for theoretical reflection on the possible replacement of capitalism by a form of society not based on the exploitation of one social group by another. According to Marx, it is

64. Marx, *Capital*, Vol. I: 874.
65. *Ibid.*: 290–1; translation amended.
66. *Ibid.*: 292.
67. Marx, *Capital*, Vol. III: 1023.

capitalism itself that generates this possibility, giving the abstraction of class phenomenal reality by 'the concentration of the means of production in a few hands', by 'the organization of labour itself as social labour: through cooperation, division of labour and the association of labour with natural science' and by the 'establishment of the world market', which by globalizing capitalism creates the preconditions for a general transformation of social relations.[68] Under conditions of acute economic crisis, he believed, with the growing inability of commodity exchange to provide for the needs of large numbers of people, the conflict between the two aspects of modern society, as mode of human reproduction and as mode of exploitation, would lead to a reconfiguration of the category of class in thought and action.

The phenomenon Marx called fetishism, the identification of relations between human beings with relations between commodities, including the ascription of social powers of production to the capital owned by employers, is a particular and central case of what seems to be a general human tendency to view historically specific institutions as inescapable features of social life. It was Marx's early view that the dynamism of capitalism would be sufficient to overcome this tendency. As a result of the 'constant revolutionizing of production', according to *The Communist Manifesto*, 'man is at last condemned to face with sober senses, his real conditions of life, and his relations with his kind'.[69] Specifically those 'real conditions' would be faced in the form of 'the commercial crises that by their periodical return put on its trial, each time more threateningly, the existence of the entire bourgeois society'.[70] In the decades between the writing of the *Manifesto* and *Capital* it became clear to Marx that the end of this process would not arrive as rapidly as he had once hoped it would. But, as I noted at the beginning of this essay, he continued to locate the point at which the necessary transformation of consciousness might occur in the situation of economic crisis.

In the meantime, he completely reconceived the nature of crisis. While the *Manifesto* still spoke in classical accents of crises of overproduction, the theory first worked out in the 1850s and spelled out in detail in *Capital* located the origin of the tendency to periodic crisis in the tendency of

68. Marx, *Capital*, Vol. III: 375; compare Vol. I: 929.
69. K. Marx, *The Communist Manifesto*, ed. F.L. Bender (New York: Norton, 1988): 58.
70. *Ibid.*: 60. Crises are described as outstanding exemplars of 'the revolt of modern productive forces against modern conditions of production, against the property relations that are the conditions for the existence of the bourgeoisie and its rule'.

the rate of profit to fall. The latter was explained as an effect of the process of capital accumulation, which by its tendency to increase the productivity of labour decreases the proportion of value-producing labour-power in the production system as a whole. The fall of the profit rate disrupts the balance between newly generated surplus-value and the existing invested capital, which dictates the minimum surplus-value requirements for continued accumulation. Thus accumulation itself generates a process that 'would entail the rapid breakdown of capitalist production, if counteracting tendencies were not constantly at work ...'.[71] Although to speak this way is to depart from Marx's usage, economic crisis might be said to be the most important of these counteracting tendencies: the devaluation of capital accomplished by deflation and bankruptcy decreases the value of invested capital relative to labour-power employed and so increases the rate of profit. In Marx's own words, crises are 'violent solutions for the existing contradictions, violent eruptions that re-establish the disturbed balance [between the production of surplus-value and the existing mass of capital] for the time being'.[72]

The historical phenomenon of crisis must therefore be distinguished from the idea of a radical breakdown of the capitalist system. Yet Marx made crisis the focus of his theory of capitalism because it embodied, he believed, the idea of a limit to capitalist development. This is what Henryk Grossmann meant when, in his study of Marx's theory of accumulation as a theory of breakdown, he emphasized that the latter is 'the necessary basis and presupposition of [Marx's] crisis theory ...'. That is, 'the crisis according to Marx represents simply a momentarily broken and incompletely unfolded breakdown tendency, thus a transitory deviation from the "trend line" of capitalism'.[73] This trend line pointed to an absolute cessation of accumulation, theoretically deducible from the value analysis of capital, in the form of what Marx termed 'an absolute overproduction of capital', a point at which 'no further additional capital could be employed for the purpose of capitalist production'. In reality, however, the crisis provoked by the approach to such a point would restore

71. Marx, *Capital*, Vol. II: 355; the passage quoted refers specifically to the centralization of capitals as a response to declining profitability. For a concise summary of Marx's breakdown-and-crisis theory, see *Grundrisse*: 750; for a clarifying contemporary account, see Paul Mattick, *Economic Crisis and Crisis Theory*, trans. Paul Mattick, Jr (Armonk: M.E. Sharpe, 1981): Chapter 2 and *passim*.
72. Marx, *Capital*, Vol. III: 357.
73. Henryk Grossmann, *Das Akkumulations- und Zusammenbruchsgesetz des kapitalistischen Systems* (Leipzig: Hirschfeld, 1929): 140.

conditions of capital expansion, 'and so we go round the whole circle once again' as 'the same cycle of errors is pursued once more'.[74]

Anton Pannekoek was therefore agreeing with Grossmann (and with Marx) when he wrote in what was intended to be a critique of Grossmann's work that 'the working class must expect not a final catastrophe but many catastrophes – political, like wars, and economic, like crises – which periodically, now regularly, now irregularly but as a whole become ever more devastating with the increasing reach of capitalism'.[75] The Marxian theory of 'breakdown', while it provides a theoretical basis for a revolutionary politics in predicting the temporality of any stabilization through expansion of the capitalist system, cannot be taken as an adequate theorization of an actual end of capitalism. With its explanation of the continuing sequence of crises that form the empirical appearance of the 'trend line' to the cessation of accumulation, the theory of breakdown itself suggests the possibility of an indefinite postponement of its endpoint. It is only the revolutionary action of the working class that can transform an economic crisis into the end of the capitalist system.

According to Grossmann, the political significance of the breakdown theory lay in its demonstration that the final goal of the abolition of capitalism is 'not an ideal imported into the workers' movement "from outside" by way of speculation, whose realization is reserved for the distant future independent of the struggles of the present' but 'the result of the immediate class struggles of everyday life ...'.[76] In this again Grossmann was true to Marx's original vision, as expressed, for example, in his wish that the First International act 'to combine and generalize the spontaneous movements of the working classes, but not to dictate or impose any doctrinaire system whatsoever'.[77] The idea was that the working class, organized by capitalism in workplaces and industries ever more interconnected by the development of the world market and the centralization of capital, would be led in the course of its efforts to improve its conditions of work and life into a final confrontation with the social system as such. The growth of capitalism spells the growth of 'misery, oppression, slavery, degradation and exploitation ...; but with

74. Marx, *Capital*, Vol. III: 360, 364.
75. Anton Pannekoek, 'Die Zusammenbruchstheorie des Kapitalismus' [1934], in Karl Korsch *et al.*, *Zusammenbruchstheorie des Kapitalismus oder revolutionäres Subjekt* (Berlin: Karin Kramer Verlag, 1973): 44.
76. H. Grossmann, *Das Akkumualtions- und Zusammenbruchsgesetz*: 602–3.
77. K. Marx, 'Instructions for Delegates of the Provisional General Council' [1866], in K. Marx, *On the First International*, ed. Saul Padover (New York: McGraw Hill, 1972): 27.

this there also grows the revolt of the working class, a class constantly increasing in numbers and trained, united and organized by the very mechanism of the capitalist process of production' until 'the monopoly of capital becomes a fetter upon the mode of production that has flourished alongside and under it'. With these words – nearly the last of *Capital* that Marx prepared for publication[78] – Marx returned to the formulation of the 'guiding thread' enunciated in the introduction to the *Contribution*, stating his subject as the theoretical analysis of the conditions of class struggle.

To comprehend both the status quo and its possible revolutionary transformation does not, as we have seen, require a distinct theory of class. This is a consequence of the fact that the exploitation relation exists in the historically specific form of the capital–wage labour relation; – an understanding of its *modus operandi* is given by the system of economic categories and its critical analysis. In Mauke's words, 'Marx's social theory, the critique of political economy, as such already contains a general theory of class in capitalism.'[79] 'Class' is the name under which the social forces that brought capitalism into being have conceptualized, in however confused a way, their mutual relations and their relations to other social systems. 'Class' therefore naturally constitutes a conceptual pole around which the exploited organize opposition to their domination by capital. But any revolutionary implications of such conceptualizations will be grasped not by (let us say, sociological) theorizing about classes but by the critical examination of 'the system of bourgeois economy' commenced by Marx in *Capital*.

78. Marx, *Capital*, Vol. I: 929. This passage comes near the end of Chapter 32, 'The Historical Tendency of Capitalist Accumulation', which is clearly the conclusion of Marx's text; Chapter 33, 'The Modern Theory of Colonization', was most likely placed at the end of the volume in order to lull the German and Russian censors, who notoriously read only the first and last chapters of books (see Karl Marx, *Oeuvres*, t. I, ed. Maximilien Rubel [Paris: Gallimard/Pléïade, 1963]: 1224, n. 2).
79. M. Mauke, *Die Klassentheorie*: 8. I am much indebted for improvements to earlier versions of this text to the participants in the International Seminar on Marxist Theory, especially Martha Campbell, Geert Reuten and Tony Smith; and to the members of the International Workers Keg Party, particularly (as usual) Jeff Wilson. I wish to dedicate this essay to the memory of Serge Bricianer.

3
Capital in General and Marx's *Capital*

Christopher J. Arthur

When Marx published the first substantial result of his studies in 1859 the title was *Contribution to the Critique of Political Economy*; Book One[1] was 'On Capital', of which 'Section One' was 'Capital in General'.[2] However, when the first volume of Marx's masterpiece appeared in 1867 the overall title was *Capital*; 'Critique of Political Economy' was reduced to a sub-title; and the term 'capital in general' had vanished. Nonetheless, it is argued below that some such *concept* was implicit in Marx's research programme. It was Roman Rosdolsky, in his path-breaking study of Marx's *Grundrisse*, the first 'rough draft' of *Capital* written in 1857–58, who discovered there the methodological importance of the idea of 'capital in general'.[3] He argued also that it retains its importance in any attempt to judge what is going on in the three volumes of *Capital* given to us. These volumes comprise what was originally intended to be covered by the topic of capital in general, and this was to be followed by studies of competition and other things, as the following plan sent to Engels in 1858 shows: '*Capital* falls into 4 sections. a) Capital *en géneral*. (This is

1. 'Book One' is a reference to Marx's intention to write *six* 'books'; 'Capital' was to be followed by 'On Landed Property', 'On Waged Labour' etc., as he explains in the Preface (K. Marx and F. Engels *Collected Works* [MECW], Vol. 29: 261).
2. MECW, Vol. 29: 269.
3. *The Making of Marx's 'Capital'* (trans. P. Burgess, 1977): 41–53.

the substance of the *first* instalment.)[4] b) *Competition*, or the interaction of many capitals. c) *Credit*, where capital, as against individual capitals, is shown to be a universal element. d) *Share capital* as the most perfected form (turning into communism) together with all its contradictions.'[5] Given the fact that an examination of the texts shows Marx used the term 'capital in general' in different ways, the main body of this chapter will be divided into two. The issues to be treated in each part are as follows:

1. The various definitions of 'capital in general' in Marx's *Grundrisse* will be disentangled.

2. My own substantive treatment of a topic arising out of one of these definitions will be given: in this I will build on a hint in the *Grundrisse* about the possibility of using Hegel's logic in articulating this idea of capital in general.

1. Marx's *Grundrisse*

The source for Marx's understanding of 'capital in general' is his *Grundrisse*. Unfortunately there is no text-book-like account; instead there are a number of different places in which he refers to the idea, with some brief indications as to its meaning. Let us examine the evidence.

4. This 'first instalment' corresponds to what is called 'Section One' in the 1859 *Critique* and to that mentioned in a letter to Lassalle: 'The first instalment ... contains 1. Value, 2. Money, 3. Capital in general (the process of production of capital; process of its circulation; the unity of the two, or capital and profit; interest). This constitutes a pamphlet [!!] in its own right' (to Lassalle, 3 November 1858, MECW, Vol. 40: 287).
5. Marx to Engels, 2 April 1858, MECW, Vol. 40: 298. I object to Rosdolsky's repeated claim that the *Grundrisse* not only has a definite structure but that it was written 'from the outset' in accordance with the four point plan in which 'capital in general' was to be followed by 'competition' and so forth (12–14; 40–1; 51). There is no textual evidence for this whatsoever. The plan concerned was communicated to Engels when the manuscript of the *Grundrisse* was almost complete. In my view 'at the outset' Marx had only a vague idea of how the research would proceed; he used simply the titles 'chapter on money' and 'chapter on capital' (Marx's *Grundrisse*, trans. M. Nicolaus, 1973). Compare the rough plans on 108, 227, 264, 275; as late as 362 he is still working with the hopelessly inadequate introductory plan of 108. The plan sent to Engels should be understood as the *result* of his investigations. Likewise the idea of three 'sections' of capital in general (corresponding roughly to the final three volumes of *Capital*) was developed during the writing and first set down subsequent to it. See the plan sent to Lassalle cited in the previous note; see also MECW, Vol. 29: 423; 511. (Clarity over the status of the *Grundrisse* is not helped by the habit of its editors of imposing these heads from *Capital* on it.)

At the outset we must register a philological problem. Where the English translations have 'capital in general' this does not always refer to the same German phrase. For the most part the equivalent is '*Capital im Allgemeinen*',[6] but occasionally it is '*Capital überhaupt*'.[7] While the first is clearly a *logical* reference, the latter is a pretty everyday sort of term: '*überhaupt*' is in fact an adverb, the first dictionary definition being 'generally'. In the following quotations the first (logical) phrase is to be assumed, except where I give notice otherwise.

The first discussion of the general concept of capital is where Marx, evidently under the influence of Part Three of Hegel's *Science of Logic,* attempts to sketch out some categories with which to grasp the dialectic of capital. He divides it into 'generality', 'particularity' and 'singularity'.[8] These are all in their turn sub-divided triadically according to the same logic.

> *Capital* I. *Generality*: (1) [*Generality of capital*] (a) emergence of capital out of money. (b) Capital and labour (mediating itself through *alien* labour). (c) The elements of capital dissected according to their relation to labour (Product. Raw Material. Instrument of labour.) (2) *Particularization of capital*: (a) Capital circulant, capital fixe. Turnover of capital. (3) *The Singularity of capital*: Capital and profit. Capital and interest. Capital as *value,* distinct from itself as interest and profit.
> II. *Particularity*: (1) Accumulation of capital. (2) Competition of capitals. (3) Concentration of capitals. ...
> III. *Singularity*: (1) Capital as credit. (2) Capital as stock-capital. (3) Capital as money market.

It will be seen that 'I. *Generality*' divides into capital's production (the *general* moment, covering some of the topics of *Capital* Volume I), its '*particularization*' (part of Volume II) and its *singularity* (profit and interest, i.e., part of Volume III). So even if all three volumes fall within capital as '*Generality*' one can still say that *relative to each other* Volume I is at the level of the general and the following volumes at the level of the particular and the singular. The next relevant passage is some 35 pages later, where Marx differentiates 'capital in *general*' (here, its *differentia specifica* as a value

6. *Marx–Engels Gesamtausgabe* (MEGA), Part II, Vol. 1: 229.
7. MEGA, Part II, Vol. 1: 260.
8. *Grundrisse*: 275. Strictly speaking the first occurrence of this idea is on 264, but I assume this unsatisfactory plan is superseded by that a few pages later, discussed here.

form) from 'a *particular* form of capital' and from 'an *individual* capital as distinct from other individual capitals'.[9] (This is again an important reminiscence of the moments of Hegel's Concept.)

Another 35 pages later, a quite different idea appears. Here 'capital in general' (*Capital überhaupt*) is identified with *'capital as such,* say the capital of the whole society'.[10] This is significant for its ambiguity: 'capital as such' *neglects* difference: 'capital of the whole society' *absorbs* difference.

However, Marx was still not satisfied and returned to the question from yet another angle: 'Capital in general ... does indeed appear *only as an abstraction* ... which grasps ... the aspects common to every capital. ... However, capital in general, as distinct from the particular real capitals, is itself a *real existence.*'[11] The example he gives of the latter is that of banking and loans, where capital 'doubles' itself into the 'general form' accumulated in banks and the particular applications for which chunks of it are lent. What is important here is that while the latter are obviously 'particular real capitals' the 'general form' too has separate 'real existence' rather than being a mental classification. He concludes the passage by making a distinction between notions of generality once more: 'while the general is therefore on the one hand only a *mental differentia specifica,* it is at the same time a *particular* real form alongside the form of the particular and individual'.[12] Marx here, therefore, explicitly recognizes that two shapes of capital in general are possible (mental abstraction and reality); but he does not go on to address their methodological pertinence. Yet it is clear enough that very different kinds of argument would be supportable on their basis.

Then the term 'many capitals' begins to show up in the text.[13] As 'real' they are contrasted with 'what they all have in common'[14] or with their 'general concept'.[15]

Finally, towards the very end, yet another concept of capital in general appears: 'capital in general is not a mere abstraction ... if I regard capital as the general economic basis of a class as distinct from another class'.[16]

So what can be made of these genial suggestions of Marx's *Grundrisse*? In my view Marx does not stop to articulate a preferred account of capital

9. *Ibid.*: 310.
10. *Ibid.*: 346.
11. *Ibid.*: 449.
12. *Ibid.*: 450; MEGA Part II, Vol. 1: 359.
13. *Grundrisse*: 414, 517, 520, 649, 651, 661, 729, 731, 760.
14. *Ibid.*: 517.
15. *Ibid.*: 520, 649.
16. *Ibid.*: 852; MEGA Part II, Vol. 1: 715.

in general, and one is forced to suppose that he thought all the accounts given have some validity. Let us list them:

1. Most obviously and unproblematically Marx makes a distinction between many capitals and 'what they all have in common' their 'general concept' or 'capital as such'. This sort of distinction is familiar to us from many sciences. It is a favourite procedure of empiricism which abstracts common elements to form a class. Here, as Marx observes, the 'real' capitals are the many and the 'general' is merely an abstract identity ('dumb generality') which is generated by the observer and granted expositional priority in a linear logic.
2. Marx says that there is a sense in which capital in general can be understood not merely as a mental abstraction from the plurality of real capitals but as itself a real existence, unlike the previous case, and he cites banking and loans.
3. A quite different approach appears in discussions in which capital in general is not so much contrasted with many capitals but appears in a tripartite division, along the lines of Hegel's logic, between generality, particularity and individuality.
4. Sometimes capital in general appears as the total social capital.
5. Capital in general appears as the economic basis of a class opposed to another.

It may be worth noting that (as far as I can discover) Marx never at any point directly counterposes capital in general and many capitals. Rather, 'capital in general' is contrasted with the individuality of capital, while many capitals contrasts with 'capital as such', what all capitals have 'in common'. (Of course Marx does contrast 'capital in general' and 'competition' and links the latter with 'many capitals'.)[17]

While I think Marx never abandoned the idea of the three volumes of *Capital* as all part of 'capital in general', at the same time I am impressed by Marx's articulation of the various levels of analysis given in the *Grundrisse* passage containing a *tripartite* scheme. In this chapter, then, I am concerned primarily with developing the sense of capital in general in which it is part of a tripartite logic in which the general contrasts with the particular and the singular.[18]

17. *Grundrisse*: 649–51, 731.
18. For a consideration of the other senses of 'capital in general' see my companion paper 'Capital, Competition and Many Capitals'. The purpose of the two papers, taken together, is to attempt a rational reconstruction of Marx's thought with a view to accommodating *all* the aforementioned characteristics of capital in general.

2. The idea of capital in general

2.1 A nine-point plan

It will be recalled that in Marx's *Grundrisse* there is a plan (given on p. 44) organised in Hegelian fashion according to the three moments of 'the Concept'. But each of these categories is further divided by Marx into three on the same principle. I call this, therefore, Marx's 'nine-point plan'.

Marx's *Grundrisse* makes continual reference to Hegel's logical apparatus.[19] While Marx never succeeded in making clear to himself just why Hegel's logic was so relevant to the dialectic of capital, I believe that the answer to this is that capital as a value-form is constituted through the abstraction from the heterogeneity of use-value inherent in commodity exchange in suchwise as to acquire an *ideal* reality which then imposes itself on *material* production.[20] (This opposition between value and use-value becomes more and more highly mediated but always threatens to burst out into open contradiction.) In my view the 'Idea of Capital' is objectively present only if, in imposing itself on production and circulation, its *logical* dimensions find corresponding material instantiations. This is why I think Marx was on the right track in borrowing logical categories from Hegel.[21] It is appropriate therefore to examine Hegel's *Science of Logic* in order to discover anything which will help to illuminate our investigation of the dialectic of capital in general and especially of a 'nine-point plan'. The key chapter for our purposes is the first full chapter of the last part entitled 'The Notion', which argues that this must be taken as the unity of its three moments (Universality, Particularity and Individuality: U, P, I for short), while, moreover, it is perfectly present in each at the same time.

Before proceeding, it is necessary to mention the problem of English translations of Hegel's categories; for in trying to compare Nicolaus's rendering of Marx's *Grundrisse* and Miller's translation of the *Science of*

19. Marx wrote to Engels, on 14 January 1858, that in leafing through Hegel's *Logic* again he found 'much to assist me as regards the *method* of treatment' (MECW, Vol. 40: 249). This was written right in the middle of his *Grundrisse* work.
20. See my paper 'From the Critique of Hegel to the Critique of Capital', in T. Burns and I. Fraser (eds), *The Hegel–Marx Connection* (2000).
21. In a review of the first volume of *Capital*, E. Dühring complained that 'Marx's strict adherence to the framework of Hegel's logic went so far that the Hegelian figures of the syllogism were used to present the concept of capital ... as the outcome of a dialectical process' (MEGA, Part II, Vol. 9: 784). So far from denying this, Marx responded by writing: 'Hegel is my teacher. ... Nonetheless I have adopted a critical attitude towards my master, stripping his dialectic of its mysticism' (*ibid.*: 787).

Logic we are handicapped by the fact that they choose different English terms for the same German one. I will not endeavour to harmonize the translations; but I give in Figure 3.1 the relevant alternatives and ask the reader to bear in mind that the English terms are to be taken as equivalent in value.

German	*Science of Logic*	*Grundrisse*
Begriff	Notion	Concept
Allgemeine	Universal	General
Einzelnheit	Individuality	Singularity

Figure 3.1 Variations in translation from German in *Science of Logic* and *Grundrisse*

As we just said Marx redivides each of these categories (U, P, I) into three again, apparently on the same principle. Marx gives no explanation of why a triple differentiation should be repeated in this way. I hold that such a complexity is required if the Idea of Capital is to be developed in two distinct dimensions, namely the differences that arise from its development within itself – in Hegelian terms its *reflection into itself* – on the one hand, and the differences that arise from its development into a system of capitals – in Hegelian terms its *reflection against itself* into another – on the other hand.[22]

Marx himself seems to have given up his nine-point plan almost immediately; but much of *Capital* is congruent with its general principle; so I believe it continued to inform his thinking. Below I reinstate it, and reconstruct it. The problem with Marx's version is that he crammed in material at different levels of abstraction; seeing no way to make it work he abandoned the experiment. But it works well enough if things are kept simple by confining the categories solely to those of industrial capital. In this plan, if the larger context is disregarded, then the three volumes of *Capital* stand to each other as universality, particularity and individuality; for while Volume I addresses the most abstract general determinations of the concept of capital, notably valorization, Volume II addresses the various particularizations of capital in its movement (e.g. the metamorphoses of capital) and Volume III addresses both the forms of appearance of capital in actuality as single sources of profit while yet bringing back these individuals to the universal through their integration in a systemically determined competitive struggle for profit. The upshot is a single totality governed by general laws of motion.

22. An Hegelian warrant for this I take to be given in the appropriate section of his *Logic*: *Hegel's Science of Logic* (trans. A.V. Miller, 1969): 604.

reflection into self ⇓ / reflection into other ⇒	Universality (commonality)	Particularity (difference)	Individuality (systemic unity)	
Universality (self-relation)	**1** The capital relation (self-valorization) (exploitation)	**2** Constant and variable capital	**3** Accumulation of capital (reserve army)	[cf. Volume I, 'The Process of Production of Capital']
Particularity (self-specification)	**4** Metamorphoses of capital	**5** 5. Fixed capital, circulating capital, turnover times	**6** Reproduction and circulation of total social capital via departments	[cf. Volume II, 'The Process of Circulation of Capital']
Individuality (as singularity)	**7** Cost price and profit (rate of profit)	**8** Branches of capital with differing organic compositions (competition, prices of production)	**9** The laws of motion of capital (falling rate of profit, crises, historical destiny)	[cf. Volume III, 'The Process as a Whole']

Figure 3.2 The Idea of Capital in General

Let us now proceed to my reconstruction, which is set out in Figure 3.2. This gives, in the form of a nine-box diagram, the categorial structure of capital, as I understand it. Before I explain the diagram in detail it should be noted that, although the moments of 'the Concept' express themselves in both dimensions just mentioned, this is in subtly different ways. The horizontal movement starts from universality considered as something capitals have in common, their abstract identity with each other, thence to a moment of particularization that allows for a set of differences to emerge such that different species or fractions of capital may be developed, and individuality here refers to the unification of the differences in a totality. The vertical movement starts from the universal in the sense of the comprehensive in which capital is self-related, the movement of particularization is one in which the core notion of capital becomes further determined through an inner movement of self-specification, and, finally, individuality here asserts the singularity of capital that allows it to be individuated as a capital. At the level of the totality this individuality makes it a single whole, a self-grounded system. As far as the Idea of Capital is concerned, the category of totality does not merely stand for a conceptual claim that all capital is a unity but addresses a material interconnection existent as the capitalist *system*.

Another way of looking at it is that the horizontal development is an unfolding of what is implicit whereas the vertical movement is one of concretion. There are, in truth, two ways of treating the particularization of the universal. For an analogy let us work them through in terms of the example of 'human being'. One can say that the most essential difference between human beings is sex; but this can be expressed in two different ways: either one can say the category 'human being' embraces both men *and* women, or one can say that each human must be a man *or* a woman (it must be one but cannot be both). Along the first – extensive – route each and every different human being is grasped as one among many, considered as *one of them*. Along the second – intensive – route a human being is individualized as the concentration of diverse determinants, male, white, bearded, etc. And *not* female, black, etc. Hence considered apart from others. On the extensive dimension all the different human beings are yet considered in their unity. On the intensive dimension a complete picture of this special person is built up.

What now of capital? In so far as capital exists as unity and difference then both these kinds of particularizations are relevant. In so far as different capitals are part of a connected system then categories which make possible difference *between* capitals must be developed and then connected (across columns). In so far as capital is a single whole its *own specifications* must be brought out and concretized, for example the general rate of profit, and its movement (down rows). The intersection of rows and columns makes the whole scheme more complex of course.

Now let us turn to the detailed exposition of the Idea of Capital outlined in Figure 3.2, beginning with Box 1: the capital relation. This represents the 'core idea' of capital. The categories in play here presuppose and incorporate earlier ones such as commodity and money, of course, but these are not categories *of* capital but of the value form, of which capital is the highest expression.[23] (We shall come back to the logical 'becoming' of capital later.) The simplest way to define capital is to say that it is ideally the movement of self-valorization and that this relation is materially grounded in exploitation. Box 1 therefore constrains the origin of the whole scheme, of the articulated idea of capital. It is the most abstract beginning in that it is determined as capital-in-general in general, so to speak. However in another sense it is nonetheless a beginning that is concrete in itself because it has the inner difference, and unity-of-difference, making up the concept of valorization. Valorization is not a simple category, for it is the outcome of the movement whereby the initial amount of money, M, generates a difference from itself, namely a surplus value, which is yet posited as an increment of M, thus identifiable with the principal and united with it in a new sum of value. Marx treats this development in these terms in the first volume of *Capital*.[24] However, this relates to the *form* of valorization; if capital is to *ground* its self-valorization it must sink into its substance, namely alienate itself in factors of production, notably labour, which is a difference from capital that remains in *contradictory* unity with it. So all these topics are subsumed in the capital relation set in Box 1.

All capitals have this capital relation *in common*, but there are within each capital two distinct fractions which play particular roles in the process of valorization. As we know, Marx distinguished these and termed them 'constant' and 'variable' capital. These we place in Box 2.

However, these are yet precisely fractions of the totality of capital which achieves its wholeness in its fully developed relation to itself in keeping within itself the valorized value it throws up, making this itself

23. ' "Capital" brings the value form dialectic to closure ... "Capital" is both a determination of the more universal category "value", and itself a universal with its own forms or determinations' (Tony Smith, *The Logic of Marx's Capital*, 1990: 99). The dialectical logic of the value form I expound in a section of my paper 'From the Critique of Hegel to the Critique of Capital' (2000).
24. *Capital*, Vol. I (trans. B. Fowkes, 1976): 256.

capital, now *accumulated* capital; thus in Box 3 is placed the category of accumulation. The general significance of valorization is that through this process capital produces itself. This is the theme of the first row; and the category of accumulation, given in Box 3, signifies that the result of its productive activity achieves its wholeness by bringing together the result of valorization within its own valorizing movement in a spiral of accumulation. Marx goes to some trouble to argue that accumulation is essential to the concept of capital, both in the sense that without it capital collapses to a mere sum of money indistinguishable from money intended as means of circulation and that capital oriented to valorization cannot be considered to have fulfilled itself in a single circuit, but must throw itself again and again into circulation together with its increment. Any deduction from profit made to defray the living expenses of the capitalist is an unfortunate contingency, however necessary to the capitalist, in which role, as consumer of capital, he acts in contradiction to his role of capitalizer. Marx also ingeniously reworks even the conceptualization of simple reproduction so as to demonstrate that the apparently eternal capital which provides the capitalist with his revenue is better conceived as itself virtually accumulated capital, for the capitalist would long since have consumed his principal had capital not been fructiferous.

Marx also demonstrates in detail the dialectic of capital and labour inherent in accumulation at the level of capital as a whole, namely the way the common drive for exploitation works itself out systematically in centralization and concentration of capital and, notably, the generation of the reserve army of labour.

The whole first row, compared with the following rows, is characterized as the universal. (So is the first column from the perspective of a columnar sequence. It will be recalled that I argued these universals are subtly different from each other. In some ways both represent determinations common to all capitals. The row categorizes the essentialities of capital as such; it is not therefore to be understood as the basis of subsequent differences that arise between capitals, but as being what capital as a whole is all about. The generality of the first column, by contrast, stands towards subsequent columns as a generality that allows for the common character to achieve distinctly different specificities.)

The second row is a differentiation of this universal into its specific moments, its movement within itself; the first row concentrates on the relation of capital to itself as a whole, issuing in a spiral of accumulation; what is left out is the inner movement that allows the result to emerge *as a result*. Accumulation requires capital to throw itself again and again into circulation; so the next turn of the categorial exposition is to consider the circulation of capital in the second row. This develops capital's inner determinations as they emerge as moments of its circulation process. (It is important to understand that there are two meanings of circulation, one narrowly defined as against production, the other – that meant here – referring to the entire round of capital's movement including the phase of production activity.) Marx refers to this sort of particularization when he mentions that such categories as fixed and circulating capital are essential particularizations posited within the concept of capital in general: capital in general is 'not an arbitrary abstraction, but an abstraction which grasps the specific characteristics of capital ... and the distinctions within this abstraction are likewise abstract particularities which characterise every kind of capital, in that it is their position or negation (e.g. fixed capital or circulating capital)'.[25] Just so all those which Marx expounded throughout Volume II, the book on particularization *par excellence*. A good case of this is the differentiation of capital into departments. These departments flow conceptually from the inner character of capital as producing itself through combining produced means of production and labour power in an exploitative process; clearly these factors point to the existence of other capitals whose circuits provide their conditions of existence.[26] The two main departments of reproduction, for example, are not to be seen as two stages of production, following the scheme that to produce (workers') consumption goods we must first produce the instruments of production. Rather they are to be grasped as *formally* different in that their outputs must be *interchanged*, such that each department absorbs output from the other.

So on my account the universal of valorization of the first row is differentiated according to formal considerations in the particularity of the second row. The second row, however, also follows the dialectic of the concept, beginning (at Box 4: the metamorphoses of capital) with the general consideration that capital moves in a circuit of forms, namely money capital, production capital and commodity capital.[27] This is a

25. *Grundrisse*: 449. See also 623.
26. To be sure, in his *Grundrisse*, after stressing that any value required entering an individual circuit as a presupposition of valorization can only be a value posited by another capital, Marx hastily backs off with the reminder that 'the discussion must not be diverted by the introduction of *many* capitals'(*ibid.*: 517; MECW, Vol. 28: 440). Yet the relevance of departments is a rather different issue; it does not address the many capitals that provide specific means of production to specific capitals, it refers to particular classes of such industries, not many capitals in the sense of individual ones.
27. These three in my view also instantiate the logic of U, P, I as I have argued in 'The Fluidity of Capital and the Logic of the Concept', in C. J. Arthur and G. Reuten (eds), *The Circulation of Capital* (1998).

concretization of Box 1 in that it unpacks the process of valorization so as to exhibit the inner articulation of capital as a circuit of phases. Marx gives a detailed treatment of the specific forms in which the circuit proceeds in Volume II and this is the foundation for what follows.

Considered as a universal, Box 4 forms the start of the dialectic of the second row. If we now look at this circuit from the standpoint of discovering the specifically different circulatory determinations that affect the telos of valorization (just as we discovered in Box 2 that constant and variable capital have a different function in the production of surplus-value) then the crucial question is the turnover time (which is just as important for accumulation as the absolute rate of exploitation); for it turns out that different fractions of capital turnover at different rates; as a crude first approximation the categories of fixed and circulating capital emerge here (at Box 5).

The category of 'reproduction of capital', set in Box 6, considers all these developments in their totality. The general notion of reinvestment of capital together with the circulation processes just analysed gives rise to the idea of capital's acquiring their inputs from each other and disposing of outputs both to each other and to the working class. From this development of the circuit of capital into a circuit of circuits, Marx created one of his most original and striking contributions: the concept of capital as the reproduction and circulation of total social capital through the interchanges between departments differentiated in form according to the destination of the outputs. For the notion of the metamorphoses of capital brings with it the relation of one circuit to others, and therewith the link to a totality of circuits, and hence the category of total social capital emerges.[28] The departments assign capitals to *different* fields (in accordance with the principle of the second row) but these are structured as differences *within* total social capital (in accordance with the principle of the third column). Box 6 also acts under the influence of the category of accumulation to generate the category of 'expanded social reproduction'.

The third row, the unity of production and circulation of capital, is our next topic, and it is to be developed as shapes of the singularity of capital, the category that concretizes capital in determinate fashion. The substantive themes of the third row are singular in that they specify in determinate fashion the way in which capital measures itself against itself, in the notion of rate of profit, general rate of profit and falling rate of profit.

28. *Capital*, Vol. II (trans. D. Fernbach, 1978): 429–30.

Box 7 contains the general idea of this: that to be capital is to have a definite rate of profit; in measuring itself against itself over time capital determines its singularity as against the general notion of its production of itself through its metamorphoses. Here the wholeness of capital is asserted over the phases of its metamorphoses while at the same time the difference that emerged from it, namely the incremental profit, is brought into relation with the principal ('cost price') to yield the defining property of capital, its rate of profit. Since this is what all capitals have in common it is at the same time the starting point of the row.

In Box 8 are the consequences of the fact that in the first instance *different* capitals have *different* rates of profit. In the column above it we find determinations of capital that have a particular bearing on how this rate of profit is determined. In this column such relevant distinctions as organic composition and turnover time are mentioned; now these are brought to bear on the process of competition (singleness reflected *against* itself) for capital, in that branches of production normally have very different organic compositions from each other, which would generate different rates of profit were a uniform rate not established through the realization of appropriate prices of production. (Notice the necessity – somewhat underplayed by Marx – to do a transformation based on turnover times as well as organic composition in the static sense.)

In Box 9 is the culmination of the scheme. When capital is treated as a single whole its systematic tendencies, its inherent laws of motion emerge. In the nine-point plan of the Idea of Capital, the third row (concrete wholeness) and the third column (systemic connection) are moments of unity. Box 9, as the unity of both these unities, is where the dimensions are brought to a focal point, the moment where the system of capital achieves its individuality. This is where 'all the action is' so to speak: along with the increasing organic composition of capital goes the tendency of the rate of profit to fall. This is also the appropriate place to consider crises and the historical destiny of capital. When capital expresses itself as a whole we gain a comprehensive idea of the laws of its motion, as the systematic interconnection of a rich variety of inner determinations reflected into each other and against each other so as to form a system. We study 'the life of capital', in which the destiny of individual capitals is only a moment in the overall growth of the whole social capital.

It is of interest to illustrate the detail of the chart by a comparison of the content of Box 6 with Box 8. The reason for this selection is that Neo-Ricardian solutions to their 'transformation problem' always conflate these two determinations of the system of capital. Both topics exhibit a combination of 'particularity' and 'individuality', while 'universality' is held in the background. Reproduction of social capital through departments (Box 6) has the logic of complementary specification (as row) within a connected system (as column), whereas the struggle over profit (Box 8) has the logic of individuation (as row) in and through external opposition (as column). In both cases 'Generality' is in the background, but as a necessary context: e.g. the first presupposes that all capitals require purchases and sales, while the second presupposes that all capitals are concerned with maximizing profit, and there is a given aggregate surplus-value. So what follows? These topics are so different they should be considered separately (as Marx did) before their integration. The chart allows the required 'logical space' to separate them.

In the same way the logical apparatus deployed here makes possible the comprehension of the transformation problem as a function of the site of intersection of row and column. Box 8 is not merely, as columnar, the emergence of *difference between* capitals, here different organic compositions and rates of profit, but, as row, it is reasserted *wholeness* over against the *inner differences* emergent between *branches* of total social capital. So, together, the immediately posited differences in rates of profit in different branches are constrained by the general rate of profit characterizing the individual whole while allowing the play of difference in competition. Thereby the positing of a uniform rate of profit identical with the general rate of profit of total social capital results in difference posited *systematically* namely the assignment of the appropriate individual prices of production.

2.2 Marx's 'Capital': a comparison

If we step back now to compare with Marx's work my reconstruction of the Idea of Capital, the following observations are in order. Following Marx the whole scheme I refer to as 'the Idea of Capital in general' in contrast to further topics such as 'competition'. Here 'capital in general' is a way of talking about the general concept of capital, of capital as such, prior to the incorporation of the developments that may arise from contingent features of the interaction of a multitude of real capitals. Like Marx I see the need to divide the material of capital in general thus defined into three books. Not only does each of the books have within it the structure of the concept (U, P, I), they stand to each other as follows: the first book – capital in general (in the Hegelian sense where generality is distinguished from particularity and individuality); the second book – capital in particularity; the third book – capital in its individuality, unifying determinations from the first two. Thus I combine in appropriate ways both of these usages of capital in general from Marx's *Grundrisse*:

capital in general as a general idea is what Marx calls capital as such, or in its concept, over against competition, but within this Idea of Capital we have its essential form-determinations comprising two dimensions of the conceptual scheme 'U, P, I'.

Substantively I follow Marx in thinking of the first book as concerned with the production of capital, and of the second book as concerned with the circulation of capital. For the third book I would be inclined to restore Marx's original rubric 'Capital and Profit'.[29] Of course, compared with Marx's original my own reconstruction allows a stronger case for this in that Marx has much else in his Volume III than is comprehended in my third row. (Some of these areas I will mention shortly when I discuss financial and commercial capital.)

Marx picks out in Volume I some systematic tendencies of capitalist accumulation which it might be thought better placed in Box 9. In particular a striking feature of Marx's first volume is the chapter on the Historical Tendency of Accumulation. Let us consider this issue. In my plan I hold it back to the end because it seems paradoxical to present the downfall of capitalism before all its structures and tendencies have been explored and its capacity to absorb and restructure emergent contradictions considered. On this basis one might conclude that Marx's Volume I, Chapter 32, is out of place and should have been held back. A possible reply to this complaint is that whatever other barriers capital confronts in its own development, its supersession can only be the outcome of the bringing to a head of those contradictions inherent in the capital relation and accumulation. Thus it is possible to present this outcome abstractly having developed those notions. Perhaps the procedure may be explained by comparison with Marx's pointing out the possibility of crisis inherent in the metamorphoses of commodities through money. In both cases it is clear that a wealth of more concrete determinations would be required to pass from the abstract anticipation to a comprehensive grounding. Thus a full treatment of the historical destiny of capital may yet be *abstractly* anticipated at the level of Volume I.

2.3 An alternative exposition

It is a formal consequence of the nine-point plan that it would be logically possible to develop its argument column by column, instead of row by row. On this basis the scheme would start with the first column and deal with the *common* characteristics exhibited by capital, beginning with valorization, ending with its rate of profit; then would follow the second

29. MECW, Vol. 33: 7, 69, 346.

column and all the *distinctions* that are relevant to the quantitative determination of this rate of profit would be addressed; and finally, using the material grouped in the third column, the *overall dynamics* of accumulation and reproduction would be treated in a book called The Process of Accumulation of Capital. Each column would traverse at its own level of analysis the phases of production, circulation and their unity.

As far as I can see the only substantive change to Marx's exposition this entails is that '*c*' and '*v*' (and their sum in cost price) would first stand for the value of means of production and the value of labour power, since their thematization as fractions of capital ('constant' and 'variable') would not occur until later when it would serve as the necessary general preliminary to the notion of the organic composition of capital, and the bearing of differences in this on profit rates. (It is worth noting that the problem of the placing of the Historical Tendency of Accumulation, considered earlier, would be obviated if the books were written column by column rather than row by row, for then it would be deferred to the third book in any case.)

The superiority of an exposition following the rows is that it moves as quickly as possible to the idea that capital is conceptually inseparable from the notion of accumulation, that it is a developing, yet contradictory, whole. For this, the notion of rate of exploitation is essential, but not immediately the notion of rate of profit.

2.4 The larger context

It is clear that the nine-point plan includes only the categories of industrial capital. There are two other dialectics relevant to this central idea: its 'becoming' and its relation to financial and commercial capital. Let us address these in turn.

First let us note an ambiguity in Marx's own comments on his 'beginning'. In the Introduction to the *Grundrisse* there is a clear statement that 'capital' as the overriding moment of the economic totality must form the beginning. Yet the *Grundrisse* itself began with Money and ends with a passage on Value 'to be brought forward', while the *Capital* will begin with the Commodity. Next it is noticeable that when Marx was struggling to draw up the plan of *Capital* he was uncertain how to present the early chapters on commodities and money: were they part of the thematization of capital itself or were they merely introductory? I refer here to the period 1858–67. In some of these plans 'capital in general' is the title for the whole of this part of his 'Critique of Political Economy' but in some other plans this title is preceded by the sections on 'value' (later 'commodity') and 'money'. The latter alternative occurs in his letter to Lassalle of 11 March 1858, and these sections are no doubt to what he referred in an earlier letter (22 February 1858) when he said the book 'On Capital' would contain 'several introductory chapters'. But in his outline sent to Engels on 2 April 1858, 'value' and 'money' are placed as chapters within 'capital in general'. However in his plan of June 1858 he reverted to the set up with introductory chapters before 'capital in general'. Then when Marx published the first instalment of his 'Critique' in 1859 both schemes were in evidence! Its content is organized in the hierarchy: On Capital, Section One – Capital in General, Chapter 1 – The Commodity, Chapter 2 – Money or Simple Circulation; but its Preface says that the first part of the first book on capital has 'the following chapters: 1. The commodity; 2. Money or simple circulation; 3. Capital in general'.[30] Moreover 'A) The Process of Production of Capital' appears in the original draft of the 1859 *Contribution* under the head of 'Chapter Three. Capital'.[31] Chapter 1 was 'The Commodity' and Chapter 2 'Money'. But in *Capital* itself these chapters are all brought within the book on 'The Production Process'.

Perhaps these textual discrepancies are of no importance. However, it might be thought important whether commodities and money are on the same *categorial level* as capital or not. A related point of interest is that in the *Grundrisse* Marx several times adverted to a distinction between 'the becoming of capital' and 'capital that has become', although the exact moment of this transition is not very clear. The passage that fits our purposes best is this:

> As a relation distinct from that of [commodity] value and money, capital is *capital in general*. ... But we are still concerned neither with a *particular* form of capital, nor with an *individual* capital as distinct from other individual capitals etc. We are present at the process of its becoming. This dialectical process of its becoming is only the ideal expression of the real movement through which capital comes into being.[32]

Another passage spells out this 'becoming':

> Since we speak here of capital *as such*, capital in the process of becoming, we are not yet concerned with anything else in addition – in that the many capitals are not yet present for us – nothing but itself and simple

30. MECW, Vol. 29: 261.
31. *Ibid.*: 501.
32. *Grundrisse*: 310.

> circulation out of which it absorbs value in the double form of money and commodity and into which it throws itself in the double form of money and commodity.[33]

Taking the above considerations into account I believe that 'introductory sections' are needed to trace 'the becoming of capital'. (Reference to 'becoming' should be understood here not in an historical but in an ontological sense, and as such 'preserved' in sublated form; for 'the becoming of capital' is a continuous process of production and circulation of commodities and money as 'moments of the motion of capital itself'.)[34] Such 'introductory sections' would trace the development of the inner 'presuppositions' of the concept of capital. These elements can themselves be conceptually ordered according to the determinations of the concept of value, namely the commodity as the particular, money as the universal, and capital as the individual.[35] The whole is grounded properly only when the 'general formula' gains an adequate content in industry, but what is produced thereby is only mediatedly commodities, for these are subordinated to the real aim: the production, circulation and accumulation of capital. Thus, if the becoming of the capital form *presupposes* circulation, capital-that-has-become *determines* the circulation of commodities and money as abstract appearances of its own movement, as necessary to its concept, not merely as presuppositions but as forms of itself.[36]

33. *Ibid.*: 729.
34. *Ibid.*: 450.
35. Compare *Capital*, Vol. I: 255. Marx applied these categories (U, P, I) even to C–M–C: 'The C at the end of the two extremes of the circuit C-M-C has a different formal relation to M. The first C is a particular commodity which is compared with money as the universal commodity, whereas in the second phase money as the universal commodity is compared with an individual commodity. The formula C–M–C can therefore be reduced to the abstract logical syllogism P–U–I; whereas particularity forms the first extreme, universality characterises the common middle term and individuality signifies the final extreme' (MECW, Vol. 29: 330–1). This use of the dialectic of 'the Concept' by Marx may not be immediately perspicuous unless it is thought of in terms of the point of the two exchanges. In the first C-M, the C as an individual has no interest for the exchanger who is endeavouring to gain money (which itself exchanges against *all* commodities); what interests him from this point of view is merely that the C be *some* particularization of the universal. In the second exchange M–C, by contrast, the point is to secure, not just any C but the *one* whose individual characteristics will satisfy a certain need.
36. *Grundrisse*: 255, 262, 358, 460.

So the logical 'pre-history' of the concept of capital has to be given before the Idea of Capital is developed.[37] This Idea is that of industrial capital. But, complementing the necessity to deal first with money and commodities, there arises as a corollary to industrial capital the *externalization* of inner moments of its circuit, money capital and commodity capital, as the separated accessories finance capital and commercial capital such that three 'persons' of capital emerge.[38] Again these are logically related according to the moments of the concept: individuality (industrial capital); universality (financial capital); and particularity (commercial capital). I call this trinity 'the expanded idea of capital'. (The reason for the 'logical' attributions is as follows: commercial capital deals with exchange-values in their existence as a range of particular *kinds* of commodities; whereas industry, as the source of them, must necessarily produce every commodity as a *single* embodiment of value, and financial capital deals strictly with the *universal* concretization of value, money.) We can therefore extend the earlier diagram backwards and forwards: see Figure 3.3.

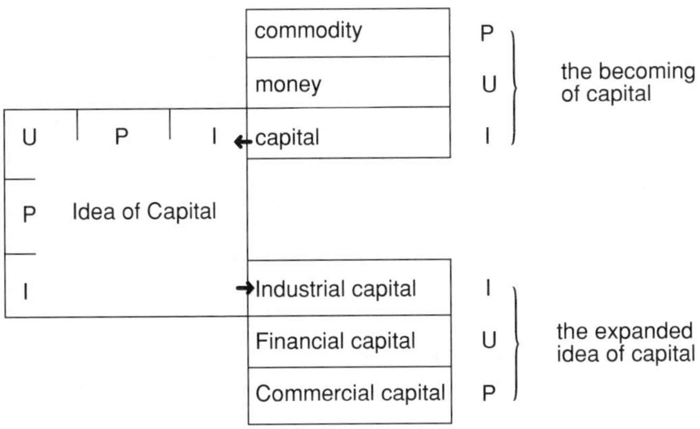

Figure 3.3 The Idea of Capital in General: its becoming and expansion

37. Tony Smith has pointed out to me that Hegel's *Philosophy of Right* contains just such an introduction (§4–29) developing the concept of right from the moments of the will. Hegel confines this discussion to an 'Introduction' precisely because the 'coming into being of the concept of right falls outside the science of right' (§2).
38. MECW, Vol. 33: 47–8, 63–4. Marx has 'externalisation' (*Veraüsserlichung*) in the title of *Capital*, Vol. III, Chapter 24: see MECW, Vol. 37: 388; Fernbach misleadingly substitutes for this the alternative 'superficial' in his translation *Capital*, Vol. III (trans. D. Fernbach, 1981): 515.

Here, then, we have a further expansion of 'the Idea of Capital in general' (as against 'Competition').

If we now glance at Marx's *Capital* again, in order to compare his arrangement with our expanded plan, we find that his first volume not only covers our first row of the Idea of Capital but that he naturally has several (introductory) chapters on commodities and money; however he does not mark these off, as he perhaps should have done, under some such rubric as 'the becoming of capital'. As things stand it appears strange that a book titled 'The Production Process of Capital' should begin with exchange and discusses production only when the chapter on the labour process is reached. (Of course the early chapters may be considered to be about the production of the *form* of capital, but this would be a slightly unusual sense of 'production'.) Once the dialectic of the value form is separated out, then the central part of Volume I is indeed about capital's production of itself through valorization, surplus-value and its transformation into capital, with the relevant circulatory moments taken as given. His second volume corresponds exactly to our second row, but his third volume contains not only our third row but what I have called the expanded idea of capital, together with rent insofar as it is influenced by the formation of a uniform rate of profit.

If we review the contents of Volume III of *Capital* according to the framework I have presented then the sequence of parts is as follows. Part One (The Transformation of the Rate of Surplus Value into the Rate of Profit) corresponds to Box 7 of my nine-point plan (see Figure 3.2); Part Two (The Transformation of Profit into Average Profit) corresponds to Box 8; Part Three (The Law of the Tendential Fall of the Profit Rate) is about one of the most important systematic tendencies that fall into Box 9.

Then Parts Four and Five (Commerce and Finance) are dealt with in my scheme under the head of the expanded Idea of Capital. In one sense they complement industry as having their own specific functions in the overall life of capital, and it might be thought that in so far as they form a triad of conceptual determinations it is wrong to give any special importance to one as against the others, just as it would also be to prioritize one of the circuits of an individual industrial capital discussed in Volume II of *Capital*. Moreover this triad is more comprehensive, it seems, than the dialectic of the nine-point-plan. The monetary moment especially seems to bulk large in both cases. For it is in money form that capital is able to measure itself, and its increment, in the form of autonomous value uncontaminated by matter. In a similar way the money market supplies finance to each industry and firm only after making such assessments. This seems the place at which the unity of the whole capitalist system posits itself explicitly and the place at which the key decisions are taken. Nonetheless, because capital as a whole cannot expand itself systematically on the basis of its mere form, industry as the site of the origin of surplus value is the truly individual moment, and the centre-piece of *Capital*.

Part Six of Volume III on Rent lies outside my conceptual scheme of capital in general because it pertains to a revenue extracted from capital on the basis of another form of property that *confronts* capital. However, Marx decided to bring the topic into Volume III 'only in so far as the treatment of the remaining themes demands' (meaning by this the dynamics of distribution of aggregate surplus value).[39]

3. Conclusion

In spite of the large claims made by Rosdolsky about the category of 'capital in general' being the key to understanding Marx's work, we find that this notion is nowhere rigorously developed in the sources. Rather Marx seems to have been using the term in a multiplicity of ways. All these play some role in his work and a reconstruction, such as that attempted here, can locate each sense in a specific context of discussion. Thus we may follow Marx in distinguishing capital in general as a topic to be addressed prior to the thematization of competition. The study of capital in general in this sense is a study of its conceptual determinations, articulating its forms with each other in a comprehensive totality. Then we may mark off another sense of capital in general in which *within* the aforementioned conceptual determinations one may contrast those which are universal, particular and individual. These very roughly correspond to much of the three volumes of *Capital* as we have it.[40] In the main part of this chapter I developed a reconstruction of this material in the form of a nine-point plan (with appropriate extensions).

I think I have done enough here to show that with certain revisions Marx implicitly followed through his intuitions about the importance of the concept capital in general, and his intuitions regarding Hegel's logic. The movement of the three volumes of *Capital* outlines the forms of 'capital in general' (in the first sense discriminated earlier) and their articulation in a systematic whole. In other words the thematization of capital in general articulates the system of 'form-determinations'

39. Marx to Kugelmann, 6 March 1868: *Letters on 'Capital'*, trans. A. Drummond, 1983: 126.
40. The only commentator to have seen this is Felton C. Shortall. See his *The Incomplete Marx*, 1994: 445–53.

structuring the capital totality.[41] At the same time the complexity of our nine-point plan allows us to say that relative to each other Volume I contains a discussion at the level of capital as universality, Volume II of capital as particularity and the first three parts of Volume III of capital as singularity. The rest of Volume III develops essential 'externalizations' and expansions of this concept of capital.

'Capital in general' drops out of Marx's writing by the time he published Capital. Why? Perhaps in the interests of popularization. The logical scaffolding which allowed the construction of the edifice was stripped away and the forms shown to move on their own basis. Here, however, I have put the logical categories back, so as to gain a clearer overview of the dialectic of the form-determinations of capital.

Bibliography

Arthur, Christopher J. (1998), The Fluidity of Capital and the Logic of the Concept, in C.J. Arthur and G. Reuten (eds), *The Circulation of Capital: Essays on Volume II of Marx's 'Capital'* (London/New York: Macmillan/St Martins Press).

— (2000), From the Critique of Hegel to the Critique of Capital, in T. Burns and I. Fraser (eds), *The Hegel–Marx Connection* (Basingstoke: Macmillan).

Hegel, G.W.F. (1821), *Elements of the Philosophy of Right* (ed. A. Wood, trans. H.B. Nisbet) (Cambridge: Cambridge University Press, 1991).

— (1812), *Hegel's Science of Logic* (trans. A.V. Miller) (London: George Allen & Unwin, 1969).

Marx, K. *Grundrisse* (trans. M. Nicolaus) (Harmondsworth: Penguin, 1973).

— *Capital* Vol. I (trans. B. Fowkes) (Harmondsworth: Penguin, 1976).

— *Capital* Vol. II (trans. D. Fernbach) (Harmondsworth: Penguin, 1978).

Marx, Karl and Engels, Friedrich *Marx–Engels Gesamtausgabe* (MEGA) (Berlin/Amsterdam: Dietz Verlag Internationales Institut für Sozialgeschichte Amsterdam).

— *Collected Works* (MECW) (London/New York/Moscow: Lawrence & Wishart/International Publishers/Progress Publishers).

— *Letters on 'Capital'* (trans. A. Drummond) (London: New Park Publications, 1983).

Rosdolsky, Roman (1968), *The Making of Marx's 'Capital'* (trans. P. Burgess, 1977), (London: Pluto Press).

Shortall, Felton C. (1994), *The Incomplete Marx* (Avebury: Aldershot).

Smith, Tony (1990), *The Logic of Marx's Capital: Replies to Hegelian Criticisms* (Albany NY: State University of New York).

41. For example Marx calls fixed and circulating capital form-determinations (*Formbestimmungen*); see MECW, Vol. 29: 11; *Grundrisse*: 623; MEGA, Part II, Vol. 1: 509.

4
Hostile Brothers
Marx's theory of the distribution of surplus-value in Volume III of *Capital*

Fred Moseley[*]

> 'Capitalists are like hostile brothers who divide among themselves the loot of other people's labour.'
>
> Karl Marx, *Theories of Surplus-Value*, Vol. II: 29

It is argued in this chapter that the main overall subject of Volume III of *Capital* is the *distribution of surplus-value*, i.e., the division of the total amount of surplus-value into individual component parts, first into equal rates of profit across branches of production and then the further division of surplus-value into commercial profit, interest and rent. This subject of Volume III is clearly stated in the following passage from the introduction of Part Seven of Volume I, which provides an succinct overview of the three volumes of *Capital*:

> The capitalist who produces surplus-value, i.e. who extracts unpaid labor directly from the workers and fixes it in commodities, is admittedly the first appropriator of this surplus-value, but he is by no means its ultimate proprietor. He has to share it afterwards with

* I would like to thank my colleagues and co-authors in this book for their many helpful comments on my chapter, both at our Amsterdam conference and in subsequent correspondence, especially Chris Arthur and Geert Reuten who disagree with me the most.

> capitalists who fulfil other functions in social production taken as a whole, with the owner of land, and with yet other people. Surplus-value is therefore split up into various parts. Its fragments fall to various categories of person, and take on various mutually independent forms, such as profit, interest, gains made through trade, ground rent, etc. We shall be able to deal with these modified forms of surplus-value only in Volume 3.
>
> Karl Marx, 1867 (1977): 709

The chapter argues further that Marx's theory of the distribution of surplus-value in Volume III is based on the fundamental premise that the total amount of surplus-value has already been determined by the theory of surplus-value in Volume I, *and is taken as given* in the Volume III theory of the distribution of surplus-value. The division of the total surplus-value into individual parts does not change the magnitude of the given, predetermined total surplus-value. The total surplus-value that is distributed in Volume III is always and by definition *the same magnitude* as the total surplus-value determined in Volume I.[1]

Contrary to the standard interpretation of Marx's theory, the total surplus-value that is determined in Volume I is *not a different magnitude*, i.e., a more 'abstract' magnitude, compared to the total surplus-value that is distributed in Volume III. Rather, the total surplus-value that is determined in Volume I is the *same magnitude* as, and is thus just as concrete as, the surplus-value that is distributed in Volume III. Both refer to the total 'income to capital' in the real capitalist economy. I argue that, in Marx's theory, this total empirical surplus-value is first determined in Volume I and then taken as given and distributed in Volume III.

I also argue that this distinction between the determination of the total amount of surplus-value in Volume I and the distribution of surplus-value in Volume III is closely related to Marx's distinction between 'capital in general' and 'competition' (or 'many capitals'). Capital in general refers to the essential properties that all capitals have in common.

1. When I say that the total amount of surplus-value is determined prior to its division into individual parts, and that this total amount is not affected by this division, I mean the determination of surplus-value within a given period. It is of course possible (and likely) that the distribution of surplus-value in a given period will affect the total amount of surplus-value produced in subsequent periods. However, the methodological principle of the prior determination of the total surplus-value still applies within a given period. I thank Tony Smith for clarifying this distinction for me.

The most important common property of capitals is their capacity for self-expansion, i.e., their ability to produce surplus-value. Since this common property is shared by *all* capitals, the analysis of capital in general is necessarily an analysis of all the capitals taken together, that is of the total social capital. Therefore, the main question addressed in the theory of capital in general in Volume I is the determination of the total amount of surplus-value produced in the capitalist economy as a whole. The theory of competition in Volume III is concerned with the relations among individuals capitals, and, in particular, to the distribution of surplus-value among individual capitals.[2 3]

Marx's theory of the production of surplus-value in Volume I is usually presented in terms of an individual capital. However, Marx's theory in Volume I is not just about the surplus-value produced by a single capital. Rather, it is about what all capitals have in common: the production of surplus-value. Therefore, any given individual capital is analysed as a

2. Parts One and Three of Volume III remain at the level of capital in general prior to the analysis of the distribution of surplus-value. The distribution of surplus-value into individual parts is not considered in these parts. Part One is a key transition from capital in general to competition that introduces the concepts of profit and the rate of profit, and will be discussed below. Part Three is, of course, about Marx's theory of the falling rate of profit. This theory clearly applies to the general rate of profit for the total social capital. Marx emphasized explicitly the tendency of the rate of profit to decline is derived prior to the division of surplus-value into industrial profit, merchant profit, interest and rent.

> We are deliberately putting forward this law before depicting the decomposition of profit into various categories which have become mutually autonomous. The independence of this presentation from the division of profit into various portions, which accrue to different categories of persons, shows from the start how the law in its generality is independent of that division and of the mutual relationships of the categories of profit deriving from it. Profit, as we speak of it here, is simply another name for surplus-value itself, only now depicted in relation to the total capital, instead of to the variable capital from which it derives. The fall in the rate of profit thus expresses the falling ratio between surplus-value itself and the total capital advanced; it is therefore independent of any distribution of this surplus-value we may care to make among the various categories.
>
> Marx, 1894 (1981): 320

Part Two is discussed after Part One because of the logical connection between 'the transformation of surplus-value into profit' in Part One and 'the transformation of profit into average profit' in Part Two. Surplus-value is first transformed into profit by relating it to the total capital, and then profit is

representative of *all* capitals and hence of the total social capital. The determination of the amount of surplus-value produced by one capital is representative of the amount of surplus-value produced by *all* capitals together, and hence of the total surplus-value produced by the total social capital. Marx expressed this representative nature of the analysis of individual capitals in Volume I in an important outline at the end of the *Manuscript of 1861–63*, as follows: 'In capitalist production [i.e., in Volume I], *each capital is assumed to be a unit, an aliquot part of the total social capital'* (Marx and Engels, 1861–63c [1991]: 299; emphasis added).

Marx's theory of the distribution of surplus-value in Volume III explains the individual parts of surplus-value – equal rates of profit, industrial profit, merchant profit, interest and rent – as the necessary 'forms of appearance' of the unifying substance of surplus value, which is produced by the unpaid labour of workers. These different forms of surplus-value appear to the agents of capitalist production – and in general also to economists – to originate from separate and independent sources (e.g., interest from capital, rent from land, etc.). But Marx's theory demonstrates that these forms of surplus-value are all derived from the same source: the surplus labour of workers. In other words, Marx's theory demonstrates the 'inner connection' of the different forms of appearance of surplus-value. Furthermore, Marx's theory explains how the illusion that these individual parts of surplus-value come from separate and independent sources is a 'necessary appearance,' i.e., an appearance that,

---

further transformed into average profit by the equalization of profit rates across industries. Marx argued that the second transformation is a necessary consequence of the first transformation. Since capitalists measure surplus-value in relation to the total capital and attempt to maximize the rate of profit rather than the rate of surplus-value, competition among capitals tends to equalize rates of profit across industries. Therefore, Part Two is discussed after Part One in order to maintain this necessary connection between these two transformations of surplus-value into profit. But the distinction between capital in general and competition would have been clearer if the order of Parts Two and Three had been reversed. Part Three will not be discussed further in this paper because it is not directly related to the distribution of surplus-value.

3. Chris Arthur has argued in his chapter 'Capital, Competition and Many Capitals' (this volume) that Volume III remains at the level of abstraction of capital in general, even though he agrees that Volume III is about the distribution of surplus-value. For the purposes of my paper, the precise meaning and boundaries of capital in general and competition is less important than the distinction between the production of surplus-value in Volume I and the distribution of surplus-value in Volume III, and the quantitative premise of the determination of the total amount of surplus-value prior to its distribution, both of which Arthur accepts.

although false, necessarily arises on the basis of capitalist production.[4] Therefore, another purpose of Volume III is to explain, not only these important phenomena related to the distribution of surplus-value, but also why these phenomena appear differently to the agents of capitalist production (and to economists). Marx announced his intention to explain these more concrete forms of appearance in the first paragraph of Volume III:

> Our concern is rather to discover and present the concrete forms which grow out of the *process of capital's movement considered as a whole* ... The configurations of capital, as developed in this volume, thus approach step by step the form in which they appear on the surface of society, in the action of different capitals on one another; i.e. in competition, and in the everyday consciousness of the agents of production themselves.
>
> Marx, 1894 (1981): 117

The overall logical structure of Volume III and its relation to Volumes I and II has hardly been discussed in the Marxian literature. Sweezy's classic *The Theory of Capitalist Development* discusses Part Two (the 'transformation problem') and Part Three (the 'falling rate of profit'), but does not discuss the rest of Volume III, and presents no interpretation of the overall structure of Volume III and its relation to the first two volumes. Mandel's Introduction to the 1981 edition of Volume III briefly mentions once, but does not emphasize, that the subject of Volume III is the distribution of surplus-value, and he does not explicitly discuss the relation between the whole and the individual parts of surplus-value. The currently dominant Sraffian interpretation of Marx's theory argues that Volume I is about the 'value system' and Volume III is about the 'price system'. However, discussion of the 'price system' is almost always limited to Part Two of Volume III only (the 'transformation problem'). Little or nothing is said about the rest of Volume III, not even Part One, which is a crucial preliminary to Part Two. Parts Four through Seven are seldom if ever discussed, and no explanation is given of how these other parts relate to Part Two. At an international conference on Volume III in 1994 in Bergamo, Italy (commemorating the 100th anniversary of the publication of Volume III), there was very little discussion of the overall logical structure of Volume III (see Bellofiore 1998). The main exceptions

4. This aspect of Volume III of explaining the 'necessary forms of appearance' of surplus-value is emphasized by Patrick Murray's chapter in this volume.

to this general neglect of the overall logical structure of Volume III and its relation to Volumes I and II have been Mattick, Rosdolsky, Foley and Dussel. But no one has yet presented a comprehensive and detailed interpretation of Volume III as a whole. That is what this chapter aims to do.

This chapter reviews the individual parts of Volume III in order to demonstrate these three main points: (1) that the main subject of Volume III is the distribution of surplus-value; (2) that the total amount of surplus-value has already been determined in Volume I and is taken as given in the Volume III analysis of the division of this total amount into individual parts; and (3) that these individual parts of surplus-value are explained as 'necessary forms of appearance' of the common substance of surplus-value, produced by surplus labour. The chapter concludes with a discussion of a very important letter written by Marx to Engels in 1868 which summarizes the overall aims and logic of Volume III and which provides further support for the interpretation of Volume III presented here. (Moseley [1997] provides further textual evidence to support this interpretation from earlier drafts of Volume III, especially the *Manuscript of 1861–63*.)[5]

The passages presented in this chapter state over and over again that the total surplus-value is determined prior to its distribution. Most of the passages do not state explicitly that the total surplus-value is determined in Volume I, or that surplus-value is determined by surplus labour, which is the theory of surplus-value presented in Volume I (although some of them do, as we shall see, including: the opening paragraph of the first two drafts of Volume III, in the *Grundrisse* and the *Manuscript of 1861–63*, several other passages from the *Manuscript of 1861–63*, and a number of passages in Part Seven of Volume III). However, if the total surplus-value is determined prior to its distribution in Volume III, where else could it be determined besides Volume I? It is not determined in Volume III. No theory of surplus-value is presented in

5. Volume III of *Capital* as we know it was written in 1864–65, just after the *Manuscript of 1861–63*, which includes the *Theories of Surplus-Value*. In this *Manuscript of 1861–63*, Marx developed for the first time his theory of the distribution of surplus-value which is presented in Volume III of Capital. The full *Manuscript of 1861–63* has recently been translated into English and published as Volumes 30–34 of the 50-volume set of the Marx–Engels *Collected Works* (MECW), by International Publishers. It is my judgement, based on the existing literature in English (Heinrich 1996–97 and Schefold 1998) on Marx's Manuscript of 1864–65, which Engels edited to make Volume III of *Capital*, that Engels's editing did not make a significant difference to the main conclusions of my chapter, or to the many passages that I cite to support these conclusions. In other words, the passages that I cite, and the conclusions that they support, reflect Marx's own thinking, not additions by Engels.

Volume III; rather the total surplus-value is taken as given throughout. Similarly, the total surplus-value is not determined in Volume II, because Volume II is about the sphere of circulation (not the sphere of production), and according to Marx's theory, no value or surplus-value is created in circulation. Therefore, if the total surplus-value is determined prior to its distribution in Volume III, then it must be determined in Volume I. This, of course, makes perfect sense, since Marx's theory of surplus-value (in the sphere of production) is presented in Volume I. Therefore, all the passages presented in this paper that state that the total surplus-value is determined prior to its distribution in Volume III also imply that the total surplus-value is determined in the theory of surplus-value in Volume I.

1. Part One: Profit and the rate of profit

Part One of Volume III provides a transition from Marx's analysis of capital in general to his analysis of competition. Before Marx analysed the division of the total surplus-value into individual parts, he first derived new 'forms of appearance' acquired by surplus-value – profit and the rate of profit. Profit is defined by Marx in terms of the surplus-value determined in Volume I. Profit is this surplus-value determined in Volume I, related to the total capital advanced (including the constant capital), rather than just to the variable capital only (which according to Marx's theory is the source of surplus-value). Profit is thus always and by definition *the same magnitude as surplus-value*, and this magnitude has already been determined by the prior analysis of capital in general in Volume I. The amount of surplus-value obviously does not change as a result of this different measure of the same amount of surplus-value in relation to the total capital as profit. The same amount of surplus-value is simply related to the total capital, rather than just to the variable capital. The rate of profit expresses this relation of the surplus-value to the total capital as a ratio, as distinguished from the rate of surplus-value which is the ratio of the same surplus-value to the variable capital only.

In the first two drafts of Volume III of *Capital* (in the *Grundrisse* and the *Manuscript of 1861–63*), Marx made it clear in the opening paragraph that, profit is defined as equal to the surplus-value that has already determined by in Volume I (the analysis of production) and that is now taken as a given (predetermined) magnitude. In the *Grundrisse*, Marx wrote:

> Capital is now posited as the unity of production and circulation; and the surplus-value it creates in a given period of time ... In a definite period of time, ... capital produces a *definite surplus-value* ... A capital

> of a certain value produces in a certain period of time a *certain surplus-value*. Surplus-value thus measured by the value of the presupposed capital, capital thus posited as self-realizing value – is profit ...
>
> Marx, 1857–58 (1973): 745–6; italicized emphasis added

And in the *Manuscript of 1861–63*:[6]

> Considered in its totality ... the movement of capital is a unity of the process of production and the process of circulation.
>
> The *surplus value* produced within a given period of circulation ... when measured against the *total capital* which has been advanced is called – *profit* ...
>
> Considered with respect to its material, profit is absolutely nothing but surplus value itself. Considered with respect to its absolute magnitude, it therefore does not differ from the surplus value produced by capital over a particular turnover time. It is surplus value itself, but *calculated* differently.
>
> Marx, 1861–63c (1992): 69[7]

In Part One of Volume III (at least as we have it from Engels), Marx did not begin with this important methodological comment. Instead, he just started right in with a specific numerical example. However, the analysis still clearly assumes that a given quantity of surplus-value has already been determined. In Marx's main numerical example, the given quantity of surplus-value is £100 (the same numerical example as in Chapter 9 of Volume I). Profit is defined in the same way as in the earlier drafts: as equal to the given predetermined quantity of surplus-value related to the total capital, rather than just to the variable capital. 'As this supposed derivative of the total capital advanced, the surplus-value takes on the transformed form of profit' (Marx, 1894 [1981]: 126). Marx emphasized further that, in these forms of appearance of profit and the rate of profit, the source of surplus-value is obscured and not recognized by capitalists

6. This very interesting draft of Parts One and Three of Volume III included in the *Manuscript of 1861–63* has recently been published in English for the first time in Volume 33 of (MECW).
7. A little earlier in this manuscript (in a part included in the *Theories of Surplus-Value*), Marx stated this important methodological point very clearly: 'When in general we speak of profit or the rate of profit, then surplus-value is supposed to be given. The influences therefore which determine surplus-value have all operated. This is the presupposition' (Marx, 1861–63b [1971]: 228).

(and economists). Profit appears to arise from both constant capital and variable capital equally. Marx argued that this illusion is not an accident; rather it necessarily appears to capitalists because capitalists make no distinction between constant capital and variable capital; to capitalists, both components of capital are equally 'costs' and therefore surplus-value appears to arise equally from both of these 'costs'.

> Profit, as we are originally faced with it, is thus the same thing as surplus-value save in a mystified form, though one that necessarily arises from the capitalist mode of production. Because no distinction between constant capital and variable capital can be recognized in the apparent formation of the cost price, the origin of the change in value that occurs in the course of the production process is shifted from the variable capital to the capital as a whole.
>
> Marx, 1894 (1981): 127

Marx's analysis of profit and the rate of profit in Part One of Volume III is presented in terms of an individual capital, as his theory of surplus-value in Volume I. However, Part One of Volume III remains at the level of abstraction of capital in general and thus is about what all individual capitals have in common. In this case, what they have in common is that surplus-value appears to be the result of both constant capital and variable capital, rather than just the variable capital alone. So the individual capital in Part One is analysed as a representative of the total social capital, or as 'an aliquot part of the total social capital', just as in Volume I. Therefore, when Marx assumes that the surplus-value has been determined, he means not just that the surplus-value produced by a single individual capital has been determined, but also that all the quantities of surplus-value produced by all capitals have been determined, and hence that the total social surplus-value has been determined. Marx expressed this point explicitly in the *Manuscript of 1861–63*:

> Just as the surplus-value of the individual capital in each sphere of production is the measure of the absolute magnitude of the profit – in so far as this is merely a converted form of surplus-value – so is the *total surplus-value* produced by the total capital the *absolute measure of the total profit of the total capital*, whereby profit should be understood to include all forms of surplus-value, such as rent, interest, etc. ... It is therefore the absolute magnitude of value ... which the capitalist class can divide among its members in various headings.
>
> Marx, 1861–63c (1991): 98

This assumption of a given, predetermined total amount of surplus-value remains the basic premise of Marx's theory of the distribution of surplus-value throughout the remainder of Volume III.

2. Part Two: The general rate of profit and prices of production

Part Two is the beginning of Marx's analysis of competition and the distribution of surplus-value. The distribution of surplus-value is first considered across different branches of production. Marx assumed more or less as an empirical fact that the rates of profit in different branches of production tend to be equalized as a result of competition among capitalists (although he certainly recognized the many obstacles to this equalization). The important point is that this empirical fact of equal rates of profit (or at least a tendency towards equality) appears to contradict the labour theory of value and surplus-value, because profit appears to arise from the total capital, rather than from the variable capital alone. This apparent contradiction between the labour theory of value and equal rates of profit was of course the main 'stumbling block' of Ricardian economics.

Marx called attention to this apparent contradiction in Chapter 11 of Volume I of *Capital*, and promised to explain this contradiction at a later stage of his analysis, according to his logical method of first determining the total amount of surplus-value and then later determining the individual component parts of surplus-value, such as the average profit collected in each industry. Marx commented that 'for the solution of this apparent contradiction, many intermediate terms are still needed' (Marx, 1867 [1977]: 421). The main 'intermediate term' that is needed for the explanation of this apparent contradiction is the determination of the total amount of surplus-value and the general rate of profit prior to the explanation of equal profit rates across industries.

The equalization of profit rates across industries is accomplished through the determination of the prices of production of individual commodities, which are different from the values of individual commodities. Therefore, Marx's explanation of the equalization of profit rates across industries is necessarily concerned with the determination of these prices of production. The key point that I wish to emphasize is that Marx's theory of prices of production and the equalization of profit rates is based on the premise that the *general rate of profit* (to which individual rates of profit are equalized) *has itself already been determined prior to the determination of prices of production*, and is *taken as given* in this determination of prices of production.

The general rate of profit (R) is defined as the ratio of the total amount of surplus-value (S) to the total capital advanced (C) in the capitalist economy as a whole:

$$R = \frac{S}{C} \tag{1}$$

The total amount of surplus-value is determined by the prior analysis of capital in general in Volume I of *Capital* and is taken as given in the determination of the rate of profit.[8]

The general rate of profit as a ratio of social aggregates depends in part on the distribution of capital across industries. Some industries have a higher 'value' rate of profit (the rate of profit that would occur if individual prices were equal to their values) than other industries, because the former industries have a higher proportion of labour for a given amount of capital (i.e., a lower composition of capital). If a given amount of capital is redistributed from industries with relatively more labour to industries with relative less labour, then, because there is now less labour in the aggregate, there is also less surplus-value produced in the aggregate, and hence a lower general rate of profit.

In order to show this dependence of the general rate of profit on the distribution of capital, Marx also expressed the general rate of profit as a weighted average of the individual 'value' rates of profit in different industries (S_i / C_i), with the weights determined by the relative size of the capital in each industry as a share of the total social capital (C_i / C), as follows:

$$R = \sum \frac{S_i}{C_i} \frac{C_i}{C} \tag{2}$$

Marx called the rate of profit determined in this way the 'average rate of profit'.

This expression of the general rate of profit as the average rate of profit obviously does not change its magnitude. Since the sums of the individual amounts of surplus-value and capital are by definition equal to the social totals, the average rate of profit is identically equal to the

8. The total capital advanced is taken as given, as the amount of money-capital (M) advanced in the first phase of the circulation of capital (M–C ... P ... C'–M') in the capitalist economy as a whole (see Moseley 1993 and 2000 for a further discussion of the initial givens in Marx's theory as quantities of money-capital).

general rate of profit as the ratio of the social totals, which can be easily seen as follows:

$$\sum \frac{S_i}{C_i}\frac{C_i}{C} = \sum \frac{S_i}{C} = \frac{S}{C} \tag{3}$$

That is why Marx used these two terms synonymously ('general or average rate of profit') in many passages throughout his manuscripts (including the title of Chapter 9 of Volume III). The average rate of profit is simply a way of showing the dependence of the general rate of profit on the distribution of capital across industries.[9]

In the *Manuscript of 1861–63*, Marx expressed the determination of the general rate of profit mostly in terms of the ratio of the total surplus-value to the total capital. To take a few examples:

> *The* general rate of profit *is formed through the total surplus-value produced being calculated on the total capital of society* (of the class of capitalists). Each capital, therefore, in each particular branch, represents a portion of a total capital of the same organic composition ... As such a portion, it draws its dividends from the surplus-value created by the aggregate capital, in accordance with its size. The surplus-value thus distributed, the amount of surplus-value which falls to the share of a block of capital of given size, for example £100, ... constitutes the average profit or the general rate of profit ...
>
> Marx, 1861–63a (1968): 433; italicized emphasis added

9. Chris Arthur has argued in his chapter 'Capital, Competition and Many Capitals' (this volume) that the average rate of profit is determined in a fundamentally different way from the general rate of profit. However, even if there were some fundamental difference in the method of determination of these two rates of profit, this difference has no effect on the quantitative determination of the rate of profit (as Arthur acknowledges). The average rate of profit is identically (i.e., always) equal to the general rate of profit, as shown in the text, because they are both derived from the same basic givens, the surplus-value produced by each and every capital.

   Furthermore, the average rate of profit is also determined prior to prices of production, just like the general rate of profit. Therefore, from a quantitative point of view, and with respect to the determination of prices of production, there is no difference between the average rate of profit and the general rate of profit.

   Therefore, I do not understand this significance of the difference between the methods of determination of the general rate of profit and the average rate of profit that Arthur alleges. Do these different methods of determination lead to different conclusions? If so, what are the different conclusions?

> The empirical, or average, profit can therefore be nothing other than the distribution of that total profit (and the total surplus-value represented by it or the representation of the total surplus labour) among the individual capitals in each particular sphere of production, in equal proportions ... It therefore represents the result of the particular mode of calculation in which the different capitals divide among themselves aliquot parts of the total profit. *What is available for them to divide among themselves is only determined by the absolute quantity of the total profit or the total surplus-value.*
>
> Marx and Engels, 1861–63c (1991): 99; emphasis added

> *Empirical or average profit ... relates the total amount of surplus-value,* hence the surplus-value realized by the whole capitalist class, *to the total capital,* or the capital employed by the whole capitalist class, in exactly this way – it relates the total surplus-value as profit to that total capital of society, without regard to the organic relation in which the individual components of that total capital have participated directly in the production of that total surplus-value ...
>
> Marx and Engels, 1861–63c (1991): 100; emphasis added

> But it was also shown that considering the sum total of the capitals which are employed in the various particular spheres of production, the total amount of the social capital, or, and this is the same thing, the total capital of the capitalist class, the *average rate of profit is nothing other than the total surplus-value related to and calculated on this total capital.*
>
> Marx and Engels, 1861–63c (1991): 104; italicized emphasis added

Marx also expressed the determination of the general rate of profit as the ratio of the aggregate totals in Volume III of *Capital*:

> The *total sum of capitals* applied in the five spheres is 500; the *total sum of surplus-value* they produce 110; the total value of commodities they produce 610. If we treat the 500 as one single capital, with I–V simply forming portions of it, ... then the average composition of the capital of 500 would be 500 = 390c + 110v, or in percentages 78c + 22v. Treating the capitals of 100 as each simply a fifth of the total capital, its composition would be this average one of 78C + 22v; in the same way the average surplus-value of 22 would accrue to each of these capitals of 100, the average rate of profit would thus be 22 per cent ...
>
> Marx, 1894 (1981): 254–5; emphasis added

> ... the average rate of profit depends on the level of *exploitation of labor as a whole by capital as a whole.*
>
> Marx, 1894 (1981): 299; emphasis added

> ... the value level of the *total capital* advanced (both constant and variable), ... [together] with a *given size of surplus-value or profit for the entire capitalist class,* determines the rate of profit ...
>
> Marx, 1894 (1981): 299–300; emphasis added

> Let us assume that the *total industrial capital* advanced during the year is 720c + 180v = 900 (say in millions of pounds sterling), and that s′ = 100 per cent. The product is then 720c + 180v + 180s. If we call this product or the commodity capital produced C, then its value or price of production (since the two coincide when we take the totality of commodities) = 1,080 and the rate of profit on the total capital of 900 is 20 per cent. This 20 per cent, as explained already, is the average rate of profit, since here we are reckoning surplus-value not on this or that capital of particular composition, but rather on the total industrial capital with its average composition.
>
> Marx, 1894 (1981): 398; emphasis added

In Volume III, Marx also emphasized the determination of the general rate of profit as a weighted average, in order to highlight the dependence of the general rate of profit on the distribution of capital:

> For the formation of the general rate of profit, therefore, it is not only a question of the difference in *rates* of profit between the various spheres of production, from which a simple average is taken, but also of the relative weight which these different rates of profit assume in the formation of the average. This depends however either on the relative size of the capital invested in each particular sphere or on which particular aliquot part of the total social capital is invested in each particular sphere of production ...
>
> The general rate of profit is determined therefore by two factors: (1) the organic composition of the capitals in the various spheres of production, i.e. the different rates of profit in the particular spheres; and (2) the distribution of the total social capital between these different spheres ...
>
> Marx, 1894 (1981): 262–3

The general or average rate of profit thus determined, it then becomes a given, a 'prerequisite' for the determination of prices of production: 'The prerequisite [of prices of production] is the existence of a general rate of profit ...' (Marx, 1894 [1981]: 257). Prices of production are then determined according to the following equation:

$$P_i = K_i + RC_i \tag{4}$$

where R is taken as predetermined by the prior aggregate analysis of capital in general, K_i is the costs of production of the given commodity (the sum of constant capital and variable capital) (a flow variable), and C_i is the total stock of capital invested in the given industry. The magnitudes of individual capitals consumed and invested in each industry (K_i and C_i) are taken as given, as the sums of money which initiate the circulation of capital in each industry. Therefore, prices of production are determined by adding the average profit to the given costs of production for each commodity, with the average profit determined as the product of the general rate of profit and the given capital invested in each industry, and the general rate of profit determined by the prior analysis of capital in general. In this way, the predetermined total amount of surplus-value is distributed such that all industries receive the same rate of profit.[10]

> The prices of production arise from an adjustment of commodity values under which, after the reimbursement of the respective capital values consumed in the various spheres of production, *the total surplus-value is distributed* not in the proportion in which it is produced in the individual spheres of production, ... but rather in proportion to the size of the capitals advanced ... It is the constant tendency of capitals

10. Tony Smith's chapter in this volume takes this interpretation of Marx's method a step further and applies it to the determination of what he calls 'prices of expanded reproduction', which differ from prices of production in that profit rates are not equalized due to the effects of technology rents, monopolies, etc. Smith's interpretation of the determination of these 'prices of expanded reproduction' is based on the same key premise emphasized in this paper – that the total amount of surplus-value is determined prior to its distribution and is not affected by this distribution. Smith adds the further corollary that the total amount of surplus-value is also not affected by the inequalities due to monopolies, etc. If monopoly industries are able to secure for themselves a higher than average rate of profit, this necessarily comes at the expense of lower than average rates of profit in competitive industries.

> to bring about, by competition, this adjustment of the total surplus-value which the total capital produces ...
>
> Marx, 1894 (1981): 895; emphasis added

The average profit included in the price of each commodity (= RC_i) will in general not be equal to the amount of surplus-value actually contained in that commodity, and hence the price of production of each commodity will in general not be equal to its value or proportional to the labour-time required to produce it. However, the total amount of surplus-value is not altered by this redistribution of surplus-value among the individual industries according to the total amount of capital invested. Taken all together, the divergences of individual profits from individual surplus-values balance out so that the sum of individual profits is equal to the total amount of surplus-value (S), as determined in the Volume I analysis of capital in general. This can be trivially shown as follows:

$$\sum RC_i = R\sum C_i = RC = \frac{S}{C}C = S \qquad (5)$$

This result follows tautologically from Marx's logical method employed in the determination of prices of production. Because the total amount of surplus-value (the 'limit') is taken as given in the determination of prices of production, the total amount of surplus-value cannot possibly change as a result of this determination (cannot 'abolish the limits').[11]

> The transformation of values into prices of production *does not abolish the limits* to profit, but simply *affects its distribution* among the various particular capitals of which the social capital is composed...
>
> Marx, 1894 (1981): 1000; emphasis added

> The equalization of the surplus-values in different spheres of production *does not affect the absolute size of this total surplus-value*; but merely alters its distribution among the different spheres of production. The determination of this surplus-value itself, however, only arises out of the determination of value by labour-time.
>
> Marx, 1861–63a (1968): 190; italicized emphasis added

11. It is just as easily shown that the sum of individual prices of production is equal to the aggregate price determined in the Volume I analysis of capital in general; see Moseley 1993. Contrary to the widely-accepted Sraffian interpretation, both of these aggregate equalities are true simultaneously, if Marx's own logical method is followed.

Please note that latter passage states that the total surplus-value 'arises out of the determination of value by labour-time', which is the theory of surplus-value presented in Volume I of *Capital*.

The equalization of profit rates across industries further obscures the origin of surplus-value. Because profit is in fact distributed across industries according to the total capital invested, and not according to the amount of variable capital, profit appears to come equally from both the constant capital and variable capital components of the total capital. Marx argued that this illusion is a 'necessary form of appearance' in capitalism because competition enforces the equalization of profit rates of across industries.

> It is now purely accidental if the surplus-value actually produced in a particular sphere of production, and therefore the profit, coincides with the profit contained in the commodity's sale price ... The actual difference in magnitude between profit and surplus-value in the various spheres of production ... now completely conceals the true nature and origin of profit, not only for the capitalist, who has a particular interest in deceiving himself, but also for the worker.
>
> Marx, 1894 (1981): 267–8

> Profit does not merely *seem* to be different, but *is* now in fact different from surplus-value ... Capitals of equal magnitude yield equal profits; in other words, profit is proportional to the size of the capital. Or profit is determined by the amount of the capital advanced. The relation of profit to the organic composition of capital is completely obliterated and no longer recognizable in all these formulae.
>
> Marx, 1861–63b (1971): 483

Marx argued that Ricardo and his followers were not able to provide a satisfactory explanation of equal rates of profit and prices of production precisely because they failed to follow the logical method of the prior determination of the general rate of profit. Instead, Ricardo simply assumed equal rates of profit and prices of production in the very first chapter of his *Principles* without first explaining how the rate of profit is determined.

> Instead of *postulating* this *general rate of profit*, Ricardo should rather have examined how far its *existence* is in fact consistent with the

> determination of value by labour-time and he would have found that instead of being consistent with it, *prima facie*, it *contradicts* it, and that its existence would therefore have to be explained through a number of intermediary stages, a procedure which is very different from merely including it under the law of value.
>
> Marx, 1861–63a (1968): 174; underlined emphasis added

The most important 'intermediary stage' omitted by Ricardo is the prior determination of the total amount of surplus-value and the general rate of profit, which is then taken as given in the subsequent determination of prices of production.

I have argued in Moseley (1993) that, if the interpretation of Marx's logical method presented here is accepted, including the key premise of the prior determination of the general rate of profit, then the following conclusions follow:

1. Marx's theory of prices of production is not 'incomplete', i.e., Marx did not fail to transform the inputs of constant capital and variable capital from values into prices of production, because these inputs are taken as given as quantities of money capital, not derived as the values or prices of production of given means of production and means of subsistence. The *same* quantities of money capital taken as given in Marx's theory of surplus-value in Volume I and in his theory of prices of production in Volume III. The only difference is that in Volume III the disaggregated quantities of constant capital and variable capital in each industry are taken as given, rather than the aggregate quantities of constant capital and variable capital, as in Volume I (the sum of the disaggregated quantities of capital is by assumption equal to the aggregate quantities of capital).
2. Marx's two aggregate equalities both are true simultaneously, as Marx himself concluded.
3. The rate of profit does not change as a result of the determination of prices of production. Instead, the rate of profit is taken as given in Marx's theory of prices of production, as determined in the prior aggregate analysis of capital in general in Volume I.
4. The labour theory of value is not 'redundant', because values as defined by Marx cannot be derived from the technical conditions of production. The prices of production as determined by Marx's theory are different from the prices of production determined by the technical conditions of production (as in the Sraffian interpretation of Marx's theory), or in Sraffian theory. The question of which of

these two theories provides a better explanation of prices of production remains, but it is not true that these two theories are the same, and therefore that value theory is redundant.

3. Part Four: Commercial profit

The next component of surplus-value explained in Volume III is commercial profit, or the profit collected by commercial capital. Commercial capital is capital which functions solely in the sphere of circulation, i.e., performs only the pure circulation functions of buying and selling, and activities related to buying and selling (accounting, advertising, credit, etc.). Since according to Marx's theory, these functions by themselves are 'unproductive', i.e., produce no value or surplus-value (see Moseley 1992, Chapter 2, for a further discussion of Marx's concept of unproductive labour), the existence of commercial profit appears to contradict this assumption of unproductive labour.

Marx called attention to this apparent contradiction between the labour theory of value and commercial profit in Chapter 5 of Volume I, and again promised to explain this apparent contradiction at a later stage of his theory, according to his logical method of first determining the total amount of surplus-value and then later determining the individual parts of surplus-value, such as commercial profit. Marx remarked that in order to explain these apparently contradictory phenomena, 'a long series of intermediate steps' is necessary, which are 'entirely absent' in the analysis so far. 'In the course of our investigation, we will find that merchants' capital and interest-bearing capital are derivative forms [of industrial capital]' (Marx, 1867 [1977]: 267).[12]

Marx's explanation of this apparent contradiction is that commercial capital receives its profit as a deduction from the surplus-value produced by industrial capital. The general mechanism through which this deduction of commercial profit from the total surplus-value occurs is through the difference between commercial capital's buying price and its selling price. Commercial capital buys commodities at less than their price of production and then sells these commodities at their price of production. This difference enables commercial capital to recover its cost and to collect the average rate of profit. In this method of determination of commercial profit, the *prior determination of the total amount of surplus-value* is very clear. Commercial profit is 'a portion of the surplus-value produced by productive capital as a whole'. The 'limits of

12. We can see from this sentence that the same method of investigation also applies to Marx's analysis of interest.

surplus-value' (i.e., the total amount of surplus-value) is given, prior to the distribution of surplus-value through competition among individual capitalists. The general rate of profit is not determined by competition, but rather by the prior analysis of capital in general.

> Since commercial capital does not itself produce any surplus-value, it is clear that *the surplus-value that accrues to it in the form of the average profit forms a portion of the surplus-value produced by the productive capital as a whole.* The question now is this. How does commercial capital attract the part of the surplus-value produced by productive capital that falls to its share? ... It is clear that the merchant can obtain his profit only from the price of the commodities he sells, and also that this profit which he makes on the sale of his commodities must be equal to the difference between his purchase price and his sale price; it must be equal to the excess of the latter over the former.
>
> Marx, 1894 (1981): 395–6; emphasis added

> Commercial capital does not have a direct effect on the creation of profit or surplus-value and it enters as a determining element into the formation of the general rate of profit only in so far as it draws its dividends from the mass of profit that industrial capital produces, according to the proportion that it forms in the total capital.
>
> Marx, 1894 (1981): 424

> If *the limits of value and surplus-value are given,* it is easy to perceive how the competition between capitals transforms values into prices of production and still further into commercial prices, transforming surplus-value into average profit. But without these limits, there is absolutely no way of seeing why competition should reduce the general rate of profit to one limit rather than to another, to 15 per cent instead of 1,500 per cent.
>
> Marx, 1894 (1981): 429; emphasis added

How then are the purchase price and the selling price of commercial capital determined?[13] With the inclusion of commercial capital, the

13. I consider here only the simple case in which there are no additional costs of circulation beyond that necessary to purchase the commodities. For a consideration of the more complicated case with additional costs of circulation, see Moseley (1997).

general rate of profit (R') is now determined as the ratio of the predetermined total amount of surplus-value to the sum of industrial capital (C_p) and commercial capital (C_c), not just to the industrial capital as before:

$$R' = \frac{S}{C_p + C_c} < R = \frac{S}{C_p} \tag{6}$$

Therefore, the general rate of profit is less than what it was in the absence of commercial capital.

Commercial capital's buying price or 'wholesale' price (WP) (or industrial capital's selling price) is then determined as follows (considering both the total industrial capital and the total commercial capital, rather than individual capitals):

$$WP = K_p + R'C_p \tag{7}$$

where K_p is the cost of production (the sum of variable capital and constant capital consumed). Since R′ < R, the average profit added to the costs of production by industrial capital is less than in the absence of commercial capital. In this way, industrial capital appropriates a smaller share of the total surplus-value.

The remainder of the total surplus-value is then received by commercial capital by adding the average profit to its buying price to determine its selling or 'retail' price, or price of production (P):

$$P = WP + R'C_c \tag{8}$$

Prices of production are now different from those determined in Part Two, because the proportion of commercial capital will vary across industries and because the addition of commercial capital reduces the general rate of profit that is taken as given.

This then is Marx's explanation of how commercial capital receives a share of the total surplus-value even though it produces no surplus-value. It is trivial to show that the sum of industrial profit ($R'C_p$) and commercial profit ($R'C_c$) determined in this way is equal to the predetermined total amount of surplus-value:[14]

14. Similarly, the sum of the 'retail' prices of commercial capital is equal to the total price of commodities determined in Volume I and the sum of prices of production in the earlier case without commercial capital.

$$R'C_p + R'C_c = R'\left(C_p + C_c\right) = \frac{S}{C_p + C_c}\left(C_p + C_c\right) = S \qquad (9)$$

The only difference is that a part of this total amount of surplus-value is now collected by commercial capital, rather than by industrial capital, by means of the above relative price mechanism. (Marx presented a numerical example of this method of determination on page 398 of Volume III, and gave a similar example in a letter to Engels [1868] to be discussed below.)

The appropriation of profit by commercial capital further obscures the origin of surplus-value. Since commercial profit receives a profit proportional to its total amount, just like industrial capital, it looks like profit is produced by commercial capital as well as by industrial capital. This illusion is enhanced by the effect that the rate of turnover of commercial capital has on the rate of profit, e.g., a faster rate of turnover of commercial capital increases the rate of profit (see Chapter 18 of Volume III). Again, these illusions arising from circulation necessarily arise in capitalism because the products of capitalism are commodities which must pass through the phases of circulation and because capital must be invested to carry out these necessary functions of circulation, even though these functions do not themselves directly product surplus-value.

> As the reader will have recognized in dismay, the analysis of the real, inner connections of the capitalist production process is a very intricate thing and a work of great detail; it is the task of science to reduce the visible and merely apparent movement to the actual inner movement. Accordingly, it will be self-evident that, in the heads of the agents of capitalist production and circulation, ideas must necessarily form about the laws of production that diverge completely from these laws and are merely the expression in consciousness of the apparent movement. The ideas of a merchant, a stock-jobber or a banker are necessarily quite upside-down.
>
> Marx, 1894 (1981): 428

4. Part Five: Interest

The next component part of surplus-value explained in Volume III is interest. According to Marx's theory, interest is simply a part of the total surplus-value which the 'functioning' capital (either industrial capital or commercial capital) has to pay to the lenders of capital for the use of the lenders' capital. Again, the total amount of surplus-value is predetermined and taken as given in the analysis of the division of this total surplus-value into 'profit of enterprise' and interest.

> *Interest ... is ... nothing but a part of the profit, i.e. the surplus-value*, which the functioning capitalist, whether industrialist or merchant, must pay to the owner and lender of capital in so far as the capital he uses is not his own but borrowed.
>
> Marx, 1894 (1981): 493

> *Where a given whole such as profit is to be divided into two, the first thing that matters is of course the size of the whole to be divided* ... And the circumstances that determine the magnitude of the profit to be divided, the value product of unpaid labour, are very different from those that determine its distribution among these two kinds of capitalist ...
>
> Marx, 1894 (1981): 482; emphasis added

> The ratio in which profit is divided, and the different legal titles by which this division takes place, already assume that profit is ready-made and presuppose its existence ... *(P)rofit is produced before this division takes place* and before there can be any talk of it.
>
> Marx, 1894 (1981): 504–5; emphasis added

> With the division into interest and profit of enterprise, the average profit itself sets the limit for the two together. *It supplies the given amount of value they have to share between them, and this is all they have to share.*
>
> Marx, 1894 (1981): 1001; emphasis added

> Interest *is therefore nothing but a part of the profit (which, in turn, is itself nothing by surplus-value, unpaid labor*), which the industrial capitalist pays to the owner of the borrowed capital with which he 'works', either exclusively or partially. Interest is a part of profit – of surplus-value – which, established as a special category, is separated from the total profit under its own name, a separation which is by no means based on its origin, but only on the manner in which it is paid out or appropriated.
>
> Marx, 1861–63b (1971): 470–1; italicized emphasis added

Please note again that the second and fifth passages above state that the total surplus-value is determined by 'unpaid labour', which is the theory of surplus-value presented in Volume I.

Marx argued that there are no general, systematic laws that determine the rate of interest, as there is with the rate of profit. Therefore, there are no general laws that determine the relative shares of 'profit of enterprise' and interest in the total surplus-value. The rate of interest is instead determined by the supply and demand for capital as loan capital. The most relevant point for our purposes is that the maximum rate of interest is the rate of profit. This maximum limit for the rate of interest follows from the prior determination of the rate of profit, before the division of the total surplus-value into 'profit of enterprise' and interest.

Marx called interest the 'most fetishistic form of surplus-value', because interest appears to arise solely from the nature of capital itself, with no necessary relation to labour or even to production. Marx argued that this fetishism necessarily arises in capitalism because of the actual emergence of loan capital and the consequent actual division of the total surplus-value into interest and profit of enterprise. Even capitalists who do not operate with borrowed capital nonetheless often divide their 'gross profit' into interest and 'net profit'.

> The division of profit into profit of enterprise and interest ... completes the autonomization of the form of surplus-value, the ossification of its form as against its substance, its essence ... [I]nterest then seems independent both of the wage-labour of the worker and of the capitalist's own labour; it seems to derive from capital as its own independent source.
>
> Marx, 1894 (1981): 968

> It is in *interest-bearing capital* – in the division of profit into interest and [industrial] profit – that capital finds its most objectified form, its pure fetish form, and the nature of surplus-value is presented as something which has altogether lost its identity. Capital – as an entity – appears here as an independent source of value ...
>
> Marx, 1861–63b (1971): 498–9

5. Part Six: Rent

The final component of surplus-value explained in Volume III is land rent. Rent is explained as a part of the total surplus-value which landlords are able, by their monopoly of the land (and other natural resources), to appropriate for themselves, rather than this surplus-value being distributed among all capitalists. In this theory of rent, the total amount of surplus-value is again taken as a given magnitude, as determined by the prior analysis of capital in general. This total amount of surplus-value is 'split' into profit and rent, and rent does not enter into the equalization of profit rates across industries.

> All ground-rent is surplus-value, the product of surplus labour.
>
> Marx, 1894 (1981): 772–3

> The analysis of landed property in its various historical forms lies outside the scope of the present work. We are concerned with it *only in so far as a portion of the surplus-value that capital produces falls to the share of the landowner.*
>
> Marx, 1894 (1981): 751; emphasis added

> In our analysis of ground-rent, we intend to proceed first of all from the assumption that products that pay a rent of this kind – which means that *a part of their surplus-value ... is reducible to rent* – are sold like all other commodities at their prices of production ...
>
> Marx, 1894 (1981): 779; emphasis added

Marx's theory of rent assumed that agriculture is organized on a capitalist basis, and that capital invested in agriculture receives the same average rate of profit as all other industries. However, agriculture is unique in that productivity differentials of different lands are due in part to unequal natural fertilities, which cannot be eliminated by competition and the transfer of capital. As a result, the price of production of agricultural goods is determined by the labour-time requirements on the least fertile land, rather than the labour-time requirements on the land of average fertility. The greater quantity of goods produced by the same amount of labour on the more fertile lands will sell at the same price as goods produced on the least fertile land. Therefore, the goods produced on the more fertile land will contain a sustainable 'surplus profit', i.e., a profit over and above the average rate of profit. This surplus profit is transformed into (differential) rent that must be paid to landlords because of the landlords' private ownership of the land and thus their monopolization of the benefits of the greater natural fertility.

> Capital-profit (profit of enterprise plus interest) and ground-rent are thus nothing but particular components of the surplus-value; categories in which this surplus-value is distinguished according to whether it accrues to capital or landed property; designations which in no way affect its essence. Added together, they form the total of

> surplus-value. Capital directly pumps from the workers the surplus labour that is expressed in surplus-value and surplus product.
>
> Marx, 1894 (1981): 959–60

The collection of rent by landlords further obscures the origin of surplus-value because it makes it appear as if surplus-value arises from the natural fertility of the land. Indeed to some, like the Physiocrats, it even appears that all of surplus-value, not just rent, originates from the natural fertility of the land.

> Finally, besides capital as an independent source of surplus-value, there appears landed property, as a limit to the average profit which transfers a portion of the surplus-value to a class that neither works itself nor directly exploits workers, and cannot even, like interest-bearing capital, launch forth in edifying homilies about the risk and sacrifice in lending capital. Since in this case one part of the surplus-value seems directly bound up not with social relations but rather with a natural element, the earth, the form of mutual alienation and ossification of the various portions of surplus-value is complete, the inner connection definitively torn asunder and its source completely buried, precisely through the assertion of their autonomy vis-a-vis each other by the various relations of production which are bound up with the different material elements of production process.
>
> Marx, 1894 (1981): 968

6. Part Seven: Revenue and its sources

We come finally to Part Seven, entitled 'Revenue and its Sources', which is seldom discussed in the literature, but which I think is very important. Part Seven provides a culmination of Marx's theory of the distribution of surplus-value in Volume III of *Capital*. It makes very clear the main points of Volume III: (1) the distribution of surplus-value into its component parts; (2) the prior determination of the total amount of surplus-value; and (3) the necessary appearance of the individual parts of surplus-value as separate and independent 'sources' of value.

The quantitative premise of the determination of the total surplus-value prior to its distribution is clearly expressed throughout Part Seven. The total surplus-value is determined by 'unpaid labour', which is the theory of surplus-value presented in Volume I. This predetermined total surplus-value is then the 'limit' of the sum of the individual parts.

> Profit (profit of enterprise plus interest) and rent are nothing more than characteristic forms assumed by particular portions of the surplus-value in commodities. The size of the surplus-value sets a *quantitative limit* for the parts it can be broken down into.
>
> Marx, 1894 (1981): 971; emphasis added

> The sum of average profit plus ground-rent can never be greater than the quantity of which these are parts, and this is already given before the division.
>
> Marx, 1894 (1981): 972

> We have thus an *absolute limit* for the value component that forms surplus-value and can be broken down into profit and ground-rent; this is determined by the excess of the unpaid portion of the working day over its paid portion, i.e. by the value component of the total product in which this surplus labour is realized. If we call *this surplus-value whose limits are thus determined* profit, when it is calculated on the total capital advanced, as we have already done, then this profit, considered in its absolute amount, is equal to the surplus-value, i.e. it is just as regularly determined in its limits as this is. It is the *ratio between the total surplus-value and the total social capital advanced in production*. If this capital is 500 ... and the surplus-value is 100, the absolute limit to the rate of profit is 20 per cent. The division of the social profit as measured by this rate among the capitals applied in the various different spheres of production produces prices of production which diverge from commodity values and which are the actual averages governing market prices. *But this divergence from values abolishes neither the determination of prices by values nor the limits imposed on profit by our laws ... This surcharge of 20 per cent ... is itself determined by the surplus-value created by the total social capital*, and its proportion to the value of this capital; and this is why it is 20 per cent and not 10 per cent or 100 per cent. The *transformation of values into prices of production does not abolish the limits to profit, but simply affects its distribution among the various particular capitals of which the social capital is composed ...*
>
> Marx, 1894 (1981): 999–1000; emphasis added

This last passage is a concise summary of Marx's theory of prices of production, in which it is clearly stated that the general rate of profit (the 'surcharge') is determined prior to prices of production, and is determined by the aggregate ratio of the total surplus-value to the total capital.

Marx's theory of the total amount of surplus-value, presented in Volume I, is, of course, based on the labour theory of value. The labour theory of value is itself based on essentially the same premise – that the total amount of value, or the total price, is determined prior to its division into individual parts, or individual forms of income. Leaving aside the constant capital component of the total price, the total new-value produced in a given period may be divided into wages plus the various forms of surplus-value discussed in Volume III. Marx emphasized repeatedly in Part Seven (and especially in Chapter 50) that the labour theory of value assumes that the total amount of new-value is determined by 'objectified social labour' prior to its division into wages plus profit plus rent, etc. A few examples:

> The distribution rather presupposes this substance as already present, i.e. the total value of the annual product, which is nothing more than objectified social labour.
>
> Marx, 1894 (1981): 961

> Apart from the confusion produced by the transformation of values into prices of production, a further confusion derives from the transformation of surplus-value into various separate, mutually independent forms related to the various elements of production, into profit and rent. It is forgotten that *the value of commodities is the basis* and that the breakdown of this commodity value into particular components, and the further development of these value components into forms of revenue, their transformation into relations that the various owners of the different agents of production have to these particular value components, their distribution among these owners according to particular categories and titles, in no way alter the value determination and its law. Just as little is the law of value affected by the fact that the equalization of profit, i.e. the distribution of the total surplus-value among the various capitals ... gives rise to governing average prices for commodities that diverge from their values. This again affects only the addition of surplus-value to the various commodity prices; it does not abolish surplus-value itself, nor the total value of commodities as the source of these various price components.
>
> Marx, 1894 (1981): 984–5; emphasis added

> The commodity value of £250 thus produced, and determined by the amount of labour objectified in it, sets the limit to the dividends that

> worker, capitalist, and landlord can draw from this value in the form of revenue – wages, profit, and rent.
>
> Marx, 1894 (1981): 994

> The value freshly added each year by new labour ... can be separated out and resolved into the different revenue forms of wages, profit, and rent; this in no way alters the limits of the value itself, the sum of the value that is divided between these different categories. In the same way, a change in the ratio of these individual portions among themselves cannot affect their sum, this given sum of value ... What is given first, therefore, is the mass of commodity values to be divided into wages, profit, and rent ...
>
> Marx, 1894 (1981): 998

Marx also contrasted his theory of value and surplus-value with essentially the opposite view held by the 'vulgar economists' – that the forms of income are first determined separately and independently and then the total amounts of value and surplus-value are determined as the sum of these individual forms of income. According to this view, the different forms of revenue – wages, profit and rent – are themselves independent 'sources' of value, rather than being parts of a predetermined total value. Marx called this opposite view the 'Trinity Formula'[15] or the 'illusions created by competition'. Another version of this opposite view is of course Adam Smith's 'cost of production' theory of value.

> [I]t is correct to say that the value of a commodity, in so far as it represents freshly added labour, is always reducible to three elements, wages, profit, and rent, which constitute the three forms of revenue, while the respective value magnitudes, i.e. the aliquot parts that these form of the total value, are determined by different specific laws that have already been developed. It would be wrong however to say that the value of wages, the rate of profit and the rate of rent are independent constituent elements of value, with the value of the commodity ... arising from their combination; in other words, it would be wrong to say that these form constituent components of commodity value or the price of production.
>
> Marx, 1894 (1981): 993

15. For a further discussion of Chapter 48 on the 'Trinity Formula', see Patrick Murray's chapter in this volume.

> Thus if the portion of commodity value representing labour freshly added ... breaks down into different portions, which assume mutually independent shapes in the form of revenues, this does not in any way mean that wages, profit, and ground-rent are now to be considered as the constituent elements, with the governing price of commodities ... itself arising from their combination or sum ... *In actual fact commodity value is the quantitative premise, the sum total value of wages, profit and rent, whatever their relative mutual magnitudes might be.* In the false conception considered here, however, wages, profit and rent are three independent value magnitudes, whose total produces, limits and determines the magnitude of commodity value.
>
> Marx, 1894 (1981): 1002; emphasis added

> This new value of 100 is all that is available for division into the three forms of revenue. If we call wages x, profit y and ground-rent z, the sum of x+y+z, in our present case, is always = 100. In the minds of the industrialists, merchants and bankers, and the vulgar economists as well, things proceed quite differently. For them it is not the commodity value that is given as 100, ... this 100 then being divided up into x, y, and z. Instead, the price of the commodity is simply put together out of the value magnitudes of wages, profit, and rent, which are determined independently of the commodity's value and of one another ...
>
> Marx, 1894 (1981): 1007

Marx argued that this illusion (the opposite view) necessarily arises in capitalism because individual capitalists, in their everyday practical calculations, do, in fact, regard these different forms of income as given and independent magnitudes, i.e., as the magnitudes then prevailing in the economy. Individual capitalists are not interested in a scientific analysis of value and distribution. They simply take the forms of income as given, as they actually exist in the economy. These forms of income appear to be determined in separate and independent ways, and the total price appears to be determined as the sum of these individual parts.

> The breakdown of surplus-value, that is, of part of the value of commodities, into these special headings or categories, is very understandable and does not conflict in the least with the law of value. But the whole matter is mystified because these different parts of surplus-value acquire an independent form, because they accrue to different people, because the titles to them are based on different elements, and

> finally because of the autonomy with which certain parts of surplus-value confront the production process as its conditions. From parts into which value can be divided, they become independent elements which *constitute* value ... How their apparent independence as conditions of the process is regulated by the inherent law and that they are only *apparently* independent, does not become evident at any moment in the course of the production process, nor does it act as a determining motive. Exactly the opposite. The highest consistency which can be assumed by this semblance of results taking the form of independent conditions becomes firmly established when *parts of surplus-value* – in the form of conditions of production – are included in the price.
>
> Marx, 1861–63b (1971): 511

Marx also argued in Part Seven that 'vulgar economics' simply took these everyday perceptions of individual capitalists as its starting point and tried to give these perceptions some coherence and profundity.

> Vulgar economics actually does nothing more than interpret, systematize, and turn into apologetics the notions of agents trapped within bourgeois relations of production.
>
> Marx, 1894 (1981): 956

> [T]he vulgar economist does nothing more that translate the peculiar notions of the competition-enslaved capitalist into an ostensibly more theoretical and generalized language, and attempt to demonstrate the validity of these notions.
>
> Marx, 1894 (1981): 338

Therefore, at the end of Volume III, Marx arrived at the point that he promised in the first paragraph of Volume III – the explanation of the different forms of appearance of surplus-value on the surface of capitalist society and in the consciousness of individual capitalists and vulgar economists.

7. 1868 Letter

There is one final piece of important textual evidence to be discussed concerning the aims and logic of Volume III: a letter that Marx wrote to Engels in April of 1868, three years after he had written the full draft of Volume III (in the *Manuscript of 1864–65*) and one year after the publication of Volume I. In this letter, Marx explained to Engels what Volume III is all about.

By this time in his life and theoretical development, Marx had a clear idea of the subject matter and the overall logical structure of Volume III, and its relation to Volumes I and II. Therefore, this letter provides very important evidence concerning the nature of Volume III. I think it should be considered Marx's final and definitive statement on Volume III. The reader is urged to read the four-page letter in its entirety.

In previous letters, Marx and Engels had been discussing the effect of a change in the value of money on the rate of profit, an issue raised and discussed by Marx in a letter of 22 April (Marx and Engels, 1868–70 [1988]: 16–18). Engels replied, in a letter of 26 April, that he agreed with Marx's analysis, but raised the following objection:

> The only thing that is unclear to me is how you can assume $m/(c+v)$ as the *rate of profit*, for *m* does not flow solely into the pockets of the industrialist who produces it, but has to be shared with the merchant, etc.; unless you are taking the whole branch of business together here, therefore disregarding how *m* is divided up between manufacturer, wholesaler, retailer, etc. In general, I am very keen to see your exposition on this point.
>
> Marx and Engels, 1868–70 (1988): 19[16]

We can see that Engels's objection had to do with the division of the total profit into different individual parts, precisely the main subject of Volume III. In order to explain this point to Engels, Marx replied in the letter of 30 April with a long and detailed summary of what he called 'Book III' (which is what we know as Volume III) (Marx and Engels, 1868–70 [1988]: 20–5; Marx and Engels, 1975: 191–5). Marx stated his intention: 'It is proper that you should know the *method* by which the rate of profit is developed' (emphasis added).[17] Marx began his summary of 'Book III' by clearly stating its main overall subject: 'In Book III, we then come to the conversion of surplus value into its different forms and separate component parts.' In other words, we come to the distribution of surplus-value.

The letter then summarizes each of the seven parts of Volume III, which correspond exactly to the seven parts of Marx's draft of Volume

16. *m* here stands for surplus-value, presumably because the German word for surplus-value is *Mehrwert*.
17. This letter is a very clear indication of how little Engels knew about Volume III.

III in the *Manuscript of 1864–65*, which Marx no doubt had in front of him as he wrote the letter to Engels. I will briefly review excerpts from this letter that are especially relevant to the main points of this chapter.

The summary of Part One begins with the main points emphasized above: that profit is only 'another name' for surplus-value, and that there is no quantitative difference between them.

> *Profit* is for us, for the time being, only *another name* for or another category of *surplus value*. As, owing to the form of wages, the whole of labour appears to be paid for, the unpaid part of it seems necessarily to come not from labour but from capital, and not from the variable part of capital but from the total capital. As a result, *surplus value* assumes the form of *profit*, without there being any *quantitative* difference between the one and the other.

After discussing the important concept of *cost-price*, Marx then summarized his analysis of the determination of the rate of profit by the rate of surplus-value and the quantities of constant capital and variable capital (i.e., the composition of capital), which Marx said 'has of course been hitherto *inexplicable* to everybody.' Then Marx made the following important methodological comment:

> The laws thus found ... hold good no matter how the surplus value is later divided among the producer, etc. This can only change the form of appearance. Moreover, they remain directly applicable if m/(c+v) is treated as the relation of the *socially produced surplus value* to the *social capital*.
>
> italicized emphasis added

In other words, the laws derived concerning the rate of profit derived in Part One apply directly to the 'socially produced surplus-value' and the 'social capital'. These laws 'hold good no matter how the surplus value is later divided among the producer, etc.'. The later division of the total surplus-value only changes the *forms of appearance* of this total surplus-value; it does not change its magnitude. Marx's theory in Part One is discussed in terms of an individual capital (see above), but this individual capital represents what all capitals have in common, and thus represents the total social capital.

Marx's summary of Part Two clearly states the determination of the general rate of profit by the ratio of the total surplus-value to the total capital, prior to the determination of prices of production.

> This rate of profit, expressed absolutely, can be nothing but the *surplus value* produced (annually) by the *capitalist class* in relation to the total of *social* capital advanced. E.g., if the social capital = 400c + 100v, and the surplus value annually produced by it = 100m, [then we have a] 20 per cent rate of profit. This is the *general rate of profit*. ... The price thus equalized, which divides up the social surplus value equally among the various masses of capital in proportion to their sizes, is the *price of production* of commodities, the centre around which the oscillation of the market prices moves.

Marx called this equalization of profit rates through prices of production a kind of 'capitalist communism', in which each capital receives a '*fractional part of the total surplus value* proportionate to the *part of the total social capital* that it forms' (emphasis added).

Marx's summary of Part Four is another clear and unambiguous statement that the total amount of surplus-value is determined prior to its division into individual parts, in this case, prior to its division into industrial profit and commercial profit. Marx extended the numerical example in his summary of Part Two (see above) to include a merchant capital = 100. Since *the total amount of surplus-value remains the same* (= 100), the general rate of profit is reduced from 20 per cent to 16⅔ per cent. This new, lower general rate of profit is then taken as given in the determination of both the selling price of industrial capital (what I have called the 'wholesale price') and the selling price of commercial capital (what I have called the 'retail price'), as discussed above.

> Until now we have only dealt with *productive capital*. Now there enters modification through *merchant capital*. ... According to our previous assumption the *productive capital* of society = 500 (millions or billions, *n'importe'*). And the formula was 400c + 100v + 100m. The general rate of profit p', = 20%. Now let the merchant capital = 100. ... So, the 100m has now to be calculated on 600 instead of 500. The general rate of profit is thus reduced from 20% to 16⅔%. The *price of production* ... now = 583⅓. The merchant sells at 600 and therefore realises ... 16⅔% on his 100, as much as the productive capitalists; or, in other words, he appropriates ⅙ of the social surplus value.[18]

18. There is one terminological difference between this letter and the 1864–5 draft of Volume III: prices of production are here defined as the selling price of industrial capital (the 'wholesale price'), rather than the selling price of commercial capital (the 'retail price'), as in the 1864–65 draft. So either Marx

The summary of Part Five is very brief, but again makes clear that the total surplus-value is determined prior to its division into profit and interest: *'Next comes the division of this profit into entrepreneur's gain and interest.'* For Part Six, there is only one phrase (perhaps Marx was running out of steam in his letter): *'Transformation of surplus profit into rent.'* This phrase by itself is not completely clear, but we know from all that has gone before that this phrase means that a part of the predetermined total surplus-value is 'transformed into rent', by the pricing mechanism discussed above.

Finally, Marx's summary of Part Seven emphasizes his critique of the 'vulgar conception', according to which each of the different forms of income (wages, profit and rent) has a separate and independent source, and the value of commodities is determined by adding up these independent forms of income. As discussed above, Marx's conception is the opposite: that the total value is determined prior to its division into individual parts, or individual forms of income. 'At last we have arrived at the *forms of manifestation* which serve as the *starting point* in the vulgar conception: rent, coming from the land; profit (interest), from capital; wages, from labour. But from our standpoint things now look different. The apparent movement is explained.' Therefore, I think this letter provides very strong evidence in support of the interpretation of Volume III presented in this chapter. The main overall subject is the distribution of surplus-value and the key quantitative premise of the prior determination of the total amount of surplus-value is clearly and unambiguously stated, especially in the summaries of Part Two and Part Four.

Conclusion

This chapter has presented a considerable amount of textual evidence to support the following conclusions:

1. that the main subject of Volume III is the distribution of surplus-value into its individual component parts;
2. that the total amount of surplus-value has already been determined by the prior analysis of capital in general in Volume I and is taken as

changed his mind, or perhaps he remained undecided about which of these two prices should be called prices of production. But the method of determination of these two prices is exactly the same, as described above, with the general rate of profit taken as given, as determined by the ratio of the total surplus-value to the total capital, now including commercial capital.

given in the Volume III analysis of the division of this total amount into individual parts;

3. that these individual parts of surplus-value are explained as 'necessary forms of appearance' of the common substance of surplus-value, produced by surplus labour.

It is hoped that this chapter will stimulate further research and discussion of Marx's logical method in *Capital*, especially the overall logical structure of Volume III and its relation to the first two volumes. With a better understanding of Marx's logical method, we should then be able to move beyond *Capital* and to further develop Marx's theory towards more concrete levels of abstraction.

Bibliography

Arthur, Christopher J. (2001), Capital in General and Marx's *Capital* (this volume).

Bellofiore, Riccardo (ed.) (1998), *Marxian Economics: A Reappraisal*, 2 volumes (London/New York: Macmillan/St Martin's Press).

— (2001), 'Transformation' and the Monetary Circuit (this volume).

Dussel, Enrique (2001), *Toward an Unknown Marx: A Commentary on the Manuscripts of 1861–63* (LondonL Routledge).

Foley, Duncan (1986), *Understanding Capital: Marx's Economic Theory* (Cambridge, MA: Harvard University Press).

Heinrich, Michael (1996–97) Engels's Edition of the Third Volume of *Capital* and Marx's Original Manuscript, *Science and Society*, 60/4: 452–66.

Mandel, Ernst (1981), Introduction to Volume III of *Capital* (New York: Random House).

Marx, Karl (1857–58), *Grundrisse* (Harmondsworth: Penguin, 1973).

— (1861–63a), *Theories of Surplus Value*, Vol. II (Moscow: Progress Publishers, 1968).

— (1861–63b), *Theories of Surplus Value*, Vol. III (Moscow: Progress Publishers, 1971).

— (1867), *Capital*, Vol. I (New York: Random House, 1977).

— (1894), *Capital*, Vol. III (New York: Random House, 1981).

Marx, Karl and Engels, Frederick (1975), *Selected Correspondence* (Moscow: Progress Publishers).

— (1861–63c), *Collected Works*, Vol. 33 (New York: International Publishers, 1991).

— (1868–70), *Collected Works*, Vol. 43 (New York: International Publishers, 1988).

Mattick, Paul, Sr (1969), *Marx and Keynes: the limits of the mixed economy* (Boston: Porter Sargent).

Moseley, Fred (1993), Marx's Logical Method and the 'Transformation Problem', in Moseley (ed.), *Marx's Method in 'Capital': A Reexamination* (Atlantic Highlands, NJ: Humanities Press).

— (1997), The development of Marx's theory of the distribution of surplus-value, in F. Moseley and M. Campbell (eds), *New Investigations of Marx's Method* (Atlantic Highlands, NJ: Humanities Press).

— (2000), The 'New Solution' to the transformation problem: a sympathetic critique, *Review of Radical Political Economics* 32(2): 282–316.
Murray, Patrick (2001), The Illusion of the Economic. The Trinity Formula and the 'religion of everyday life' (this volume).
Rosdolsky, Roman (1968), *The Making of Marx's 'Capital'* (London: Pluto Press, 1977).
Schefold, Bertram (1998), The Relationship between the Rate of Profit and the Rate of Interest: A Reassessment after the Publication of Marx's Manuscript of the Third Volume of *Das Kapital*, in Bellofiore (ed. 1998, vol. 1): 127–43.
Smith, Tony (2001), Surplus Profits from Innovation. A missing level in *Capital III?* (this volume).
Sweezy, Paul (1942), *The Theory of Capitalist Development* (New York: Monthly Review Press).

5
'Transformation' and the Monetary Circuit
Marx as a monetary theorist of production

Riccardo Bellofiore

> 'In fact, the seller of labour-power, like the seller of any other commodity, *realizes its exchange-value*, and *alienates its use-value*. He cannot take the one without giving the other. The use-value of labour-power, in other words *labour*, belongs just as little to its seller as the use value of oil after it has been sold belongs to the dealer who sold it. The owner of the money has paid the value *of a day's labour-power*; he therefore *has the use of it for a day, a day's labour belongs to him*. On the one hand the daily sustenance of labour-power costs only half a day's labour, while on the other hand the very same labour-power can remain effective, can work, during a whole day, and consequently the value which its use during one day creates is double what the capitalist pays for that use; this circumstance is a piece of good luck for the buyer, but by no means an injustice towards the seller.'
>
> Karl Marx 1976 (1867): 301; emphasis added

1. Introduction

One of the more debated issues in Marxian theory is the relationship between Volume I and Volume III of *Capital*. Indeed, since the publication of Volume III, the thesis according to which there is a 'contradiction' between the two books has been one of the favourite arguments of Marx's critics. The main point is, of course, Marx's presumed failure to 'transform' exchange-values into prices of production.[1] The charge has been repeated again and again over the last century, beginning with Bortkiewicz and Dmitriev and ending with contemporary Neoclassicals like Samuelson, or Neo-Ricardians like Steedman. While Marx thought that exchange-values were the necessary starting points in the deduction of prices of production, these critics maintain that exchange-values are redundant. Prices, including a uniform rate of profit among industries, can be reached directly with the technological matrix and the real wage taken as givens.

A second contradiction between the two volumes can be detected – a contradiction which has been little explored in associated literature, as it is less evident. What I am referring to is the notion of money which Marx puts forward in the first chapters of Volume I, as against the notion of money underlying Volumes II and III. In Volume I, money is introduced as a special commodity, a product of labour. In these early chapters Marx's inquiry is concerned with the general exchange of commodities from which he derives money as the universal equivalent. In Volume III, the cycle – or circuit – of capital has as its first step the financing of industrial capitalists' production by monetary capitalists. Yet, a heterodox tradition in monetary thought dating back to the beginning of the century, and having among its prominent advocates Wicksell, Schumpeter and Keynes, states that money opening the circuit of capital cannot have the nature of a commodity, but is rather that of a pure symbol.[2] Today, this sign-money is bank money created *ex nihilo*. However, even gold money of the good old days had to be interpreted, to quote Keynes's well-known dictum, as 'a banknote printed on gold'.

Since the 1970s, the first contradiction has produced an uninterrupted and unending flood of books and papers, mainly by Neo-Ricardians, all scrutinizing *Marx after Sraffa*. The usual outcome is that the labour theory of value must be rejected. Although a divide exists between those like Garegnani, who hold that giving up the labour theory of value does not damage Marx's conclusions, and those like Steedman, who hold that the questionable theory is fundamental to Marx's edifice which – as a

1. In this chapter, exchange-values are defined as the money prices of commodities as long as they reflect the social labour directly and indirectly embodied in them, i.e., labour-values. This situation is sometimes referred to as a condition of 'equal exchange' (Foley 1986), and exchange-values are often labelled as 'direct' (Shaikh 1977) or 'simple' prices (De Vroey 1981). This *absolute* notion of exchange-values is the ground for the definition of the *relative* exchange value of two commodities as the ratio between their labour-values.
2. A review of this stream in monetary theory is given in Bellofiore (1992).

consequence of Sraffa's 1960 book – crumbles together with its faulty foundations and must be rebuilt from scratch. Both positions entail a negative judgement of the labour theory of value as a theory of exploitation (Volume I) – needless for Garegnani, wrong for Steedman – and as a theory of production prices (Volume III) happily rescued by Sraffa, who goes beyond Marx's errors. Alternatively, the second contradiction has been underlined in the 1980s by those who, like the present writer, insist upon the utility of reading *Marx after Schumpeter* – embracing, especially, the credit theory of money spelled out in his *Theory of Economic Development.*[3] According to this minority view, sign-money can be reconciled with the labour theory of value. The argument requires clear qualification, against parallel monetary readings of Marx's *oeuvre*. These other readings – while shifting the focus of attention from production prices to market prices, and hence reducing the emphasis on the first contradiction – end up claiming that a rejection of Marx's commodity theory of money empties his notion of exploitation of any meaning.[4]

In the course of this chapter I definitely will not establish what Marx 'really' meant. On the contrary, my point of departure is that Marx's project cannot be defended as it stands, and that some of the contradictions on which the critics have insisted are really there in *Capital*. What I want to show is that, in spite of the presence of some breaches in Marx's project, a 'core' in his critique of political economy – which is also a critical political economy – can be picked out, and that a firm grasp of this core enables Marx's progression from Volume I to Volume III to be reestablished on a sound theoretical basis. The core is the labour theory of value as a theory of the *origin* of capitalist surplus *before* it is a theory of price determination. This theory is strengthened, rather than weakened, by the shift to a monetary theory of production where the cycle of capital is seen as a monetary sequence opened by bank finance, even if this move does compel us to revise some steps in Marx's original train of thought.[5] I will specifically show how a (bank) *credit theory of*

3. Indeed, 'Marx after Schumpeter' was the title of a paper of mine published in *Capital and Class* (Bellofiore 1985a), following a close inspection of the Schumpeterian system which ended with a detailed confrontation between the Austrian economist and Marx (Bellofiore 1985b).
4. A survey of these debates encompassing the 1970s and the 1980s, with a full list of references, may be found in Bellofiore (1989): the path leading many authors from a criticism of Neo-Ricardianism to the abandonment of the quantitative (if not also the qualitative) side of the Marxian labour theory of value is summarized in sections 2 and 3: 5–9.
5. I am referring to the so-called 'circuit theory of money'. For a short description, see Bellofiore and Seccareccia (1999), where some basic texts are quoted in the bibliography.

exploitation allows us to regain the priority of exchange-values in the determination of prices of production for *methodological* reasons, thus paralleling Marx's approach to the transformation. Contrary to some 'new approaches', this reading of Marx highlights that the rate of surplus-value in Volume I before the transformation is the same as the rate of surplus-value in Volume III, but is different from the (gross) money profits/money wages ratio (as a ratio between the labour equivalents of these money magnitudes) after the transformation.

2. The origin of surplus-value

A good place to start is Part Three, Chapter 7 of *Capital*, Volume I. The sale and purchase of labour-power is over, and we now enter into the capitalist labour process as the arena where value and surplus value are created. To understand how the valorization process goes on, Marx follows a form of reasoning based on the *method of comparison*. Since the matter is a controversial one, it is best to quote Marx at length.

Marx shows us an amusing dialogue of 'our would-be capitalist' with himself. The givens in the argument are the methods of production, the level of employment, the intensity and productive power of each worker, and the real wage. To begin with, imagine that a capitalist makes wage-earners work just the time needed to reproduce their labour-power, including the replacement of the means of production. At this point, '[o]ur capitalist [says Marx] stares in astonishment. *The value of the product is equal to the value of the capital advanced.* The value advanced has not been *valorized*, no *surplus-value* has been created, and consequently *money has not been* transformed into *capital*' (Marx 1976 [1867]: 298). Please note that in this quote and those following, I've reintroduced italics missing from the original English translation. Two pages later he goes on: 'The capitalist paid to the worker a value of 3 shillings, and the worker gave him back an exact equivalent in the value of 3 shillings he added to the cotton: he gave him value for value' (*ibid.*: 300). But the capitalist's surprise is short-lived: indeed, it was a joke:

> Let us examine the matter more closely. The *value of a day's labour-power* amounts to 3 shillings, because on our assumption *half a day's labour* is objectified in that quantity of labour-power, i.e. because the means of subsistence required every day for the production of labour-power cost half a day's labour. But the past labour embodied in the labour-power and the living labour it can perform – the daily cost of maintaining labour-power and its daily expenditure in work – are two totally different things. The former determines the exchange-value of

> the labour-power, the latter is its use-value. The fact that *half a day's labour* is necessary to keep the worker alive during 24 hours does not in any way prevent him from working *a whole day*. Therefore the *value* of labour-power, and the value which that labour-power *valorizes* in the labour process, are two entirely different magnitudes; and this *difference* was what the capitalist had in mind when he was purchasing the labour-power.
>
> *Ibid.*: 300 [a minor error of translation has been amended].

What matters here is the analytical distinction between labour and labour-power, the pivot of Marx's critique of Classical Political Economy. It is thanks to this distinction that the *origin* of the capitalist surplus – that I've called the 'originary' profits elsewhere[6] – may be explained: '[o]ur capitalist foresaw this situation, and that was the cause of his laughter. The worker therefore finds, in the workshop, the means of production necessary for working not just 6 but 12 hours. ... The trick has at last worked: *money has been transformed into capital*' (*ibid.*: 301). The process of valorization

> is nothing but the *continuation* of the [process of creating value] beyond a definite point. If the process is not carried beyond the point where the value paid by the capitalist for the labour-power is replaced by an exact *equivalent*, it is simply a process of creating value; but if it is continued *beyond that point*, it becomes a process of valorization.
>
> *Ibid.*: 302

In Marx's argument, we compare two very different outlooks. The *first* is the situation where *living labour*, i.e., the abstract labour which is going to be embodied in the output, does not exceed *necessary labour*, i.e., the abstract labour embodied in the equivalent of the wage goods given over to workers. Though hypothetical, this situation is *meaningful* and *real* since a vital capitalist production process needs to reintegrate the capital advanced to reproduce the working population at the historically given standard of living. In this Marxian analogue of Schumpeter's 'circular flow' there would be no surplus-value and hence no profits, and commodities would exchange at relative ratios given by their relative exchange-values. When Marx proceeds to the *second* term of the

6. Cf. Bellofiore and Finelli (1998: 56–9).

comparison – which corresponds to what *actually* happens *in production* during the current period's valorization process, as a result of the antagonism between capital as a whole and the working class – he examines the *lengthening* of the working day beyond the point that is necessary according to the first outlook. Living labour now surpasses necessary labour as the abstract labour *embodied* in 'the means of subsistence required every day for the production of labour-power'. As a consequence of surplus labour, the capitalist surplus-value sees the light of day. Not to muddle up his inquiry into the *origin* of surplus-value in the capitalist labour process with his inquiry over its *redistribution* among the industries where it was extracted – redistribution which is due to competition between single capitals – Marx sticks to the same rule governing relative prices within the circular flow. Hence, both outputs and inputs are, for the moment, computed from exchange-values, 'attaching' simple prices to the various commodities.

It is crystal clear that this view has nothing to do with the idea that the labour theory of value gives an adequate picture of a 'simple commodity production' stage historically preceding the capitalist stage. Rather, the (abstract) labour theory of value is a *logical* device Marx adopts to show why surplus value is nothing other than surplus labour. The comparison Marx makes is not between a situation where the wages of petty commodity producers exhaust income, and a situation where capitalists are present and making profits out of a proportional reduction in wages. It is rather between two actual *capitalist* situations, where the *determining factor* is the 'continuation' of the social working day (holding constant the given price rule).[7] There is however, in a

7. Because *both* terms of the comparison are *essentially* capitalist, *both* are *real* and *both* affect *production*, my interpretation is different from Rubin's reading of the relationship between value and production price (Rubin 1973 [1928]: 221–57), which from other points of view may be seen as an anticipation of the line proposed here – especially for the stress on the 'method of comparison'. According to Rubin, the 'first' comparison is between a *simple commodity* economy and an *embryonic capitalist* economy abstracting from competition, where capitalists take the place of petty commodity producers and there is a parallel reduction in the income of 'direct producers', i.e. workers. In fact, Rubin sees the labour theory of value as a theory of the capitalist economy only inasmuch as it is a theory of a *commodity* economy where production relations are mediated by *the market*. On the contrary, I see the labour theory of value as a theory of the extraction by total capital of labour and surplus labour (and thereby of value and surplus-value) from the whole working class, thanks to the form-determination of the capitalist production process which empowers capital to overcome the potential resistance of workers to valorization (cf. Bellofiore and Finelli, 1998: especially 59–63; and Bellofiore,

very special sense, a 'historical' element behind Marx's argument, but not the one stressed by Engels, nor the 'historical transformation problem' advanced by Meek and others. It is rather the *sequential* nature of the capitalist monetary process within each period – that is, the time implicit in the chain of successive phases going on during the monetary circuit. I will say more on this later. What is important now is to understand that Marx's comparison is effected not only when absolute surplus value is first pumped out, but at the end of each capitalist monetary circuit – and that this compels us to go back to exchange-values as the ruling prices.

The crucial role of the 'method of comparison' we are referring to may be measured also by the central role it plays in Marx's critique of Ricardo in the *Theories of Surplus Value*, Volume II, Chapter 15. In Part A, Section 2, called 'Surplus value'. Marx writes:

> The total working-day is *greater* than that part of the working-day which is required for the production of the wages. Why? That does not emerge [in Ricardo]. The *magnitude of the total working-day* is therefore wrongly assumed to be *fixed* ... But it is equally obvious, that [if] with a given labour-time (a given length of the working-day) the productivity of labour [may be very different], on the other hand, with a given productivity of labour, the labour-time, the length of the working-day, may be very different. Furthermore, it is clear that though the existence of *surplus-labour* presupposes that the productivity of labour has reached a certain level, the mere *possibility* of this surplus-labour (i.e. the existence of that necessary minimum productivity of labour) does not in itself make it a *reality*. For this to occur, the labourer must first be *compelled* to work in excess of the [necessary] time, and this compulsion is exerted by capital.
>
> Marx 1975 (1861–63): 406

1999, sections 5 and 6). In *this* sense, the theory of value is not a 'first' approximation to capitalist reality, but rather its only *fully* adequate theoretical picture; though, of course, it needs to be complemented by an analysis of competition among capitals. A similar point is made by Arthur (1999). For analogous reasons, my view of Marx's 'method of comparison' is still farther away from Croce's early Neo-Kantian approach (cf. Croce 1966 [1900]: 60–6). Croce confronts capitalist value with some theoretical standard – a 'type', as he calls it – which is not, as in Rubin, a generalization of one aspect of capitalist society, but rather a picture of an imaginary *non*capitalist society. Croce's perspective has been recently revived by Bellanca (1997).

The passage quoted suggests that in each valorization process, the mere possibility of surplus labour given by some 'presupposed' level of the productive power of labour, becomes a reality only through capitalist control; i.e., it must be realized through a 'social' element, the *forced* and *other-directed* nature of the living labour of wage workers. I cannot pursue this thread here to show that in the Marxian argument, with the real subsumption of labour to capital, the 'technical' possibility of surplus labour is shown to depend on – to be the 'posit' of – the 'social' condition of labour in the production process (for a development of this argument, see my papers quoted in footnote 7).

In Volume I, each firm is seen as just a fraction of total capital. The pumping out of living labour in each capitalist labour process leads in the aggregate to a division of the social working day into two magnitudes: the *necessary labour* hidden behind the *wage goods* which are made available to the working class, and the *surplus labour* hidden behind what we may call *profit goods*, the capital goods or the consumption goods taken over by the capitalist class. This macro social sharing of the current 'value added' by workers is accurately reflected in the rate of surplus value as the ratio of the simple price of profit goods over the simple price of wage goods – that is, in the ratio of the surplus labour *embodied* in profit goods over the necessary labour *embodied* in wage goods which are the result of *production*.

3. The value of money and the value of labour-power

It looks like quite a clear-cut argument. It isn't. I have omitted essential elements in Marx's approach. So let us then complete the picture. The first qualifications touch on the problematic identity between embodied labour coefficients and magnitudes of value we posed before. The problems here are two. The first is that the living labour of wage-workers is, before exchange, only a potential value. At the beginning of *Capital*, when the analysis is still limited to the 'presupposition' of a general exchange of commodities, abstract labour is private labour *becoming* social labour on the market. When the unfolding of the argument shows that exchange may be general only with capital, the private labours externally connected in actual exchange are shown not to be the labours of private independent producers but the labours organized by capitalist firms. The capitalist organization of production marks out abstract labour as a 'bet' on sociality made by the individual industrial capitalist, a *precommensuration* of labour in advance of final exchange which in its turn has to be *ante-validated* by the monetary capitalist in advance of production. That bet, of course, has to be submitted to the further, eventual, validation of the commodity market.[8] Not only does the labour time spent in production count in so far as it is the 'socially necessary labour time' for the production of use values: it must also correspond to social need. Marx assumes all along in Volume I – and for much of the other two volumes (including the transformation problem) – that the potential value in production will be really 'actualized' in final exchange. On the basis of this hypothesis, the living labour of the wage-worker spent in the sphere of production, which strictly speaking is only 'potential' abstract labour, is considered to be fully 'realized' on the commodity market.

The second problem concerns the unity of production and circulation. Again in the first chapters of *Capital*, before introducing capital into the picture, the metamorphosis of abstract labour into social labour is not effected through the direct exchange of the commodity against other commodities, but through the indirect exchange of the commodity with money as the universal equivalent. Money here is considered as a very

8. The precommensuration of labour before final exchange is explicitly stressed by Reuten and Williams (1989), but a similar notion is implicit in Napoleoni (1975 [1973]) and in Rubin (1973 [1928]). The idea of ante-validation is indebted to De Brunhoff's (1967) writings on Marx's monetary aspects. Rubin (1973 [1928]) wanted to ground labour as 'potential' social, abstract, simple and socially necessary before exchange, as a particular phase of the process of capitalist reproduction (among the many possible quotes, see those on 70, 128, 149–50, 154–5). He didn't fully succeed because in his approach the monetary sanction of social equalization was only *ex post*, through the acquisition by the commodity of the form of value *on the commodity market*, when labour is already *dead* labour. This of course contradicts his efforts to anticipate some 'preliminary', 'ideal' social magnitude in the phase of exchange as such. Once the 'initial finance' is interpreted as I interpret it in this chapter – that is, as the ante-validation of the *living* labour of the wage workers through the mediation of financiers' and entrepreneurs' expectations: so that the actual labour *in motion* within the capitalist labour process, labour as *activity*, can be qualified as *at the same time* concrete and latently abstract – it is possible to take up again Rubin's Hegelian standpoint. According to Rubin, in Hegel the content is not in itself something to which form adheres from outside. Rather, through its development, 'the content itself gives birth to the form which was already latent in the content. Form necessarily grows out of the content itself. This is a basic premise of Hegel's and Marx's methodology, a premise which is opposed to Kant's methodology. From this point of view, the form of value necessarily grows out of the substance of value. Therefore, we must take abstract labor in all the variety of its social properties as characteristic of a commodity economy, as the substance of value' (117–18). This last passage must be read, contrary to a widespread myth, as saying that for Rubin the character of abstract labour – though not in the full sense of the word – is there *already* in the process of direct production. Further considerations are in Bellofiore and Finelli (1998: 51–6).

'special' commodity. Once more, it is important to quote Marx's own words at this stage:

> *[p]roducts of labour* would not become commodities, were they not products of separate *private labours*, carried on independently of one another. The *social interconnection* of these private labours exists materially, insofar as they are *members of a* [*natural-spontaneous*] *social division* of labour and hence, through their products, satisfy wants of different kinds, in the totality of which the similarly [*natural-spontaneous*] *system of social wants* consists. This *material* social interconnection of private labours carried on independently of one another is however only *mediated* and hence is realised only through the *exchange* of their products. The product of private labour hence *only* has *social form* insofar as it has *value-form* and hence the *form of exchangeability* with other products of labour. It has *immediately social form* insofar as its own bodily or natural form is *at the same time* the form of its exchangeability with other commodities or *counts as value-form for other commodities*. However, as we have seen, this only takes place for a product of labour when, through the *value relation of other commodities to it*, it is in *equivalent-form* or, with respect to other commodities, plays *the role of equivalent.*
>
> Marx 1978 (1867): 140, italics in the text

Gold as the 'product of labour' which plays the role of the *universal* equivalent 'counts as the value-form for other commodities', and hence it 'has immediately social form'. The inner opposition between use-value and value within the commodity develops into an *external* opposition: the equivalent-commodity counts as value-form, the shape of exchange value, while the other commodity counts as the shape of use value. As a consequence, the *concrete* labour producing money as a commodity is *immediately* not private but *social* labour: it is *the form of actualization of abstract labour*. Gold as money is a commodity in the sense of being produced by labour. It is not a commodity in the sense of 'having' value (though Marx often uses this expression). Value is private labour validated in exchange, whereas money does not need to be validated almost by definition: rather, money as the *material* symbol of abstract labour 'represents' value in its own 'bodily or natural' form. Major consequences follow from this view of value and money. The magnitude of (potential) value within a commodity can be traced back to 'embodied' labour *merely as a share of the labour producing money as a commodity*. On the market, the *monetary expression of labour time* tells us how many units of money, and hence of *directly social* labour, a unit of (*private, indirectly social*) labour time spent in producing commodities is able to buy. It is the sum of prices divided by the labour time pumped out in production. The *value of money* is the reciprocal, i.e., the amount of (*directly social*) labour embodied in the production of money as a commodity. This allows Marx to translate labour embodied in commodities into observable money magnitudes in the market (as the quotes in the second section of this chapter make clear).

Marx's commodity theory of money is relevant also to understanding his notion of the *value of labour-power* in *Capital*, Volume I. Marx is well aware that the wage is paid in *money* by the capitalist to the worker before entering production, and that the latter has to wait after the end of production until he will spend the wage on the commodity market, confirming the *real* wage. The labour embodied in the real consumption basket of the worker is, therefore, unidentified *before* the valorization process. Marx, however, claims the opposite: the owner of money, he stresses, has *already* paid the value of labour-power on the labour market. Marx is quite right in taking this position. Variable capital is money-capital which may be thought of as gold, that is, an amount of (*directly social*) labour *embodied* that is *given* before the valorization process. If the real wage is at the 'subsistence' level – a level which is determined by 'historical and moral elements' and hence by class conflict – the labour embodied in the gold buying labour-power at the beginning corresponds to a given amount of the abstract labour embodied in the wage goods bought by the worker. There is a bi-directional mapping between the money *equivalent* of labour-power and the value of labour-power, both being reducible to embodied labours.

As a consequence, in this *monetary* perspective Marx's application of his 'method of comparison' appears to have this structure: (1) at the beginning of the circuit the 'would-be' capitalist advances the value of labour-power in *money* (i.e., gold) with a given labour content, which corresponds to the value of labour-power because the capitalist class will in fact supply on the market at the end of the circuit the *subsistence* wages the working class expects; (2) if the labourers' work lasts until their living labour reaches the necessary labour embodied in the *money* (i.e., gold) advanced, the owner of money would not become a capitalist; exchange-values would be the ruling prices; (3) the 'would-be' capitalist is actually a smart capitalist: he compels workers to expend living labour exceeding the necessary labour embodied in the *money* (i.e., gold) advanced, hence creating surplus abstract labour; (4) when the capitalist goes to the commodity market he gets back a *larger sum of money*, hence a larger amount of labour embodied in gold as the universal equivalent: the surplus-value is nothing other than the 'surplus labour' contained in the extra money, and corresponds to a certain amount of actualized abstract labour coming from production; (5) the real wage gained by the worker after production is equal to the value which the 'special' commodity labour-power deserves in this mode of production because it is the labour time needed for the production and reproduction of this specific article: a value which, according to Marx, in a given country and in a given period is a *datum*. Beware of the causality chain: the value of money is *given* at the beginning of the circuit; it is because the value of money is *already* given that variable capital may be expressed *both* in labour and in money *before* production, and that the living labour of wage-workers may be expressed *both* in labour and in money *before* the final exchange on the commodity market.

Two objections may be raised against this train of thought. Let's start from the end. The correspondence of the labour embodied in money as a commodity with the labour embodied in the consumption bundle of the wage-worker we mapped in the previous argument is, of course, valid only within 'equal exchange' – namely, with relative prices proportional to relative exchange-values, or with money prices at simple prices. When production prices diverging from simple prices emerge, the labour *bought* on the commodity market by the money wage paid in gold and the labour *embodied* in the production of wage goods will not, in general, correspond. Here we come up against a consequence of the first contradiction we recalled in the Introduction of this chapter: I shall return to it in the next section. The other charge goes to the heart of the matter: can money be coherently depicted as a *product of labour* – as a 'special' commodity – in a monetary production economy like Marx's capitalism? My answer is negative. In a monetary economy based on wage labour, the production both of consumption goods and of capital goods must be financed with money.[9] The *sequence* is *opened* by the exchange between capital and labour on the *labour market*: firms buy the labour-power they need in view of the output they plan to sell after production. The dealing between firms and workers is a standard labour contract in money, and the general means of payment to firms to fulfil their obligation is

9. This point, and more generally the view on money adopted in this section and in the sixth section of this chapter is heavily dependent on the writings of Augusto Graziani (1989 and 1997).

provided by the banking system. *Production* is the *intermediate* step and it *takes time*: for the sake of simplicity, I assume that production begins at the same moment and lasts one period for each firm. After production, at the *closing* of the circuit, the *commodity market* opens. Consumption goods are sold to the workers against their money wage, whereas the rest of the output remains inside the firm sector, either as capital goods for productive use or as consumption goods for personal use.

Thus, in a closed economy, *initial finance* from banks is necessary in order that firms are able to acquire labour-power and intermediate goods – the expenditure for intermediate goods disappears in aggregate for firms, and the initial finance needed by the capitalist class reduces to the *wages bill*. If money is the outcome of this production process – the 'gold producer' – where does the money financing the production of money as a commodity come from? This question, and the related one – where should the extra money paying for surplus-value come from? – was posed by Rosa Luxemburg, with good theoretical insight. Unfortunately, she lost her way in the fog of the gold producer on the former question, and gave only a partial and incorrect answer to the latter question, referring to the money coming into the commodity market from 'external' sources. As Schumpeter clearly saw, and Wicksell before him, the problem can be satisfactorily answered only if finance to production means bank loans created *ex nihilo*, with money interpreted as a *pure symbol*.

The second contradiction recalled in my Introduction reappears. If money has no labour content, then the Marxian notion of exploitation may seem to get into trouble. Without money as a commodity, it is impossible to establish the labour counterpart of variable capital as an advance of money *before production*, and to calculate *before final exchange* the amount of the surplus labour embodied in the extra money the firm is struggling for (indeed, the very notion of extra money becomes dubious, for reasons I will not go into now). From production we can grasp only living labour as indirect social labour: to know the division of the social working day, we have to wait until (gross) profits and wages are spent on the commodity market. In an inconvertible paper money system, the value of money and the value of labour-power will be fixed only at the end of the monetary circuit. Hence critics argue, Marx's chain of causality collapses.[10]

10. An extensive review of the (mainly French) literature criticizing Marx's value theory from a noncommodity money approach is De Vroey (1985). An interesting commentary on all these difficulties is Messori (1997 [1984]).

4. The transformation of exchange-values into prices of production: another interpretation

I don't think that replacing Marx's money as a commodity with a credit theory of money gives such negative results. Before trying to solve the second contradiction, however, we need to deal with the first one: namely, the claim put forward by Neoclassicals and Neo-Ricardians alike that the shift from 'equal exchange' to 'unequal exchange' *dissolves* the labour theory of value. In this section, I intend to show how the transformation can be seen as the *consequential logical development* in Volume III of the theory of value interpreted as a theory of the origin of surplus-value developed in Volume I; and that a reappraisal of the transformation a century later disproves the positions of critics and Fundamentalists alike. In the following section, I'll refer to the so-called New Interpretation, underlining how particular definitions of the value of money and of the value of labour-power break with crucial points in Marx's argument. Then, in the sixth section of this chapter, I'll return to the issue of exploitation within the capitalist monetary sequence, and discuss to what extent the notion of surplus labour as the ground of the capitalist surplus is fully confirmed by the theory of the monetary circuit, with a logical *prior* determination of the rate of surplus-value relative to the rate of profit.

Let us go back to the argument that Marx uses to explain the birth of surplus-value from surplus labour. In the *logical* order of that argument, capital cannot be presupposed in itself. As reference to the 'method of comparison' shows, Marx has to start from a situation where surplus-value is assumed away. At the same time, in the *temporal* sequence of the capitalist process the metamorphosis between labour and capital on the labour market precedes the production of capitalist commodities to be sold on the market. Hence, exchange on the labour market *constitutes* the capitalist process in a double meaning. Being introduced before capital is explained, the inputs to the valorization process have to be considered as *mere* commodities, and this affects also the valuation of the wage goods that make up the subsistence bundle (those wage goods which determine the value of the labour-power at the beginning of the circuit). Commodities may be deduced as *capitalist* commodities only *after* exchange on the labour market: it is as a *consequence* of the *double* social relationship in the labour market *and* in the capitalist labour process that capital is *produced*; the former alone is not enough, consideration of the latter is essential. To have capital *as the output* of the production process, the inputs bought by money capital have to be initially conceived as *not* capitalist commodities.

This two-step argument in *Capital*, Volume I, which explains the origin of surplus-value and thereby of capital, is prolonged in the two-step transformation Marx suggests in Volume III. As I've shown in the second section of this chapter, Volume I relative prices are equal to relative exchange-values, and money prices to simple prices: because these are the prices proper to the situation of circular flow (the first side of the comparison), and because when the ideal lengthening of working time gives way to surplus value (the second side of the comparison, which is nothing other than the actual situation), surplus-value is not immediately redistributed to individual industries. When we go on to the analysis of the redistribution of surplus-value among competing capitals, we need to take into account that the individual capitalist is interested in the ratio between the excess in the value of a product over the capital advanced, and that a tendency towards the formation and equalization of the *profit rate* is immanently built into the abstract nature of capitalist wealth. Our inquiry must then deal with the issue of the determination of relative prices which allow for an equal rate of profit, and of money prices as production prices; and to ask if those relative prices (which in general differ from relative exchange-values) and those production prices (which in general differ from simple prices) are compatible with the labour theory of value.

The deduction of prices of production is, in Marx, effected once again through a *mediation* which, first of all, aims at explaining the formation of the category in question – the general rate of profit – and afterwards look at the feedbacks of the new category on the theoretical structure. The *formation* of the general rate of profit is tackled by Marx in strict continuity with the first two-step comparison in Volume I. He starts by asking how prices of the capitalist *output*, allowing for an equal rate of profit, are determined. Since in Volume I the inputs had to be accounted for as mere commodities when explaining the origin of surplus-value, Marx begins his construction of the general rate by connecting *total* surplus-value with *total* capital advanced, the numerator and the denominator still being computed in simple prices. This is the general rate of profit as it is introduced in Volume III, Part Two, Chapter 9. Through the application of this rate of profit to advanced capital computed at simple prices Marx reaches, for the first time, a capitalist price for output. Thus, the same commodity has a *double exchange-ratio*: it is valued at simple prices when it is looked at as an input, and at production prices when it is looked at as an output. To examine the *feedbacks* we must subsequently apply the capitalist price of the outputs to the inputs, as Marx himself suggests. If we iterate the procedure, we reach the Sraffian simultaneous solution for a reproduction 'equilibrium' where relative prices which include a uniform profit rate reestablish the 'originary' distribution of the commodities. Now input prices and output prices are the same.

Before making further comment on Marx after Sraffa, let me stress that here we have another application of the 'method of comparison'. The *first* step of this second comparison, where the rate of profit *à la* Marx and the prices of capitalist output are set, is another theoretical construction whose function is to provide a bridge between the first comparison in Volume I – which discovers surplus labour behind the capitalist surplus – to the *second* step of the second comparison – which 'extends' the transformation to the inputs, as suggested in Volume III. It is possible in this way to *isolate* the object of analysis of Volume I, the production of surplus-value (the origin of the capitalist surplus), taking fully into account the *unity* of production and circulation and without *severing the links* with the redistribution of surplus- value in circulation. Once again, this theoretical construction in the second comparison is expressing something hypothetical but *real*, the 'value' rate of profit hidden behind its surface modified expression as the 'price' rate of profit.

Thus, the method whereby Marx tackles the problem is such that we move *sequentially* along two routes, whose order cannot be reversed. We begin with an argument tracing capital back to labour: it is a *linear*, one-way road. Labour *originates* capital because capital compels labour-power to perform a living labour greater than necessary labour. Capital here is the outcome of the argument, not the starting point. It is then justified, theoretically, to recognize the logical priority of labour over capital and, therefore, recognize that inputs are not immediately taken to be capitalist commodities; hence, the first valuation of the elements of constant and variable capital at simple prices. In this view, the determination of the general rate of profit in the way Marx accomplishes it in Volume III is quite straightforward. Subsequently, we must include the means of subsistence as well as the other inputs and also outputs of capital's *circular* process. Once the 'originary' profits have seen the light, and the formation of the uniform rate of profit has been accounted for, prices of production and the general rate of profit must be *simultaneously* determined on the commodity market, at the end of the circuit.

This methodical sequentiality is fundamental to Marx. The rate of profit of the simultaneous solution would be meaningless if it were not grounded in the dynamics of production as the centre of the valorization process, through the 'value' rate of profit in Chapter 9. If this point has been totally overlooked by the Neo-Ricardians, where is the problem for the Fundamentalists? The problem is that Marx is not at all clear that the rate of profit as he computed it in Chapter 9 was not the end of the story, e.g., that it was *different* from the one reached by iterating his procedure, and converging to the simultaneous solution. He rather seems to assume that the two are identical. Moreover, contrary to Marx's strictures, after Seton and Sraffa we know that prices of production can be set *directly* without starting from exchange-values: an accounting of the conditions of production at simple prices is redundant – in the precise sense that the last stage of the deduction of the prices of production *cancels* traces of all the previous steps. Finally, the simultaneous solution cannot confirm in one stroke the two famous equalities – between the total value added in prices of production and in exchange-values, and between (gross) profits and surplus-value – through which Marx intends to show that 'price' changes merely redistribute 'value' magnitudes, and that the total of (gross) profits is merely the phenomenal form of the total of surplus labour. According to Marx, not only is the rate of profit before and after the 'correction' to inputs the same: but also the rate of surplus-value and the (gross) money profits/money wage ratio (as a ratio between the labour equivalent of these monetary magnitudes) should be equal.

This last charge has been countered by the New Interpretation proposed by Duménil and Foley.[11] Now I would like to take a closer look at the latter.

5. The New Interpretation

We saw in the third section of this chapter that Marx's argument in *Capital*, Volume I, was framed in a monetary sequence economy, where money was understood as a money-commodity. Before going into the details of the New Interpretation of the transformation of simple prices into prices of production, it may be helpful to sketch out how consideration of the monetary nature of Marx's first comparison affects the issue.

If we move from 'equal' to 'unequal' exchange – that is, if prices diverge from simple prices – after the transformation, an hour of labour embodied in money as a commodity (i.e., an hour of directly social labour) *buys* in exchange a different magnitude of abstract labour (i.e., a different amount of indirectly social labour) than before. The two definitions of the value of labour-power given by Marx in Volume I – labour *bought* for a *given* amount of the universal equivalent and the labour *embodied* in

11. Cf. Duménil (1980) and Foley (1986). The considerations in the text apply more to Foley's version of the New Interpretation than to Duménil's.

production in the *given* amount of the means of subsistence – become contradictory. It is of course, quite meaningful to say that in both schemes there *is* an amount of labour contained *both* in money as a commodity *and* in the wage goods bought by workers. But we reach different results in the transformation if either the former or the latter are held constant.

We are indeed compelled to make a choice: either we take as given the variable capital in *money* (i.e., the hours of labour embodied in money as a commodity buying labour-power), or we take as given the *elements* of variable capital (i.e., the hours of labour embodied in the production of the wage goods workers are able to buy). If we assume that finance to production is unchanged from the 'price' to the 'value' scheme, and if prices of production are higher (lower) than simple prices, the amount of commodities bought by a given money wage will be lower (higher) after the transformation. The necessary labour embodied in the means of subsistence will then be known only after the transformation or, if you like, the real wage now becomes an endogenous variable. Following this route, the hours of labour embodied in money as a commodity are the datum in the transformation, whereas the hours of labour embodied in the production of the wage goods the worker can buy are a function of the purchasing power of money as a commodity at the new prices. On the other hand, if we stick to the real wage as the exogenous variable, the hours of labour embodied in the production of the wage goods the worker can buy are the datum in the transformation, since the wage bundle is given, and the amount of money advanced as variable capital must then be adjusted to allow workers to buy the wage bundle in both schemes.

The New Interpretation is, in a sense, a generalization of the first route, the one in which the money wage is given, leading to a situation where money may not be a product of labour. In their solution, the *normalization constraint* is that the value added by actual living labour remains the same both in exchange-values and in prices of production. The sum of variable capital and surplus-value is therefore, by definition, identical to the sum of (gross) profits and wages in money. What is essential to Marx, it is argued, is that the value added exactly represents (indirectly) social labour time – a point on which, by the way, I fully agree. To express this view, the equation where living labour's monetary expression is set equal to the price of the 'net product' takes the place of the Volume III equality between total 'values' and total 'prices'. The *value of labour-power* is here meant to be the *labour time equivalent of the money wage*. We then need to know the *value of money* to know the value of labour-power. Since money is not a commodity, the value of money bears no relation whatsoever to any notion of labour embodied in the universal equivalent, as it was for Marx. The value of money is now simply *the amount of (indirectly) social labour time a unit of money represents*, a magnitude which is indeed nothing more than the ratio of living labour over the value added in 'prices'. This means two things: that the value of money in this approach is set only *at the end* of the monetary circuit, when the 'net product' meets the demand for commodities (consumption goods and new capital goods) derived from money income (wages and profits); and that the aforementioned normalization constraint holds the value of money *constant*.

At this point in the New Interpretation, we are able to decipher the value of labour-power as the *money wage multiplied by the value of money*. It is the amount of (indirectly) social labour time bought by the money wage or, what is the same thing, *the share of the value added going to money wages*. Since *surplus-value* is defined as the *value added less the value of labour-power*, surplus-value is *just another name for (gross) money profits*. Surplus-value reduces to *unpaid labour time*: not, to be sure, the labour time embodied in the remainder of the 'net product' after a given subsistence is granted to workers; but rather, the labour time *bought* by nominal profits in exchange, *the share of living labour which does not go back to workers as an expenditure on wages*. According to this approach, the equality between (gross) money profits and surplus-value is said to confirm another essential claim of Marx's – a point which follows directly from the definitions used and on which, by the way, I disagree as a fair interpretation of the core of Marx's theoretical project.

The New Interpretation has been a tremendous advance in Marxian economics. It breaks, however, with Marx's chain of causality. The value of money and the value of labour-power are no longer given *before* the production process.[12] Moreover, surplus-value and the rate of surplus-value are no longer determined before the general profit rate resulting

12. Fred Moseley (e.g., Moseley 1993: 169–70) sidesteps this difficulty by simply *postulating* that the value of money is *already given* at the beginning of the circuit: which to the present writer appears to be no solution at all, but simply amounts to a *petitio principii*. Moseley's value of money is in fact the same as that of the New Interpretation, Foley's version. As Foley himself recognizes, the New Interpretation's definitions are *ex post accounting identities* and his approach borders on a *circulation-based view of price* (Foley 2000: 28, 30). Inasmuch as the value of money is determined only by looking at the capitalist process once the economic circuit is closed, there cannot but be a *simultaneity* of determination between prices of production and the general rate of profit. The same conclusion follows from the consideration that in Moseley's interpretation of Marx's transformation the givens from Volume I

from the transformation, and before the exchange on the commodity market. The supporters of the New Interpretation may retort that the approach they follow is compulsory, once we recognize that money may not be a commodity and that with 'unequal exchange' the dual definitions of the value of labour-power present in Volume I cannot be held together. I would like to prove the opposite in the next section.

6. Transformation in a sequence monetary economy

Let us go back to Rosa Luxemburg's fundamental question: from where does money *enter* the capitalist process? This issue is still embarrassing for 'bourgeois' general equilibrium theory, as the debate running down from Patinkin to Arrow-Debreu-Hahn to Clower to overlapping generation models shows very clearly. It also seems neglected in recent Marxian economic thought, as the exclusive and prior focus on money as a measure of value and as means of exchange confirms. Money is always thought of as being *already* there.

I have implicitly given a possible answer at the end of the third section of this chapter.[13] Money comes in through banks' initial *finance to capitalist production*. Thanks to their privileged access to money capital lent by banks, industrial capitalists hold a power not only over the determination of the level but also over the *composition* of output. The capitalist class decides how many workers to employ, and where to *allocate* them. In this *macrosocial* view, once firms as a whole have (unconsciously) chosen the share of the total labour-power going to produce wage goods

are the aggregate quantities of constant and variable capital and surplus-value *in money*: this seems to suggest that these magnitudes buy the *material* elements of constant and variable capital at their prices of production so that money givens are actually *after* the transformation. This contrasts with Moseley's assertion that his interpretation maintains Marx's priority of the 'value' rate of profit over prices of production, and that his general rate of profit is different from Sraffa's. In my view, the real need for a break with Sraffian economics has to do not with what Sraffa's *Production of Commodities by Means of Commodities* took as its object of analysis, i.e., price-determination 'after the harvest', but with what was out-of-sight in that book: money (as capital) and living labour (as source of value and surplus-value), and the internal connection between these two essential moments of capitalist reality. Whether Sraffian economics is faithful to Sraffa's original perspective is a different question. A preliminary assessment is in Bellofiore (1996). The Sraffa papers in the Cambridge archives promise to widen the gap between the two.

13. Some elements in what follows have been more fully developed in other papers written jointly with Riccardo Realfonzo: Realfonzo and Bellofiore (1996), Bellofiore and Realfonzo (1997), and Bellofiore *et al.* (2000).

and the share going to produce profit goods, the *real* consumption of the working class *is set*. At the beginning of the monetary sequence, money capital, though valueless, is nevertheless a *command over workers' labour time*. Because of this monetary ante-validation, living labour is 'latently' social even before the final exchange on the commodity market and the metamorphosis of commodities into the universal equivalent (see footnote 8). The value of money in this first step of the monetary circuit is the number of workers a unit of bank finance is able to buy. Given the methods of production and the productive power per worker, the length and intensity of the working day, and the employment level, we also know the living labour pumped out from these workers. I suggest calling the value of money *as capital* the ratio of living labour over the wage bill (variable capital in money). From aggregate production we can also establish the abstract labour embodied both in the profit goods and in the wage goods produced according to firms' decisions about the composition of output and the allocation of workers.

All this happens *before*, and *irrespective* of, any transformation of simple prices into prices of production, simply because the transformation problem 'opens up' after the conditions of production – the inputs and outputs – are set. The transformation problem is entirely placed at the level of *dead* labour, while the command of money capital affects *living* labour. The reference to labour 'in motion' is necessary for Marx to explain how in capitalism, as the monetary economy *par excellence*, the surplus is extracted from workers. In this view, the given in the transformation issue should be the aggregate *real* wage. Of course, workers' real wages will be known only *post factum*, on the commodity market. We may, as Marx did, proceed on the assumption that firms as a *whole* let workers take an *aggregate* subsistence wage bundle, in which a certain amount of abstract labour time is embodied during its production (this I would suggest calling the *value* of labour-power); we may then follow Marx in treating the value of labour-power as given before the production process 'in a given country at a given period'. Or we may consider the possibility that firms as a whole fix an aggregate real wage different from the subsistence bundle, in which a different amount of abstract labour is embodied during its production (this I suggest calling the *price* of labour-power). The necessary labour for the working class is the labour embodied in the wage goods *actually* consumed by workers. With the price equal to the value of labour-power, necessary labour is just the labour *embodied* in the subsistence bundle: '[t]he value of labour-power can be resolved into the value of a definite quantity of the means of subsistence', i.e., 'the quantity of labour-time required to produce them'

(Marx 1976 [1867]: 276). Hence, we now know the rate of surplus-value for the capitalist process as a whole as the ratio of surplus labour embodied in the production of profit goods over the necessary labour embodied in the production of wage goods; and we know this rate *prior to* production prices and the rate of profits. This rate of surplus-value is computed according to a definition of the value of labour-power at exchange-values.

When we go on to determine prices of production, we must take into account what happens to the value of money as capital, and what happens to the value of labour-power. Let me start with the latter. The methods of production, the intensity and productive power of each worker and the real wage, but also the length of the social working day and the conditions of production (the level and composition of output, and the inputs actually employed) are now the givens of the problem. With production prices different from simple prices, workers can consume the same wage bundle only if the value of labour-power is *reevaluated* at the new prices. This means that the variable capital in money has to change: if the price of production of wage goods is higher (lower) than their simple price the wage bill will increase (decrease), as if banks' initial finance is going up (down). Since the wage bill is the denominator of the value of money as capital and since living labour, the numerator, is unchanged, the value of money as capital in the 'price' scheme is lower (higher) after the transformation. It seems strange, but it is not. In fact, we are holding constant in the transformation *both* the *purchasing power* of initial finance in terms of the total living labour *and* the *real cost* of labour-power needed by total capital to extract that living labour. This necessarily implies a change in the *nominal* magnitude of initial finance relative to the 'value' scheme. In other words, money capital's command over labour time in Volume III has to based on two *givens* – the total social working day and necessary labour – which are the *results* of the inquiry in Volume I into the capital-labour class struggle within production and the labour market. But of course this imposes the development of a new category: the *transformed* value (or, *mutatis mutandis*, the *transformed* price) of labour-power, e.g., the real wage accounted in 'prices'.

Let us look at this point from another angle. Wage workers sell their labour-power against the wage bill. There is then a certain sum of money the working class will spend on the commodity market. If we accept the normalization constraint of the New Interpretation, we require the constancy of what Foley originally called the value of money (and that I prefer to qualify as the value of money *spent as income*, to distinguish it from the value of money as capital). However I give a *double* valuation of labour-power – first at exchange-values, then at prices of production. Why? With the former valuation I obtain the (macro) rate of surplus-value as the ratio between the abstract labour *embodied* in the production of profit goods over the abstract labour *embodied* in the production of wage goods. With the latter valuation I get the (gross) profit/wage ratio as the ratio between the abstract labour *represented* in the money buying the profit goods over the labour *represented* in the money buying the wage goods. The meaning is quite clear. When wage goods are sold at the end of the circuit, they gain an amount of (indirect) social labour expressed by the wage bill *after the transformation* multiplied by the value of money as income. Since exchange is 'unequal', this amount is divergent from the abstract labour embodied in the production of those wage goods themselves – which may be also resolved in the amount of (indirect) social labour expressed by the wage bill *before the transformation* multiplied by the same value of money. The latter reveals what is obscured in the former, the *division of the social working day among classes.* The real wage of the working class expressed at exchange-values is more *fundamental* than the same real wage at prices of production. It is the end-result of class struggle in the valorization process, which is hidden behind the circulation and distribution of commodities.[14]

14. This view of the *duality* of the accounting systems by which to compute the value of labour-power and the consequent *duplication* of the rate of surplus value from the ratio of the labour equivalent of (gross) money profits over the labour equivalent of money wages has also been proposed in Bellofiore (1989: 16–17). In that paper the rate of surplus value was labelled as the 'value' rate of exploitation, and the ratio of the labour equivalent of (gross) money profits over the labour equivalent of money wages as the 'price' rate of exploitation 'in circulation'. An interpretation of the role of 'exchange-values' versus 'prices of production' and of the rate of surplus value very similar to the one put forward in the present chapter seems to be suggested by Robert F. Brinkman in an unpublished paper summarized in Foley (2000: 26): 'Brinkman proposes to distinguish "essential prices" (money prices divided by the monetary expression of labour time [the New Interpretation's 'value of money']) and "labor values", that is embodied labor coefficients. He argues that embodied labor coefficients are the appropriate accounting system to distinguish in general between necessary and surplus labor time, but that essential prices are the appropriate accounting system to distinguish between paid and unpaid labor time. Profit and the wage bill are always equal to paid and unpaid labor time, but paid and unpaid labor time are equal to necessary and surplus labor time only under special assumptions that guarantee the proportionality of embodied labor coefficients to prices of production.'

Conclusion

What is the relationship between this interpretation of the transformation and Marx's own approach? On the view I have proposed here, the argument in exchange-values is foundational because it gives an *explanation* of how the capitalist surplus stems from a *prolongation* of labour over the necessary labour embodied in the *production* of wage goods, as in Volume I. The transformation of simple prices into production prices in Volume III means that the sole external input for firms as a whole – labour-power – has to be valued according to a *double* exchange ratio to get the phenomenal (gross) profits/wage ratio (as a ratio of labour equivalents) without losing sight of class relations in production. The *logical* priority of this macro analysis of the pumping out of labour and surplus labour over the micro determination of prices – linked as it is to a *temporal* sequence within the monetary circuit from finance (labour-*power*) to production (*living* labour) to exchange (*dead* labour) – is what I see as the 'core' of Marxian value theory. This core is fully respected in the alternative perspective I am proposing. What is lost is the neat correspondence in Marx's argument between the rate of surplus-value in the class economy as a whole and the rate of surplus-value in each valorization process, since the latter changes if, within the given aggregate wage bundle, we allow workers the freedom to choose their personal consumption basket.

Neo-Ricardians and Fundamentalists alike may retort that the eventual shape of the transformation in my view is, once again, the simultaneous solution – loved by the former, hated by the later. So what? The determination of prices on the commodity market *is* simultaneous. Value theory was for Marx *also* a theory of price determination: but this is a *secondary* aspect, the *fundamental* aspect being value theory as a theory of the *origin* of the capitalist surplus. Marx surely did not intend that the last stage in the transformation should cancel the previous one. But is it not a spectacular corroboration of his theory of fetishism that there is no trace of the reification process in the reified, so that we have the picture of a 'production of commodities by means of commodities'? That capital as a *circular* process, where current labour is already *dead* in the 'things' and *included* as the 'means of subsistence', *conceals* capital as the *linear* process where *living* labour *produces* the 'originary' profits and hence capital itself?

Bibliography

Arthur, C. (1999), Napoleoni on Labour and Exploitation, *Rivista di Politica Economica*, April–May: 141–63.

Bellanca, N. (1997), *Economia politica e marxsmo in Italia.Problemi teorici e nodi storiografici 1880–1960* (Milano: Unicopli).

Bellofiore, R. (1985a), Marx after Schumpeter, *Capital and Class,* 8 (24): 60–74.

— (1985b), Money and Development in Schumpeter, *Review of Radical Political Economy,* 17 (1–2): 21–40.

— (1989), A Monetary Labor Theory of Value, *Review of Radical Political Economy,* 21 (1–2): 1–25.

— (1992), Monetary Macroeconomics before the *General Theory*, the circuit theory of money in Wicksell, Schumpeter and Keynes, *Social Concept*, 6 (2): 47–89.

— (1996), Sraffa in context, *Research in Political Economy*, 15: 305–14.

Bellofiore, R., Forges Davanzati, G. and Realfonzo, R. (2000), Marx Inside the Circuit: Discipline device, wage bargaining and unemployment in a sequential monetary economy, *Review of Political Economy*, 12 (4): 403–17.

Bellofiore, R. and Finelli, R. (1998), Capital, Labour and Time, The Marxian Monetary Labour Theory of Value as a Theory of Exploitation, in R. Bellofiore (ed.), *Marxian Economics: A Reappraisal* (London/New York: Macmillan/St Martin's Press): 48–74.

Bellofiore, R. and Realfonzo, R. (1997), Finance and the Labor Theory of Value, Toward a Macroeconomic Theory of Distribution from a Monetary Perspective, *International Journal of Political Economy*, 17 (2) (special issue, Marxian theory: the Italian debate – ed. R. Bellofiore): 97–118.

Bellofiore, R. and Seccareccia, M., Monetary Circuit, in P.A. O'Hara (ed.), *Encyclopedia of Political Economy* (London: Routledge): 753–6.

Brunhoff, S. de (1967), *La monnaie chez Marx* (Paris: Editions Sociales).

Croce, B. (1966 [1867]), *Historical Materialism and the Economics of Karl Marx* (London: Frank Cass & Co.).

Duménil, G. (1980), *De la valeur aux prix de production* (Paris: Economica).

Foley, D. (1986), *Understanding Capital: Marx's Economic Theory* (Cambridge, MA: Harvard University Press).

Foley, D. (2000), Recent Developments in the Labor Theory of Value, *Review of Radical Political Economics*, 32: 1–39.

Graziani, A. (1989), The Theory of the Monetary Circuit, *Thames Papers in Political Economy*, Spring.

— (1997 [1986]), The Marxist Theory of Money, *International Journal of Political Economy*, 17 (2) (special issue, Marxian theory: the Italian debate – ed. R. Bellofiore): 26–50.

Marx, K. (1975), *Theories of Surplus Value* (London: Lawrence & Wishart).

— (1976 [1867]), *Capital, A Critique of Political Economy*, Vol. I (Harmondsworth: Penguin).

— (1978 [1867]), The Value-Form, *Capital and Class*, 2 (4): 130–50.

— (1981 [1894]), *Capital, A Critique of Political Economy*, Vol. III (Harmondsworth: Penguin).

Messori, M. (1997 [1984]), The Theory of Value Without Commodity Money, Preliminary Considerations on Marx's Analysis of Money, *International Journal of Political Economy*, 17 (2) (special issue, Marxian theory: the Italian debate – ed. R. Bellofiore): 51–96.

Moseley, F. (1993), Marx's Logical Method and the 'Transformation Problem', in F. Moseley (ed.), *Marx's Method in 'Capital': A Reexamination* (Atlantic Highlands, NJ: Humanities Press): 157–83.

Napoleoni, C. (1975 [1973]), *Smith Ricardo Marx* (Oxford: Blackwell).
Realfonzo, R. and Bellofiore, R. (1996), Marx and Money, Il terzo libro del Capitale di Marx, *Trimestre*, 29 (1–2) (special issue, – ed. M. L. Guidi): 189–212.
Reuten, G. and Williams, M. (1989), *Value-Form and the State: the tendencies of accumulation and the determination of economic policy in capitalist society* (London/New York: Routledge).
Rubin, I. (1973 [1928]), *Essays on Marx's Theory of Value* (Montreal: Black Rose).
Shaikh, A. (1977), Marx's Theory of Value and the 'Transformation Problem', in J. Schwartz (ed.), *The Subtle Anatomy of Capitalism* (Santa Monica: Good Year Publishing Co.): 106–49.
Vroey, M. de (1981), Value, Production and Exchange, in I. Steedman *et al.*, *The Value Controversy* (London: Verso): 173–201).
— (1985), La théorie marxiste de la valeur, version travail abstrait, Un bilan critique, in B. Chavance (ed.), *Marx en perspective* (Paris: Editions de l'Ecole des Haute Etudes en Sciences Sociales): 385–417.

6
Capital, Competition and Many Capitals

Christopher J. Arthur

The three books of *Capital* given to us were intended to cover the topic of 'capital in general'; and they were originally to have been followed by a study of 'competition or the interaction of many capitals'.[1] Several issues arise for consideration already. Did Marx stick to this plan or was material brought forward from the never-to-be-written book on competition into Volume III? Is a study of 'many capitals' (distinguished from 'capital in general' in Marx's *Grundrisse*) equivalent to the planned book on competition, or does the concept 'many capitals' raise other additional issues? Is it possible to discuss capital in general without saying something about competition?

In Chapter 3 of this book I investigate the occurrences of the term 'capital in general' in Marx's *Grundrisse*. There are no less than five different senses in which Marx used the term. The earliest of these was part of a tripartite distinction between generality, particularity and singularity, organized on Hegelian lines. This aspect I have taken up and developed in Chapter 3. But this relatively 'narrow' definition of 'capital in general' is ignored here. In this paper I shall be concerned with the other senses of the term 'capital in general' occurring in the *Grundrisse*, and, in particular to elucidate the way in which 'many capitals' are counterposed to it. Corresponding to Marx's above-mentioned plan (communicated to Engels just after the writing of the *Grundrisse*) there

1. Marx to Engels, 2 April 1858; Marx–Engels Collected Works (MECW), Vol. 40: 298.

is indeed to be found in the *Grundrisse* a distinction between 'capital in general' and competition that is part of a distinction between 'capital as such' or 'in its concept' and 'many capitals';[2] in fact there are two kinds of abstraction here: 'taken as general as opposed to in specific' and 'taken in isolation as opposed to in relation'; most of the time Marx takes the level of many capitals to be of interest because it introduces interaction. In another place it is stated that 'capital in general' is not a mere abstraction (as in the previous case), but has 'a real existence' of its own;[3] finally there is a reference to the way 'capital in general' as 'total social capital' appears as the economic basis of a class as distinct from other classes.[4] To begin with I shall be using 'capital in general' and 'many capitals' in the first sense and I will bring in the others at the appropriate point.

This chapter will treat the following topics:

1. The place of Volume III in Marx's scheme 'capital in general and competition'.
2. A careful analysis of the content of the key chapters of Volume III for our purposes, those that appear to raise the topic of competition, namely Chapters 9 and 10 on the formation of an equal rate of profit and the transformation of values into prices of production.
3. My own substantive treatment of some issues involved in capital, many capitals and competition.

It is argued that the reality of the General Rate of Profit is underlain by an understanding of capital as a totality. At the same time considerable confusion is likely in sorting out Marx's problematic if it is not understood that the concept of capital includes the *form* of competition and the dialectic of 'many capitals'. In both his *Grundrisse* and *Capital*, Volume I, Marx makes reference to the essential role of competition, and in discussing its role he talks of the 'repulsion and attraction' of capitals. This peculiar jargon provides a clue to the philosophical background of his thought, for these terms occur in Hegel's logic in close connection with his discussion of the logic of 'one and many'. Accordingly the chapter gives an account of relevant passages in Hegel's logic and considers competition in this light.

2. Marx, *Grundrisse* (trans. M. Nicolaus, 1973): 414, 517, 520, 649, 651, 661, 729, 731, 760.
3. *Ibid.*: 449.
4. *Ibid.*: 852.

1. The text of Volume III

I do not believe that Marx abandoned his plan to write a separate book on competition, having done all that was necessary in Volume III. In Volume III itself there are numerous references to it. Just one example: 'Further details on this fall outside our limits, since they are to be developed in the treatise "On Competition"'[5] – and this in a chapter headed precisely 'Competition'! We shall address this contradiction shortly. But, taken together with other similar remarks in the third volume (see 177, 205, 342, 422, 426, 970), the unavoidable conclusion is that in 1865, while writing Volume III, Marx still planned a book on competition. It seems logical to conclude from this that he thought himself still to be working within capital in general. A letter of 1868 gives a hint to the resolution of the problem posed by references to 'competition' in Volume III. Marx writes of what became Volume III: 'there is also an analysis, amongst others, of land ownership, and of *competition only in so far as the treatment of the remaining themes demands*.'[6]

For solving this problem about the occurrence in Volume III of reference to 'competition', it is necessary to make a distinction between the introduction and employment of a *concept* and a study of the *phenomena* peculiar to that domain in all their detail. If it is of the very nature of capital that it is *constituted* as 'many capitals' this does not mean that the entire content that is so structured has to be dealt with in Volume III; there it is necessary to look at competition in concrete terms only in so far as the essential forms of distribution are concerned and to combat resulting illusions in the consciousness of the capitalists concerned. According to this argument there is no contradiction in Marx's still speaking of a forthcoming treatise 'On Competition' while yet referring to competition as essential to capital in general, and concretizing this in the treatment of certain themes of Volume III. For general characteristics of a system based on many capitals confronting one another may be *abstractly* treated at the level of a study of capital in general. Questions arising from the specific differences contingently

5. K. Marx, *Das Kapital. Drittes Buch. Die Gestaltungen des Gesamtprozesses*: K. Marx and F. Engels, *Gesamtausgabe* (MEGA), Part II, Vol. 4.2, (1992): 270. This is the original manuscript of *Capital*, Vol. III, composed by Marx in 1864–65. Here the manuscript is more definite on the projected book than is Engels's edition; see *Capital*, Vol. III: 298. Note that this and all subsequent references in the text itself to Volume III are given to the following translation: *Capital*, Vol. III (trans. D. Fernbach) (Harmondsworth: Penguin, 1981).
6. Marx to Kugelmann, 6 March 1868; *Letters on 'Capital'* translated A. Drummond, 1983: 126 (my emphasis).

present in this plurality may be postponed until these more general determinations have been elucidated.[7]

Let us now examine the argument in *Capital* more closely and see precisely how 'competition' arises within Volume III. A very interesting methodological consideration adduced by Marx there is as follows: 'In a general analysis of the present kind, it is assumed throughout that actual conditions correspond to their concept' so that 'actual conditions are depicted only in so far as they express their own general type' (242). This is by no means a Weberian ideal-type method, because what is at issue here, when deviations from the 'concept' are concerned, are those arising from 'local obstacles' which it is in the nature of capital to iron out with the progressive subordination of all actual conditions to the universalizing tendencies of capital as a real force. Thus differences in the wages of simple labour, for example, are contrary to the concept of capital, and to be disregarded in a study of capital in general (275). The thematization of capital in general articulates the system of form-determinations structuring the capitalist totality. On this basis it is possible to distinguish what capital essentially is, compared with obstacles it encounters in its extensive and intensive development due to contingencies in its field of operation.

It should be stressed that this 'idealization' of actual conditions is very differently justified than is any abstraction from concrete differences that are *not* contrary to the concept. For example in considering exchange at value one abstracts from different organic compositions even though there is nothing about the concept of capital that would tend to render these uniform; likewise one discusses prices of production even though it is known that these are necessarily superseded by market prices. But these necessary differences may give rise to new forms to be situated at a more concrete level of exposition of capital in general.

It is this issue that structures the transformation of surplus-value into profit; a move to the concretion of the concept of capital brings new essential forms to light. The problem to be treated is the fact that, given different branches of production, different organic compositions of capital coexist, and that these would have different rates of profit if there were no means of equalization of profit rates. The result is to show that such a rate obtains when values are transformed into prices of production.

7. For example, I suggest such problems as 'comparative advantage' and 'geographical distantiation' could be included in a book on competition. The most important consideration Marx himself adduces in Volume III is the degree of mobility of capital and labour (298).

To begin with, let us just note that Marx assumes that he can talk of the organic composition prevalent 'in a specific *branch* of production'; that is to say, he is not concerned with '*chance differences* between individual capitals invested there' (243). This distinction maps onto that on which we have based our argument that Volume III is still at the level of capital in general; for the above mentioned 'chance differences' affect capitals as a plurality, but here we are concerned with an inner *essential* difference when we recognize the necessity for capital to integrate *branches* of production.

Now it might be argued that, since there is nothing in the concept of capital that demands uniformity in organic compositions, then analysis of the consequences of differences in this respect takes the argument into the sphere of many capitals and their competitive struggle. However this view fails to grasp the importance of organic composition as a form-determination. In Volume I differences in organic composition are set aside in order to study in its purity the form of exploitation. But, given the fact that surplus-value appears phenomenally as a profit rate, Volume III articulates this new form around such notions as cost price and organic composition. In this context there appears a contradiction between the value theory of Volume I and the appearance that all capital is equally fructiferous, and its profit therefore to be calculated in relation to cost price. 'There is no doubt ... that in actual fact ... no ... variation in the average rate of profit exists between different branches of industry. ... The theory of value thus appears incompatible with the actual movement, incompatible with the actual phenomena of production' (252).

This is a somewhat unfortunate way of stating the problem; for 'in actual fact' there are variations to be seen. The point is rather a *conceptual* one: that any variation should be temporary because in *form* all capitals are absolutely identical and ideally should therefore realize the same rate of profit. Thus it is part of the nature of capital that there is a contradiction between value created proportionately to labour and value 'created' in proportion to cost price. 'The difference is not only *numerical* but also conceptual, essential. This difference ... expresses a new characteristic relation of capital, the creation of a new form.'[8] This misleading form of appearance of capital is intrinsic to the very structure of capital. Marx writes

> Because the rate of profit measures surplus-value against the total capital and the latter is its standard, surplus-value itself appears in this

8. MECW, Vol. 33: 70; the whole passage 69–77 is of exceptional importance; it is the first version of the beginning of Volume III.

> way as having arisen from the total capital, and uniformly from all parts of it at that, so that the organic distinction between constant and variable capital is obliterated in the concept of profit.
>
> 267

What happens with the establishment of a uniform rate of profit is that

> ... this idea is completely confirmed, reinforced and hardened by the fact that the profit added to the cost price is not actually determined, if the particular spheres of production are taken separately, by the value formation that proceeds within these branches, but on the contrary established quite externally to them.
>
> 268

At the level of concretion reached in Volume III all capital appears as fructiferous because its identity in form occludes the only concrete content that supports systemic profit. This theme is therefore an appropriate subject to be addressed at the level of capital in general. The point is that we are not dealing here with a movement towards concretion, consisting in refinement of price determination; rather we have an essential contradiction between all capital as fructiferous in appearance, and a quite different reality where only variable capital counts in so far as it secures the value producing agency. It is absolutely necessary to 'save the appearances' for the theory to have any scientific credence. Thus the fact that in Volume III 'competition' has to be introduced in this specific limited context as the mediation whereby the tendency towards a uniform rate is secured (253) does not mean that Marx is addressing the phenomena he always intended to leave to a particular treatise on competition.

Let us now turn to the key chapters covering these matters, namely Chapters 9 and 10. The first point to address is the apparent identity of 'average' and 'general' rates of profit. This occurs at the outset, in the very title of Chapter 9, and I do not think that Marx ever, at any point, makes a distinction between them and to all intents and purposes treats these terms as synonyms. This is a pity. For they are not. Furthermore they could usefully be so defined as to refer to distinctly different concepts as follows:

1. The notion of a 'general rate' implies that we have here something determined by *other generalities*. Of course, even in this case, there would remain a real process whereby a uniform rate of profit would

become actual, in tendency at least, through the mediation of competition; the point, however, would be that the resulting rate would be logically determined in advance, resulting, in effect, from the posited general determinations. Competition would merely work within this constraint to make the general rate visible.

2. The notion of an 'average rate' implies an average of *prior differences*; hence leading to a *re*distribution (of something created in particular sites) as a result of the interrelations of *individual* capitals, that is to say, as a result of competition. An average can of course also be worked out in advance *theoretically* but this is of no consequence; the total would be merely the theoretical sum of the individually determined outputs and it would be reallocated through competition; in *reality* it is a question of the conditions of competition and whether they really tend to form a uniform profit rate across the capitals concerned.

Because Marx treats these different concepts as identical it is not at all clear how he thinks the rate in question is determined. Sometimes the text can be read as if he held only the second notion, whereby the individual rates are prior to their average, and ironed out by competition (253, 273–4). (But in one place where he speaks of 'the average rate of profit' he really seems to mean 'general' in our sense. For he says that it is determined by 'the level of exploitation of labour as a whole by capital as a whole' [299].) Sometimes the text seems to favour the first interpretation: for example Marx speaks of 'total social capital', and of individual capitals as simply 'aliquot parts' of it (258ff). Indeed he does not hesitate to speak of these capitals as 'shareholders' in a 'common enterprise' which naturally accrue returns *pro rata*; hence such a return 'is governed not by the mass of profit that is produced by this specific capital in its specific sphere of production, but by the mass of profit that falls on average to each capital invested, as an aliquot part of the total social capital invested' (258–9). However, the imagery of 'shareholding' seems on the face of it thoroughly misleading when it is recalled that these capitals necessarily confront one another in competitive struggle. Indeed Marx's real position seems put beyond doubt when he begins his chapter on 'the equalisation of the general rate of profit through competition' (273). He says that, while it is easy enough in theory to carry through an equalization of the rate of profit conserving total value and total surplus, 'the really difficult question' is how exchange and competition effect it, since 'a general rate of profit ... is evidently a result and cannot therefore be a point of departure' (274). So in this passage it appears that Marx is committed to the view that a general rate of profit is established in reality as a *result* of competition between individual capitals, and has no logical priority.

However, Marx makes every effort to assimilate all capitals to each other by arguing that they equally care for nothing but profit, that conversely labourers are indifferent to the specific character of work, being prepared to 'be flung from one sphere of production to another' (297). This identity in the essential nature of capital means that 'migration' of capitals will equalize profit rates if there is no obstacle they encounter, if capital 'subjects all the social preconditions that frame the production process to its specific character and immanent laws' (298). In an exceptionally important passage Marx says that equalization depends on the *mobility of capital and labour* (298) and he shows how social determinants accomplish this. One key institution making capital more fluid is the credit system which concentrates the available social capital and puts it at the disposal of the individual capitalists (298). Marx then argues that exploitation is itself socially determined; it is a matter of class against class 'not just in terms of class sympathy, but in a direct economic sense' (298–9); for each capital 'has the same interest in the productivity of the social labour applied by the total capital', while 'the particular interest that one capitalist ... has in exploiting the workers he directly employs is confined to the possibility of taking an extra cut, making an excess profit over and above the average' (299).

The general drift of these closing pages of Chapter 10 tends to qualify the assertion at the beginning that the general rate of profit is a result of competition, not a point of departure. For here he says that 'the average rate of profit depends on the level of exploitation of labour as a whole by capital as a whole' (299). To be sure, this is mediated case by case, as individual capitals attempt to squeeze out that bit 'extra'. But the general conditions of the class struggle are prior to this.

Having examined carefully the text of Volume III, one might draw out two approaches to the problem of the rate of profit:

1. One approach to the problem would take it that the determination of profit is peculiar to the ability of each capital to squeeze out a surplus from its own work force, and that the tendency towards a uniform rate of profit kicks in subsequently as a *result* of the pressure arising from systematic competition and of capitals migrating whither returns seem greater.
2. Another approach to the problem would take the equalization achieved through competition as realizing a general rate of profit whose essential determinants are equally general, that the aggregate

value and surplus-value arise from system-wide determinations effective at the level of the capitalist totality (which presupposes that 'capital in general' has a real existence and is not merely a tool of theory) and then allocated to 'aliquot parts' of it.

I want to harmonize these two approaches. I aim to explain how capital can be both so *unitary* it makes sense to treat single instances merely as 'aliquot parts' of the whole aggregate capital, yet so *competitive* that each strives to do better than others at gaining surplus profit.

2. Hegelian logic

The first thing to observe is that value theory does not get very far with the standard empiricist account of the relation between the general and the many. This is based on the abstraction of a common element to group cases into the class of which they count as cases. Here the 'real' is the fully individuated being and the general notion simply a convenient classification. Marx appears to use in one of his definitions of capital in general this method: where capital 'in its general concept' is investigated it is contrasted with 'real capitals, as the interaction of many capitals on one another'.[9]

However, capital as such is a value-form and hence, like the commodity form, involves a distinction within it of use-value and value; capitals are engaged in particular spheres of useful production but are interested in this for the sake of valorization. Now it is important to attend to the fact that there is a curious discrepancy between these two aspects when a concept of capital as such is produced through abstraction. Use-value behaves in the normal way; although we know capitals produce ships or sealing wax or shoes these differences are abstracted from and it is stated as a condition that capitals produce something or other marketable. The 'something or other' is clearly an unreal notion adopted for purely methodological reasons to avoid getting bogged down too soon in difference. With the value aspect matters stand very differently. We are supposed to abstract from how capitals differ as value producing. *But they do not differ!* Value is *already* abstract. Unlike use-value, value is not a concept produced by the theorist for methodological reasons; it is produced in *reality* through exchange relations and posited by capital – all and every capital – as its aim. The *identity* of capitals is *already present* in this respect and does not need to be theoretically produced by thought alone, as when it constructed a notion of utility. So we have a peculiar

9. Marx, *Grundrisse*: 649.

methodological problem to confront in the case of capital; for it is *itself* grounded in a systematic abstraction yielding value, albeit value existing as a universal only on the foundation of the materially distinct bearers.

Of course capitals do differ *quantitatively* in the amount of value invested and in their rate of return. But this is clearly a difference of a lesser order than their lack of qualitative difference. Also commonality is already present in that this quantitative difference is uniformly marked in money terms. What this means is that the identity of capital as a social *form* of value does not differentiate itself qualitatively but only quantitatively; so it is *as if* there were a single homogeneous social capital that divided itself into fractional parts. But how is this 'as if' supplanted by the reality of many capitals competing against one another? Warrant in Marx for turning to Hegel for illumination is provided by his unmistakable allusions to Hegel's peculiar turns of phrase. In his *Grundrisse*, Marx refers to 'many capitals' as follows: 'The essence of capital ... *is* something which repels itself, *is* many capitals mutually quite indifferent to one another. ... Since value forms the foundation of capital, and since it therefore necessarily exists only through exchange for *counter value*, it thus necessarily repels itself from itself. ... The reciprocal repulsion between capitals is already contained in capital as realised exchange value.'[10] Moreover exactly these terms occur when Marx discusses the 'general law of capitalist accumulation' in the first volume of *Capital*: 'This fragmentation of the total social capital into many individual capitals, or the repulsion of its fractions from each other, is counteracted by their attraction.'[11]

The reference to 'repulsion' here is without doubt one to Hegel's dialectic of 'one and many' in his *Logic*, which is discussed in terms of 'repulsion and attraction'. An additional point is worthy of note about the *Grundrisse* passage: that since capital as a form-determination is itself value, it incorporates in its own logic its abstract beginnings in the dialectic of exchange value. If we look at what Hegel has to say about *Individuality* the following remarkable parallel is to be found. 'The individual ... is the abstraction that determines the Notion according to its ideal moment of *being* as an *immediate*. In this way, the individual is a qualitative *one* or a *this*. With this quality it is first, repulsion of itself from *itself*, whereby the many *other* ones are presupposed; secondly, it is now a negative relation towards these presupposed others, and the individual is in so far *exclusive*.'[12] We see here that, just as Marx refers

10. *Ibid.*: 421n.
11. Marx, K., *Capital*, Vol. I (trans. B. Fowkes, 1976): 776–7.
12. Hegel's *Science of Logic* (trans. A.V. Miller, 1969): 621.

capital back to its foundation in the self-repulsive character of value, Hegel refers the concept of individuality back to the primitive moment of immediate being where it appeared simply as 'one' among 'many'. Without further ado, therefore, I shall embark on an exegesis of the dialectic of 'one and many' in Hegel, remembering our intention is to read into it subsequently the dialectic of commodity exchange.

Hegel's *Encyclopaedia Logic* starts with the bare notion of *Sein*, 'Being', and then concretizes it as *'Dasein'*, a 'being-there', determined through its 'being for another' such that it has its 'being in itself' within the limit that posits it as other than the other. But defining it in relation to this other generates an infinite regress. If something defines itself in relation to another, and this other in turn to yet a third, there is no stopping the endless regression. What Hegel calls 'true infinity', by contrast, returns to itself having grasped itself *in* its other, that it is one and the same in both cases. But the 'being for self' thus developed is contradictory: it is *self-related* because it is negatively related to its other as well as finding itself in it. It is 'one' which *excludes* other ones yet is not distinguishable from them; they are all one and the same, having no inner specificity.[13] Hegel argues that their numerical distinctness is sustained therefore only by continual *'repulsion'* of one another, 'a process of reciprocal *excluding*'.[14] The 'one' determines its being through the negative relation to other such ones, yet this relation necessarily connects it indissolubly *to* its others; this is a force of 'attraction', he says.[15]

In his *Science of Logic* Hegel goes further than the *Encyclopaedia* in this dialectic to argue that a resolution of this opposition between repulsion and attraction is not a static equilibrium but a positing of the notion of the 'one One', a unitary principle in relation to which the many ones are its mere 'extension'; it is thus their 'realised ideality'.[16] This universal attractor does not *absorb* all the many ones because it remains rooted in the primal repulsion; it itself therefore stands in a relation of exclusion to the ones it yet represents. He remarks of this one One: 'Since it contains repulsion in its determination, this latter at the same time preserves the ones as many in it; through its attracting, so to speak, it acquires something for itself, obtains an extension or filling.'[17]

13. G.W.F. Hegel, *The Encyclopaedia Logic* (trans. T.F. Geraets *et al.*, 1991): §96.
14. *Ibid.*: §97.
15. *Ibid.*: §98.
16. Hegel, *Science of Logic*: 173–4.
17. *Ibid.*: 174. (It is best to think of this category as an anticipation of the category of 'Essence'.)

Now let us see how this logic informs the development of the value form, and then how it may be 'scaled up' to illuminate the logic of capital. The 'cell-form' Marx begins with is the commodity which defines itself as having the quality of 'exchangeability'. But to be actual this requires the commodity to have others against which it may exchange. It is only in so far as C acquires C* that its exchangeability is demonstrated. But that this exchangeability has yet been retained, and not dissipated in its realization, is shown if C* in turn proves itself 'of worth' through exchanging against C**, and so on. An ever-changing series of commodities passes before us endlessly. This is what Hegel called the 'bad infinity'. But Hegel's genuine infinity is posited when the category of exchangeability *by itself* (exchange-value) is generated in so far as the other commodities are grasped only as other forms of the first in a closed system in which all commodities refer to each other.

For the exchangeability of C to manifest itself, C is translated into C*. From this point of view we can borrow Hegel's terms and say C* is in effect the *repulsion* of C's value from itself; therewith the value of C is excluded from it and posited as C*; then it is reflected back onto the original C. C* is excluded from C just so as to be a vehicle for the actualization of C's power of exchange, and yet C's exchange-value is registered only *as* this other C. It gains actuality in this form. Because this *relation* implies 'attraction' in Hegel's sense, there is no difference between the sides as equivalents of one another, and all commodities are posited on this basis abstractly as a set of identical *value bodies*. Thus the *difference* here is wholly abstract, just numerical difference (repulsion) which is at the same time a relation of *identity* in value (attraction).

Thus we can see commodities as simply the *extension* of the category of 'value' (the 'one One' in Hegel's sense). But this account leaves 'value' hovering as an insubstantial transcendent category, unifying the many commodities in a quasi-Kantian ideal synthesis. The imputed value dimensionality of commodities will be *concretely* actual in their relation to the universal equivalent they *mutually exclude* from themselves, namely money. However, money has this dialectic within itself: just in so far as it is excluded from commodities as their posited value, it *attracts* them to realize themselves as commodities in exchanging against it. Equally the 'universal attractor' money 'contains' the mediation of 'repulsion'; without any opposed commodities it could not be their 'realised ideality', and would have no determinate value form. Money is inherently pure *universal* value; the *individual* instances of value are commodities; although materially different they may be called 'values' in the plural just in so far as they are posited as such through money in the price form. They are its extension, and money is their intension objectively posited.

To sum up: we have now established the commodity as 'one' among 'many'. This expresses itself in the coexistence of 'repulsion' and 'attraction', which is itself posited more concretely with the doubling of commodities into commodities and money; now the commodities both repel money from themselves so as to establish a universal equivalent and yet at the same time achieve an adequate expression of value (namely price) only in so far as money is their common attractor.

The argument of Marx's *Grundrisse* passage cited above is that the same dialectic of repulsion and attraction obtains when simple commodity circulation is superseded by that of capital. However, a very important additional point about this dialectic is made there.

> Since value forms the foundation of capital, and since it therefore necessarily exists only through exchange for *counter value,* it thus necessarily repels itself from itself. A *universal capital*, one without alien capitals confronting it, with which it exchanges – and from the present standpoint, nothing confronts it but wage labourers or itself – is therefore a non-thing.[18]

(Here 'universal capital' is in English; while 'non-thing' is '*Unding*'.[19]) So a capital exists only in relation to other capitals, and hence a universal capital taken abstractly (i.e., without its inner repulsion into many capitals) is a thing of thought, a non-thing. (We shall return to this problem of the '*Unding*' in the final section of this paper.) This is why competition is of the essence of capital: 'Conceptually, competition is nothing other than the inner nature of capital, its essential character appearing in and realised as the reciprocal interaction of many capitals with one another, the inner tendency as external necessity.'[20] Moreover: 'Competition is nothing more than the way in which the many capitals force the inherent determinants of capital upon one another and upon themselves. Hence not a single category of the bourgeois economy, not [even] the most basic, e.g. the determination of value, becomes real [other than] through free competition.'[21]

A key conceptual point follows from Marx's argument here: competition is *internal* to the very notion of capital; thus it should not be

18. *Grundrisse*: 421n.
19. K. Marx and F. Engels, *Gesamtausgabe* (MEGA), Part II, Vol. 1.2, 1981: 334.
20. *Grundrisse*: 414.
21. MEGA, Part II, Vol. 1.2: 534; MECW, Vol. 29: 39; *Grundrisse*: 650–1.

taken to be some external context, or force, that capital encounters; capital expresses its own essence in the struggle between its instances. It is because *in form* capitals are identical in substance, i.e., value, and identically oriented to appropriating value, any value, all value, that they are structured competitively; they each can have no special aim or preferred site, but are all ambitious in the same way and on the same terrain.

3. The general and the particular

The main purpose of this chapter is to address and resolve two contradictory discourses in Marx. The one asserts that total capital is an effective power and individual capitals simply replicate its categories as aliquot parts of it, picking up their share of the total surplus-value as if they were merely shareholders in a single enterprise. The other discourse insists that capital necessarily exists as many capitals *confronting* one another in competitive struggle, that only thus are the determinations of capital in general enforced on each.

Now how is this competitive struggle structured as one between *materially different* capitals? This takes us to *another* level of concretion. Just now I have been stressing that as pure *form* capitals are abstractly identical as valorizing bodies while numerically distinct. Now in *further* specifying them we must take into account that capital *includes* both money and commodity in its circuit. Capital unites the universal moment (monetary self-expansion) with the particular use-values it invests in, so as to achieve its individuality. At one level this unity is achieved for each and every capital singly, e.g., this particular factory is constituted as a capitalist enterprise. At another level, however, all these instantiations of capital are subsumed formally under their abstract universal essence just as money stood for this identity in essence of commodities. If we set aside their material integument and concentrate attention on their substance, as value capitals differ only in amount. In this way, capitals subsist only in the dialectic of their concept, which has its universal and individual aspects. They subsist only in their inner relation rather than bumping up against one another, as it were, in purely external relations. But, at the same time, if such relations of 'repulsion and attraction' are required to constitute them (there has to be some determination that prevents them collapsing together, e.g., private property, differentiated ownership), their dependence on this dialectic means the several capitals are not fully individuated beings and hence liable to coalesce again very easily.

While it is essential to capital that it is many, these as pure value in process are qualitatively identical, differing only as quantities and thus capable of immediate comparison and merging. But requiring material bearers and even more as requiring material sources of surplus-value they are determined materially as different, and thus not aggregatable, contrary to their form as value. This is a central contradiction in the Idea of Capital.

Capitalist firms are specified formally as 'lumps' of capital. In such a light the material side appears rather as a predicate of such inner essence. But capital must always be materially instantiated; hence as tied to specific sites of enterprise it must appear as many single capitals. Capital is the unity of identity (capital-value) and nonidentity (its use-value material). The material content introduces a ground for *qualitative* difference and relation, while as pure form the only difference which counts is in *amount*. It follows there are two possible modes of particularization: the material and the formal.[22]

Since capital as self-valorizing value *doubles* into itself (value in motion) and its other (the material in which it invests itself), in the constitution of individual capitals *two kinds of particularization* are simultaneously realized: on the one side, the formal existence of capital as value must be *quantitatively* determined as an *amount* of capital; on the other side, the material existence of capital invested in commodities (notably means of production and labour-power) must be *qualitatively* determined, and situated in specific *sites*. Particularizations of value, because value is pure quantity, can only be particular amounts of value, and the individual capitals are differentiated in this respect only in virtue of such quantitative differences. But, while one has the same capital whether one puts it 'into' shoe factories or shipyards, with regard to the material particularization of capital, the resulting technical composition is the root of the transformation problem. For these qualitative differences between capitals with regard to their technical composition cannot but have consequences for their quantitative differences with respect to their value composition, inducing comparatively different rates of return that are contrary to the concept of capital as an identity in form. To quote Marx: 'use-value itself plays a role as an economic category' for its particularity is here 'determinant of the *form* and the action of capital ... as particularizing it'.[23] This is the logic underlying the requirement for the effectuation of the transformation of values into prices of production that realize a uniform rate of profit.

22. It is relevant to the above discussion to notice a remark thrown out by Hegel in his *Encyclopaedia Logic*: that where 'external' considerations are involved 'particularity presents itself as doubled' (§230 Addition); I relate this to the 'two judgments' mentioned in §223.
23. *Grundrisse*: 646; see also *Capital*, Vol. II (trans. D. Fernbach, 1978): 470.

So far in this section the two kinds of particularization internal to the concept of capital (namely the formal and the material) have been explicated. Now a new twist in the development of the concept of capital must be considered, which brings us to the notion of the *real existence* of capital in general. Just as the universality and individuality of value (money and commodities) are brought into the structure of every capital, so they are *externalized* again. Now these distinctions within capital reappear as distinctions within the capitalist totality, as complementary branches, the individual side appearing dominant in industry and the universal side appearing dominant in the *money market*.[24]

In the money market capital in general achieves, as Marx says in his *Grundrisse*, a 'real existence' alongside that of the 'real' individual capitals.[25] Capital markets spring naturally from the identity in form of all capitals. Marx says: 'in the money market, capital is posited in its totality.'[26] The totality has ontological priority over the individual elements just in so far as the system is totally permeable, i.e., capital can move, and in which every instance can be shown to be ahead or behind the game through the concrete existence of a general rate of profit established in the money markets. As Marx says: 'The general rate of profit reappears in the average rate of interest as an empirical fact, even though the latter is not a pure or reliable expression of the former' (487). He goes on to discuss some of the differences involved (488–91), but it is clear that he thinks it significant that capital in the money market exists 'as the *common capital of the class* ... under the control of the bankers as representatives of social capital' (490–1). It follows that:

> Capital in this *general form*, although belonging to individual capitalists, in its elemental form as capital, forms the capital which accumulates in the banks or is distributed through them ... in accordance with the needs of production. ... It is a law of capital in general that, in order to realise itself, it must posit itself doubly.[27]

If capital is to act in accordance with its concept there has to be a place where it is fixed (industry) and a place where it is in solution (the money market).

24. Strictly speaking the externalization of the moments of the capital circuit results in a triplicity, including commercial capital: see 'the expanded Idea of Capital in General' in Chapter 3, pp. 61–3.
25. *Grundrisse*: 449.
26. *Ibid.*: 275.
27. *Ibid.*: 449.

> [In] money capital ... all capital's determinations are dissolved and its real elements are invisible. Money is in fact the very form in which the distinctions between commodities as different use-values are obliterated, and hence also the distinctions between industrial capitals, which consist of these commodities and the conditions of their production; it is the form in which value – and here capital – exists as autonomous exchange-value. In the reproduction process of capital, the money form is an evanescent moment, a moment of mere transition. On the money market, on the contrary, capital always exists in this form. (517)

Thus we do not only have separate capitals generating separate rates of return we have global capital flowing until its general rate of profit becomes the real uniform rate (566). The general rate of profit is the moment where total social capital establishes its unity with itself. This is implicit in the movement of industrial capital and represented explicitly in capital markets. The financial institutions of capital provide both a rough measure of the overall rate of profit and the facilities whereby capital can be mobilized from one sphere of production to another accordingly.

Before moving on it is worth adding a point on the nature of the individuality of capital. In my view the individuality of every capital is realized as such, not in the person, or persons, of the capitalist. Marx is not entirely clear on this. For he thinks joint stock companies constitute 'the abolition of the capitalist mode of production within the capitalist mode of production itself' (569). This confuses the individuality of capital with the individual capitalist. In fact, to be sure it acted in accordance with its concept it is better if the capital is not owned by a private individual; for the subjectivity of the latter may well not be totally colonized by the imperative of valorization and he may make 'irrational' decisions such as refusing to employ children. The joint stock company is in fact the apotheosis of capital not its negation.[28] While it is true that the small shareholders are ripped off by the directors, this inner tension does not affect the functioning of capital itself, as Marx noted (514).

4. Total social capital

In the remainder of this chapter, the argument comes back to Marx's point cited above that if 'universal capital' has no object it is a non-

28. See *ibid.*: 657–8.

thing (*'Unding'*). For in all volumes of *Capital* Marx *does* refer to 'total social capital'!

In Volume I, as we noted earlier, there is an important passage in which Marx first speaks of individual capitals growing 'in the proportion in which they form aliquot parts of the total social capital'; yet at the same time he speaks of the 'fragmentation of the total social capital into many individual capitals', and their 'repulsion' and 'attraction'.[29] This poses anew the question of whether capital acts as one or as many.

'Total social capital' also appears in Marx's *Capital* in the Introduction to Part Three of Volume II in which he says 'each individual capital forms only a fraction of the total social capital, a fraction that has acquired independence and been endowed with individual life'.[30] Is this open to Marx's objection to 'universal capital'? If one attends more closely to the objection, it is clear that he is worried about 'the fallacy of composition' that lies in moving from the observation that each individual capital traces a *circuit* in its action to the assumption that total social capital performs such a circuit. Such a conclusion is conceptually incoherent. That *a circuit* (rather than a *system* of circuits) of total social capital makes no sense is obvious as soon as we see that the very notion of a circuit involving purchase of inputs and sales of outputs logically presupposes the separateness of capitals, each having their own circuit but necessarily interlocking with others. At the macro level a good part of aggregate capital (viz. constant capital) never leaves the hand of capital so does not circulate (in the sense required) *as an aggregate* but is only conceivable as circulating when capital is *disaggregated*. If we return now to Volume II it emerges that, so far from Marx taking total social capital as performing a circuit, the whole point is to emphasize that it consists of a *system* of circuits: 'the circuits of individual capitals are interlinked, they presuppose one another and condition one another, and it is precisely by being interlinked in this way that they constitute the movement of the total social capital'.[31] There is no question here therefore of Marx taking total social capital to act as a single aggregate.

However, there *is* in Volume III clear reference to such aggregation. For example he says that each capital secures 'only the surplus-value and hence profit that falls to the share of each aliquot part of the total social capital, when evenly distributed, from the total social surplus-value or profit produced in a given time by the social capital in all spheres of

29. *Capital*, Vol. I: 776–7.
30. *Capital*, Vol. II: 427.
31. *Ibid.*: 429.

production' (258). Indeed he then goes out of his way to invite a charge of committing the fallacy of composition: 'the various different capitals here are in the position of shareholders in a joint-stock company, in which the dividends are evenly distributed ... according to the size of the capital they each of them has put into the common enterprise' (258). But surely there *is* no 'enterprise' harmoniously carried on in common! Even if it is possible to calculate the general rate of profit, capitals do not tamely queue up for their appropriate ration. They remain within the totality as competitors always looking for surplus profit.

Let us remind ourselves what the *Grundrisse* passage said: 'A *universal capital*, one without alien capitals confronting it, with which it exchanges – and from the present standpoint, nothing confronts it but wage labourers or itself – is therefore a non-thing.' In that very passage, while concentrating on the exchange between capitals, he remarks in passing that capital also confronts 'wage labourers'. This is important, and it is explicitly acknowledged as such by Marx when he says that 'If I regard the total capital of e.g. a nation as distinct from total wage labour (or, as distinct from landed property), or if I regard capital as the general economic basis of a class as distinct from another class, then I regard it in general.'[32]

Capital as-a-whole confronts the labourers-as-a-whole. But there is no fallacy of composition in considering all the interchanges between capital and labour at a global level. Indeed there is every reason to believe that class relations fundamentally condition individual transactions. While it is true that the self-repulsive character of capital gives rise to intense competitive struggle between capitals, they are 'as one' in their concern to confront globally their 'other' (298–9). Moreover capital is *constituted as a social power* in this global relation to labour. It is therefore logically prior to the disputes among capitals over how to share out what has been won from exploiting labour. This relation *between classes* at the level of total social capital generates the general rate of profit which is logically prior to the way the distribution of capitals across industries determines the average rate of profit *between them*. Thus, I claim that the general rate of profit and the average rate of profit are *semantically* distinguishable even if they are *numerically* the same. The reason for this is that the 'general' rate of profit has an ontological reality that the term 'average' does not connote. There has to be a relation where capital acts 'as One', as universal capital, this is against labour, but at the same time another relation where it acts as 'many', i.e., upon itself through competition.

32. *Grundrisse*: 852.

Thus the definition of capital in general as 'total social capital', specified in opposition to labour, is merely a *partial* definition because the notion of capital in general includes the conception of capital as necessarily appearing as many capitals imposing the inner determinations of capital upon each other through competition.

In its primary aspect total social capital may *itself* be viewed as an Individual. Capital is 'the enemy' in a different sense than that in which Disease is an enemy. The latter is a personified class name for empirically distinct diseases which have enough in common to group and personify. But Capital has a reality as an individual whole. It is not just a class name for Ford, Shell, ICI, etc. These are not so much members of a set as they are capital's own concretizations in numerically separable shapes which nonetheless are constituted as organic parts of a systematic totality and move within it. Capital is an Individual, determined in its unity of many capitals by its negative relation to the working class.

5. Conclusion

While Marx's distinction between the three volumes of *Capital,* together comprehending the theme of 'capital in general', and a further book on 'competition' dealing with the interaction of 'many capitals', holds up, in so far as capital is formed as many capitals it is the case that certain essential form-determinations of capital are structured by competition, and that is why within *Capital* itself it had to be considered so far as these themes demanded it.

In Marx's work on the formation of a general, or average, rate of profit, two discourses were in play; one which took this rate to be determined systemically, and one which took it as a mathematical reference point for the migration of individual capitals. The reconciliation of these discourses was achieved by arguing that capital, in its nature, is a single individual totality and yet necessarily composed of many capitals subject to a dialectic of 'repulsion and attraction'.

The root of the transformation problem is that the general concept of capital is particularized in two dimensions: as a quantitative amount of value, and as a qualitative selection of use values. While the result of such particularization is obviously 'particular real capitals', the 'general form' too has separate 'real existence' in banking and loans, where capital 'doubles' itself into the 'general form' accumulated in banks and the particular applications for which chunks of it are lent to firms.

The question whether total social capital can exist, not merely as system, but as a single *aggregate* was addressed. It was argued that in such an interpretation there is a clear danger of falling into a fallacy of composition in that features common to single capitals are transferred illogically to the aggregate. However, the class relation is not so compromised by aggregation. On the contrary, this relation exists as a reality at the level of the social whole.

Corresponding to this reality Marx was right to speak of a general rate of profit in the strong sense of the term. Moreover he was equally right to treat the quantitative mass of surplus-value created as logically prior to its distribution to individual sites in accordance with the relations of capitals to each other through such mediations as prices of production. As they participate in total social capital, at this level of abstraction it is legitimate to treat them as aliquot parts of it for this purpose. But at the same time the reality of many capitals makes the actualization of a uniform rate of profit a matter of a *process* of competitive adjustment of capitals to each other.

In so far as capital may be considered as the economic basis of a class as against another class, it achieves an actuality as an individual over against its determinate other, the labouring class.

Bibliography

Hegel, G.W.F. (1812), *Hegel's Science of Logic* (trans. A.V. Miller) (London: George Allen & Unwin, 1969).

— (3rd edn 1830), *The Encyclopaedia Logic* (trans. T.F. Geraets *et al.*, (Indianapolis: Hackett, 1991).

Marx, K. (1867), *Capital*, Vol. I (trans. B. Fowkes) (Harmondsworth: Penguin, 1976).

— (1885), *Capital*, Vol. II (trans. D. Fernbach) (Harmondsworth: Penguin, 1978).

— (1894), *Capital* Vol. III (trans. D. Fernbach) (Harmondsworth: Penguin, 1981).

— (1939), *Grundrisse* (trans. M. Nicolaus) (Harmondsworth: Penguin, 1973).

Marx, K. and Engels, F., *Gesamtausgabe* (MEGA) (Berlin/Amsterdam: Dietz Verlag/Internationales Institut für Sozialgeschichte Amsterdam, 1976).

— *Collected Works* (London/New York/Moscow: Lawrence & Wishart/International Publishers/Progress Publishers, 1975).

— *Letters on 'Capital'* (trans. A. Drummond) (London: New Park Publications, 1983).

7
Surplus Profits from Innovation
A missing level in *Capital III*?

Tony Smith

Is there any object of social inquiry more immense, complex, obscure and ominous than capital? In the course of the three volumes of *Capital* Marx investigates a tremendous number of topics and employs a wide variety of methodological approaches and rhetorical tropes. It would be foolhardy to claim that a single framework could possibly capture this vast multiplicity. Every proposed interpretation is a *reconstruction* of Marx's masterwork, emphasizing certain themes and downplaying others. In the reading proposed here, *Capital* consists of a systematic ordering of categories proceeding simultaneously along two distinct – if ultimately inseparable – dimensions. I shall argue that these two dimensions come together in Volume III in a manner that requires us to introduce a distinct theoretical level in Marx's theory, defined by the category 'surplus profits due to innovation'.

1. The two dimensions of *Capital*

Marx begins Volume I with what he takes to be the simplest and most abstract manner of categorizing capital: it is a system of generalized commodity exchange. This implies both that production is undertaken privately, and that the social necessity (the 'value') of any act of production can only be established subsequently, through sale of the produced commodities for money. Money is thus the ultimate form of value, the sole socially objective representation of socially necessary labour (Campbell, 1993; Murray, 1993). When this is the case, 'value' necessarily becomes an alien pseudo-subject, subjecting every nook and cranny of social life to the imperatives of valorization (Arthur, 1993).

The development of Marx's value theory consists of a systematic ordering from the relatively simple and abstract categories of 'commodity' and 'money' to determinations that are progressively more complex and concrete (Reuten and Williams, 1989; Arthur, 1997; Smith, 1990, 1993, 1999). The first dimension of this ordering emerges in the following manner. After we have introduced the notion of valorization, the next most complex and concrete way of categorizing capital as a totality is in terms of a M–C–M′ process on the level of total social capital. How are we to explain surplus-value, that is, the difference between M′ and M? In answering this question Marx explicitly takes as his unit of analysis a single period of accumulation, abstracting from any imbalances between supply and demand (Marx, 1867: 201; Moseley, 1995). This is a very violent abstraction from the very factor that defines value theory, the possibility that privately undertaken labour may prove to be socially wasted. It is, however, completely justified, allowing Marx to consider the above question without irrelevant distractions.

Marx argues that valorization on the level of total social capital rests on the exploitation of industrial wage-labourers by the class that owns and controls the means of production. The dominance of value as an alien pseudo-subject is thus identical to the reproduction of the capital/wage labour relation (Mattick 1991–92). In Volume I Marx attempts to establish this thesis both through direct arguments in its favour and through criticisms of alternative explanations, such as appeals to the abstinence, effort, or risk taking of capitalists. It is important to recognize, however, that much of Volumes II and III constitutes an extended argument for the theory as well. This argument takes the form of replies to three apparently compelling counterexamples to the claim that surplus-value stems from the exploitation of wage labour. First, the time spent in circulation outside of the labour process appears just as important to capital accumulation as the labour process itself. Second, it is manifestly not the case that industrial sectors employing greater numbers of wage-labourers tend to enjoy a higher rate of profit than other sectors, as would seem to follow if the exploitation of wage-labourers were the sole source of profits. Finally, if profits rest on the appropriation of surplus-value produced by industrial wage-labourers, how can we account for the profits of commercial and financial capitals, or the appropriation of rents by landowners? One extended line of argument in *Capital*, then, attempts to establish that these alleged counterexamples can be accounted for in a manner consistent with the theory of surplus-value.

In Volume II Marx argues that circulation costs outside of the labour process impose a deduction from the surplus-value that could potentially be accumulated in any given period. Reductions in circulation time that lower these costs thus tend to increase the accumulation of surplus-value, despite the fact that time spent in the circulation process outside of production does not itself produce surplus-value.

Marx's response to the second alleged counterexample comes at the beginning of Volume III, where total social capital is disaggregated into a multiplicity of sectors with different value compositions of capital, that is, different ratios between the amount of money capital invested in the purchase of means of production ('constant capital') and the amount invested in the purchase of labour-power ('variable capital'). He notes that if commodities exchanged at cost prices plus the surplus-value produced in the given sector (C+V+S), different industries would have wildly divergent rates of profit, total investment and the rate of exploitation assumed equal. Specifically, sectors with a relatively high value composition would have a low rate of profit and vice versa.[1] Capital mobility and inter-capital competition, however, generate a tendency for rates of profit to equalize across sectors.[2] Capital investment tends to flow away from sectors with lower rates of profit, and towards sectors where profit rates are higher. Competitive pressures tend to lessen in the former industries and increase in the latter, generating a tendency for rates of profit to increase in the former and decrease in the latter. This implies that in any given period commodities produced by industrial capitals will tend to sell at prices of production P = (C+V)(1+R), with *R* defined as the rate of profit tending to hold equally across sectors.[3] These prices of production are conceived as centres of gravity around which market prices revolve, depending on temporary contingencies of supply and demand.

1. An analogous point holds for sectors with equal levels of capital investment and exploitation but different rates of turnover (Marx, 1894: 250).
2. Other factors are relevant here as well, including labour-power mobility, a reserve army and the credit system (Weeks, 1981: 162; Marx, 1894: 566, 742).
3. R = S/(C+V) with *S*, *C*, and *V* defined with reference to the total social capital (Moseley, 1993b: 172). According to this formula, units of capital in sectors with a higher than average value composition of capital (C/V) will tend to have prices of production that exceed C+V+S, while those in sectors with a lower than average composition of capital will tend to have prices of production below the sum of the cost price and the produced surplus-value.

On this level of abstraction profits tend to be proportional to the size of the capital invested. It thus appears as if capital investment were productive of surplus-value in itself. But while the connection of profits to the exploitation of wage labour may be more opaque on this level of analysis, the connection remains nonetheless. Prices of production are the result of a (logical) redistribution of surplus-value within the given period; total profits equal total surplus-value (Moseley, 1993b).

With the progression to the yet more complex and concrete levels of commercial and financial capital in Volume III, capital fetishism attains yet higher forms. Owners of both commercial capital and financial capital obviously enjoy returns on their investments. This fact blatantly appears to contradict the claim that profits rest on the appropriation of surplus-value produced by industrial wage-labourers. The profits that result from the M–M' circuit of financial capital in particular appear to challenge the Marxian theory of exploitation at its very roots. Profits appear to arise here solely from capital itself, as if capital were in and of itself productive of value even in the absence of any tie to production. The phenomenon of rent appropriated by landowners raises an equally serious problem. It appears to establish conclusively that land too is productive of economic value in and of itself. For Marx, however, the profits of commercial and financial capital, and the rents enjoyed by owners of land, also derive from a (logical) process of redistribution of the surplus-value resulting from the exploitation of wage labour by industrial capital.

There is thus an extended line of argument devoted to the defence of the theory of surplus-value and the critique of various forms of fetishism (see Murray, Moseley, this volume). This line of thought takes as its object of analysis the reproduction of the total social capital in any given period. It explains this reproduction through the production of surplus-value by wage-labourers, the deductions from potential surplus-value imposed by circulation costs, and the logical redistribution of surplus-value among capitals (and between capital and landowners). This entire line of argument, however, makes up only one dimension of Marx's theory of capital. It is accompanied throughout by a second dimension, concerned with the dynamism of capital from one period to the next (Smith, 1997).

On the most simple and abstract level of Marx's theory, the dynamism of the value form stems from the way innovations may better the odds that privately undertaken labour will prove to be socially necessary. On the level of the relationship between the capitalist class as a whole and the class of wage-labourers as a whole, the main topic of Volume I, Marx derives a tendency for technological and organizational innovations at the point of production that increase the rate of surplus-value. In Volume

II Marx shows that the drive to introduce innovations reducing circulation time is also inherent in the capital form. A systematic tendency towards innovations reducing constant capital costs is derived at the beginning of Volume III. Finally, one implication of the later parts of Marx's third volume is that the drive for innovation in the commercial, financial and agricultural sectors is no less intense than in the industrial sector.

Both dimensions of value theory are equally significant. Both dimensions are required to comprehend the historical specificity of capital. Capitalism is similar to other forms of class society in that it too ultimately rests on exploitation; but commodity fetishism, money fetishism and capital fetishism mask class relations in a manner that is historically unique. Capitalism also exhibits unprecedented dynamism; it is the first form of society capable of establishing the material preconditions for socialist democracy.[4] Marx's explanation of the production and distribution of surplus-value in any given period establishes the former; his account of the tendencies for innovation that hold in the transition from any one period to the next establishes the latter.

The topic of this chapter, surplus profits appropriated as a result of innovation, has not yet been mentioned. It is now time to address this neglect. Our first task will be to sketch the role this form of surplus profits plays in *Capital*.

2. The role of surplus profits from innovation in Marx's presentation

Unlike 'money', 'exploitation', or 'prices of production', the category 'surplus profits from innovations' does not define a particular theoretical level in the three volumes of *Capital* that have come down to us. Nonetheless, this notion plays a crucial role in both Marx's extended defence of the theory of surplus-value and in his account of the dynamism of the value form. We may consider the latter first.

In Volume I Marx notes that innovations increasing the rate of relative surplus-value further accumulation on the level of the total social capital. Innovations furthering productivity in sectors devoted to goods and services consumed by wage-labourers are thus functional for the capitalist class as a whole. But Marx was well aware that we cannot simply assume

4. This does not imply that all instances of innovation in capitalism are to be applauded, whatever their human and environmental costs. But the justified rejection of 'productionism' should not lead us to neglect the world historical significance of advances in labour productivity. These advances are necessary for socialist democracy to be more than an abstract utopian ideal.

that individual units of capital automatically act in a manner that furthers the interests of capital as a whole. And so he discussed how individual units of capital that improve productivity are able, *ceteris paribus*, to appropriate surplus profits, thereby motivating the behaviour that furthers the interests of capital as a whole (see Marx, 1894: 299–300). This consideration holds throughout Marx's discussion of the systematic tendencies for innovation necessarily given with the capital form. Innovations that lessen circulation time, reduce constant capital costs and improve productivity in the commercial capital, financial capital and agricultural sectors also tend to further accumulation on the level of the total social capital. But they are not pursued by individual units of capital because they are functional for capital as a whole. They are pursued because individual units hope to appropriate surplus profits for themselves.

In contrast, Marx explicitly abstracts from the appropriation of surplus profits by individual units of capital throughout most of his development of the theory of surplus-value. Individual capitals are simply taken as 'an aliquot part' of either the total social capital (on the level of 'capital-in-general' in Volumes I and II), or of a particular sector (on the level of 'many capitals' in Volume III). The following passage from the discussion of cost prices is representative:

> For this whole investigation, when we speak of the composition or the turnover of capital in a specific branch of production, it should be clear enough that we always mean the normal, average situation for capital invested in this branch of production, and refer always to the average of the total capital in the sphere in question, not to chance differences between individual capitals invested there.
>
> Marx, 1894: 243

In the initial derivation of prices of production the same abstraction from innovation is presupposed: 'Marx's concept of the price of production shows how profit rates in a capitalist system of production can be equalized *when all the capitalists have access to the same techniques of production*' (Foley, 1986: 106; emphasis added).

Similar remarks could be made regarding Marx's subsequent dismissal of the claim that commercial capital, financial capital, or land are productive of surplus-value. Here too individual units of capital are taken as representative ('average') units of the particular sector being considered, and here too Marx abstracts from innovations from one period to the next.

When we examine the theoretical level defined by the category 'prices of production' a bit closer, however, matters become more complicated. As we have already seen, Marx introduces the mobility of individual units of capital and the pressures of capitalist competition. Capitalist competition at first has to do with the allocation of capital to various sectors in response to price signals. This sort of competition results in a logical redistribution of surplus-value from some sectors to others, thereby granting all units of capital a share in the appropriation of surplus-value proportional to their size, regardless of differences in the value composition of capital, the direct exploitation of wage labour, or turnover time (Marx, 1894: 258). All units of capital remain standing at the end of this logical redistribution of surplus-value that were present initially. For this reason we may term this form of competition 'weak competition'. But Marx's account of prices of production in Volume III also invokes what may be termed 'strong competition': 'The capitalist who employs improved but not yet universally used methods of production sells below the market price, but above his individual price of prouction; his profit rate thus rises, until competition cancels this out' (Marx, 1894: 338). Here we have a war unto death, a war in which size is no guarantee of survival, let alone a guarantee of a proportional share of surplus-value. In strong competition innovations are crucial weapons in the war of all against all. 'Victory' is defined as winning surplus profits while forcing devaluation upon one's opponents, and 'loss is divided very unevenly ... one capital lies idle, another is destroyed' (Marx, 1894: 362).

Nonetheless, as the notion of 'cancelling out' at the conclusion of the next-to-last quotation suggests, 'surplus profits from innovations' remains a subordinate category in this discussion. The story underlying the tendency for rates of profit to equalize across sectors of industrial capital is merely fleshed out, not essentially revised and modified. This tendency remains dominant throughout Marx's subsequent discussion of the (logical) redistribution of surplus-value to commercial capital, financial capital and landlords.[5] And so from the standpoint of this dimension of *Capital* it is also the case that the category 'surplus profits from

5. For Marx, there is a systematic tendency for the rate of profit to equalize between industrial and commercial capital (Marx, 1894: 429). The cases of financial capital and rent are somewhat more complex. Interest rates, for example, are the contingent result of the particular balance of supply and demand for money-capital holding in the given period. So the rate of return on loans of money-capital may not equalize with the rate of profit holding in sectors of industrial capital (Itoh and Lapavitsas, 1999: 70–1). Similarly, the amount of rent appropriated by landlords is affected by a myriad of

innovation' does not define a distinct stage in Marx's own systematic presentation of his theory.

In the reconstruction of Volume III of *Capital* proposed here, however, a notion of surplus profits from innovation is explicitly assigned a distinct place in the ordering of the essential determinations of the capital form. In contrast to Marx's usage, which refers to intrasectoral differences among individual units of capital, this notion will be taken below to refer to differences among sectors. The case for this proposed reconstruction must now be presented.

3. Leading sectors in capitalist development

Marx's account of the production and distribution of surplus-value in any given period takes prices of production as the long-run centres of gravity for market prices. But reflection on the dynamism of the capitalist mode of production suggests that this holds true only on relatively abstract theoretical levels. Marx's own account of stages in capitalist development provides a first approach to this issue.

In Volume I Marx interrupts his systematic progression with a digression on the historical development from the early factory through manufacturing to machinofacture. The early factory arose when a number of wage-labourers were placed under the direct supervision of a capitalist or his representative. In manufacturing this 'formal subsumption' of wage labour under capital gave way to a 'real subsumption' in which control of the labour process was taken away from the worker. The labour process was fragmented whenever possible, with each distinct part assigned to a separate worker (the 'detail labourer'). The process of real subsumption was then continued with the rise of machinofacture ('big industry'). Many of the mechanized activities of wage-labourers were now taken over by steam-driven machines, to whose rhythms the work force had to adjust.

For our purposes the point to note regarding this (overly?) schematic narrative is that *the transition from one stage to the next does not occur uniformly in all industries*. New industries emerge in the middle of a given period, consolidate as that period declines, and then become hegemonic in the succeeding period, even as the dominant industries from the

contingent matters, including especially the level of demand for agricultural commodities relative to the level of agricultural productivity on different lands. Here too there is no systematic necessity that the rate of returns to landlords will tend to equalize with the rate of profit of sectors of industrial capital. But Marx does assume that there is a tendency for rates of return to capitalist agriculture undertaken on rented lands to equalize.

previous stage continue to operate. This implies that we cannot assume that prices of production are the centres of gravity for market prices throughout this extended transition. For if firms in both leading and declining industries enjoyed the same rate of profit throughout, if they both received returns directly proportional to the size of their capital investments, then investment capital would not flow towards the one and away from the other over this extended period. We then would not be able to account adequately for the transition from one epoch in capitalist development to the next. We would, in brief, be unable to account adequately for the dynamism of the capital form.

This problem can be introduced from a second perspective as well. Consider the following passage from Volume I, in which Marx refers to the process whereby 'the form of a machine becomes settled':

> It is only after a considerable development of the science of mechanics, and an accumulation of practical experience, that the form of a machine becomes settled entirely in accordance with mechanical principles, and emancipated from the traditional form of the tool from which it has emerged.
>
> Marx, 1867: 505

The sequence of innovations in machinery introduced by various units of industrial capital thus has a basic trajectory.[6] This pattern is a function of material (use-value) considerations, including both the principles discovered in the course of scientific labour and the practical experience of workers at the point of production. These use-value considerations clearly possess a value dimension as well:

> If the productivity of labour has increased in the place where these instruments of labour are constructed (and it does develop continually, owing to the uninterrupted advance of science and technology), the old machines, tools, apparatus, etc. will be replaced by more efficient and (considering their increased efficiency), cheaper ones ... Like the increased exploitation of natural wealth resulting from the simple act of increasing the pressure under which labour-power has to operate,

6. The notion of 'technological trajectories' or 'paradigms' is central to the work of contemporary Neo-Schumpeterians. In this view, technologies 'develop along relatively ordered paths shaped by the technical properties, the problem-solving heuristics, and the cumulative expertise embodied in *technological paradigms*' (Dosi and Orsenigo, 1988: 16). As the passage in the main text shows, this concept is already explicit in Marx.

> *science and technology give capital a power of expansion which is independent of the given magnitude of the capital actually functioning.* They react at the same time on that part of the original capital which has entered the stage of renewal.
>
> Marx, 1867: 753–4; emphasis added

The key point to make here is that there is no systematic reason whatsoever to assume that innovation trajectories will tend to be the same in all sectors. There is every reason to think that they will be 'steeper' in some sectors than others, as 'science ... and an accumulation of practical experience' uncover a wider range of possibilities for innovation (Marx, 1894: 894).

Another notion relevant to the present discussion can be termed 'technological systems'. This notion refers to cases where technical advances originating in one sector can be employed to improve productivity or quality levels in a number of different sectors. The significance of this phenomenon was fully grasped by Marx. Regarding the diffusion of innovations that reduce constant capital costs he wrote,

> [T]he development of the productive power of labour in *one* branch of production, e.g. of iron, coal, machines, construction, etc., which may in turn be partly connected with advances in the area of intellectual production, i.e. the natural sciences and their application, appears as the condition for a reduction in the value and hence of the costs of means of production in *other* branches of industry, e.g. textiles or agriculture. This is evident enough, for the commodity that emerges from one branch of industry as a product enters another branch as means of production. Its cheapness or otherwise depends on the productivity of labour in the branch of production from which it emerges as a product, and is at the same time a condition not only for the cheapening of the commodities into the production of which it enters as means of production, but also for the reduction in value of the constant capital whose element it now becomes, and therefore for an increase in the rate of profit.
>
> Marx, 1894: 174; see also 175, 177, 179, 266

We surely cannot assume that innovations in all sectors have the same importance for the system of capital accumulation as a whole. Innovations arising in certain sectors will have profound positive spillover effects for units of capital dispersed throughout the economy.

Innovations in other industries will lack these consequences, however successful they may be on their own terms (Freeman *et al.*, 1982; Rosenberg and Frischtak, 1983; Kleinknecht, 1987).

If we combine these notions of innovation trajectories and innovation systems the problem considered above arises once again. If prices of production were, in fact, the final long-run centres of gravity for market prices such that all sectors enjoyed equal rates of profit, then there would be no systematic drive to invest in sectors with steep innovation trajectories, or with huge potential implications for the system of accumulation as a whole, rather than in sectors with less steep trajectories and fewer system implications. Yet the dynamism of capital demands that flows of investment capital *not* be indifferent to the fact that innovation frontiers do not tend to expand at the same rate in all industries at all times. Different industries have different 'warranted rates of growth' due to their material differences (Walker, 1988: 169–72). Units of capital operating in sectors with a greater horizon of scientific-technological possibilities and a greater potential to improve productivity in numerous industries will tend to accumulate capital at a faster rate than other units of capital over an extended period of time.

This issue of time is obviously crucial. Marx himself certainly recognized that different sectors have different warranted rates of growth, and thus different rates of profit:

> Since the development of labour productivity is far from uniform in the various branches of industry and, besides being uneven in degree, often takes place in opposite directions, it so happens that the mass of average profit (= surplus-value) is necessarily very far below the level one would expect simply from the development of productivity in the most advanced branches ... [T]he development of productivity in different branches of industry does not just proceed in very different proportions, but often also in opposite directions ...
>
> Marx, 1894: 368–9

Marx, however, seems to have assumed that the different warranted rates of growth in different sectors are short-to-medium-term phenomena, and so do not force us to modify the medium-to-long-term tendencies holding on the level of prices of production:

> Something that must also be considered here, however, is the cycle of fat and lean years that follow one another in a given branch of industry

> over a particular period of time, and the fluctuations in profit that these involve. This uninterrupted emigration and immigration of capitals that takes place between various spheres of production produces rising and falling movements in the profit rate which more or less balance one another out and thus tend to reduce the profit rate everywhere to the same common and general level.
>
> Marx, 1894: 310

But if our unit of time is, say, the extended transition from the high point of the period of the early factory to the height of manufacturing, or from there to the height of big industry, there is no reason whatsoever to posit a tendency for the profit rate to reduce 'everywhere to the same common and general level'. The industries associated with a preceding period and those associated with a succeeding period surely tend to enjoy quite different rates over the long term. Similarly, differences in the slope of innovation trajectories and in the impact of innovations on the economy as a whole are *not* necessarily short-to-medium-term phenomena. The most dynamic sectors of the economy generally enjoy advantages in these two areas that last throughout an extended historical epoch, a 'long wave'.[7]

It is, once again, perfectly legitimate to abstract from such matters when we consider the production of surplus-value and its (logical) redistribution among capitals and landlords in a given period. But once we move to a more concrete and complex stage in the dialectic of capital we cannot continue to abstract from differences in the warranted growth rates of different sectors. The emergence and persistence of such differences are essential features of capital's dynamism. They are not mere contingencies of history, mere 'inessential, accidental circumstances

7. Long wave theory is a quite contested area in social theory. An adequate account of long waves would obviously require much more complex and concrete determinations than those available on the levels of abstraction with which Volume III is concerned. For our purposes we do not have to take a stand on many of the issues in dispute, such as the relative roles in the explanation of long waves of capital expansion and decline of 'technology push' (Schumpeter, 1939), 'demand pull' (Schmookler, 1966), class struggle (Mandel, 1972: 130 ff.) and the state (Arrighi, 1994). It is not even necessary to assert that long wave theory provides the best framework for comprehending capitalist economic history (see Webber and Rigby, 1996: Chapter 3). It is sufficient to note that all of the contending parties in these disputes grant that new periods of expansion are associated with the rise of new industries enjoying higher than average rates of growth for an extended time.

that cancel each other out' (Marx, 1894: 252). They are tendencies that necessarily arise from the essential determinations of the capital form.

If this is granted, then it follows that we need to introduce explicitly a theoretical level in the systematic ordering that 'transforms' the tendencies regarding profits and prices holding on more abstract and simple levels. The two dominant tendencies on the level of prices of production are for rates of profit to equalize and for prices of production to serve as centres of gravity for market prices. These tendencies are not modified with the introduction of the logical redistribution of surplus-value between industrial capital and commercial capital, financial capital and landlord rent. But with the move to the level of surplus profits due to innovations in leading sectors, where notions such as 'innovation trajectories', 'technology systems' and 'warranted rates of growth' have their proper systematic place, rates of profit do not tend to equalize in the relevant time period. And prices of production [P = (C+V)(1+R)] are not the centres of gravity for market prices.

On the relatively abstract level of prices of production the flow of capital into higher profit areas tends to equalize profit rates, and unequal profit rates reflect barriers to capital mobility. On the level of surplus profits from innovation, in contrast, capital investment unlocks the growth potential in certain industries, a growth potential that is not identical across sectors (Marx, 1894: 166). And so the mobility of capital investment now necessarily tends to lead to uneven rates of growth in the economy, reflected in different rates of profit across sectors.[8] This is a *transformation*, not a mere complication, of the general tendency holding on the level of prices of production and retained in Marx's subsequent discussion of the logical redistribution of surplus-value between industrial capital and commercial capital, financial capital and landowners.

If the dominant tendencies regarding profits are transformed, this has implications for the theory of prices as well. Once we drop the assumption that warranted growth rates and profit rates are identical in all sectors, we must also drop the assumption that market prices revolve around prices of production P = (C+V)(1+R). On a more concrete stage

8. This point is missed by Weeks: 'Competition tends to equalize returns by industry and also to generate unequal returns within industries ... The tendency for the rate of profit to equalize hides a fiercely competitive struggle within industries between the strong and the weak' (Weeks, 1981: 172). Reflection on innovation trajectories and technological systems suggests that there are strong and weak *sectors*, and not just strong and weak individual units of capital within sectors.

of the dialectic of capital market prices instead revolve around a different centre of gravity, which Walker terms 'prices of expanded reproduction'. While prices of production involve a redistribution of surplus-value towards those units of capital operating in sectors with a higher than average value composition of capital (or longer than average turnover time), prices of expanded reproduction redistribute surplus-value to units of capital with an above average rate of warranted growth and an above average profit rate. For any sector i, the formula for prices of expanded reproduction will be $P_i = (C_i+V_i)(1+R_i)$; as profit rates differ, so too do these prices.[9] As far as I can see, Walker's reasoning here is compelling:

> I suggest the term *prices of expanded reproduction* to capture the dynamic element. That is, centres of gravity are now set by long run conditions of uneven growth in different industries, which are determined by the real terms of production, but in a way that includes change. Unit costs (and behind them, labour-time) are still the foundation for price formation, but in a way that combines both levels in the present and change over time. Surplus-value is still generated from labour and reallocated among industries, not just in terms of already invested capital and its composition, but in terms of *future* build up of production in faster- and slower-growing industries. Because of the latter, prices of reproduction are a *third approximation* to market prices.
>
> Walker, 1988: 167[10]

Industries with higher growth trajectories thus have higher prices (relative to unit costs), not so much because of their present value composition, but because they are able to generate revenues for future expansion. Weak competition, which tends to lower prices (relative to unit costs) in higher profit sectors, does not dominate here. In the most dynamic sectors unit costs may fall quite rapidly, so prices can remain high relative to unit

9. Unlike prices of production, this formula for prices of expanded reproduction is general enough to be modified on later stages of the theory, where others factors systematically affecting prices are introduced, such as monopoly power, state taxes and subsidies, unequal exchange across national borders and so on. None of these modifications calls into question the central claim that 'taking all other circumstances as given ... the average rate of profit depends on the level of exploitation of labour as a whole by capital as a whole' (Marx, 1894: 299).
10. This perspective contrasts with the received view in Marxian theory that 'the law of value achieves its fullest development under capitalist conditions' with prices of production (Itoh and Lapavitsas, 1999: 40).

costs and yet still be falling in absolute terms. Prices may not even fall at all if the new products produced in these sectors are so attractive to buyers that the units of capital in question operate in the inelastic portion of demand curves (Walker, 1988: 172). This is generally the case for innovations that play a crucial role in technology systems, that is, innovations that have a significant impact on productivity throughout the economy. Also, the most dynamic industries in capitalism are often more concerned with creating new markets than with meeting preexisting market demands. Price competition is secondary to new use-value considerations in such cases.

This concludes the case for granting the category 'surplus profits from innovation' a distinct place in the systematic ordering of the essential determinations of the capital form. Two questions remain. First, is there any empirical evidence that the tendencies derived above actually hold? Second, if we accept the arguments for granting this category a place, where exactly does it fall within the general framework of Marx's theory?

4. A note on empirical evidence

> 'The concrete is concrete because it is the concentration of many determinations, hence unity of the diverse.'
>
> Marx, 1939: 101

This implies that the attempt to find concrete empirical confirmation of tendencies derived from a given determination of the capital form can be exceedingly complicated. A wide variety of distinct tendencies derived on quite different levels of abstraction will always be in play simultaneously, making the concrete a realm of contingency and path dependency. In a given case some of these tendencies will modify others, or even nullify them, while in a different case the modifications and nullifications may go in opposite directions. In specific, the derivation of a tendency for unequal profit rates across sectors due to innovation certainly does not remove the tendency for rates of profit to equalize. That tendency remains in force, and will surely be the dominant tendency in many regions and many periods of capitalist history.[11] But the fact that the tendency to equalization remains in force and can be documented empirically surely does not imply that other tendencies pointing in a contrary direction ought to be overlooked.

11. For example, we can expect the equalization tendency to dominate towards the end of 'long waves' of expansion, as established leading sectors decline and new ones have yet to emerge.

Semmler (1984) and Webber and Rigby (1996: Chapter 8) both provide extensive empirical evidence of persistent divergences in profit rates across sectors. Explanations of these divergences, however, must take into account a variety of factors beyond the appropriation of surplus profits due to innovation, such as barriers that hinder the free flow of capital between industries and regional differences. The differences with which we are concerned here result from flows of investment capital into leading sectors, not from barriers preventing such flows. And geographical differences stemming from the clustering of sectors are matters for a yet more concrete and complex theoretical level.

To my knowledge the most extensive attempt to provide empirical data substantiating the claim the profit rates tend to diverge among sectors over the course of a 'long wave' due to innovation was made by Alfred Kleinknecht. He summarizes the results of his study of German industry after World War II as follows:

> The study reveals quite remarkable sectoral differences in the rates of growth of industrial production between sectors and shows that this corresponds with a one-tailed sectoral distribution of innovations ... [T]he study ... suggests that it is appropriate to separate manufacturing industry roughly into two parts:
> 1. 'Highly innovative growth industries' which performed a locomotive function in the postwar upswing: chemicals petroleum refining, rubber and asbestos, cars, aircraft construction, electrical equipment, precision engineering, plastics manufacturing.
> 2. 'Traditional industries' with more moderate growth rates and weaker innovation performance: mining, building materials, iron and steel, non-ferrous metals, saw-mill and timber processing, woodworking/cellusose and paperboard, steel construction, machinery construction, shipbuilding, hardware and metal goods, fine ceramic, glass, wood manufacture, musical instruments/toys/jewelry, paper and board manufacture, printing and duplicating, leather manufacturing, leather processing, shoes, textiles, clothing, food/tobacco and beverages ... [D]uring the postwar Kondratieff-upswing a rising share in industrial innovation was taken by the group of eight high growth industries; correspondingly, there was a considerable decline of the relative contribution of the older, traditional sectors.
>
> Kleinknecht, 1987: 139–40

Kleinknecht cites a National Science Foundation study of six Western countries between 1953 and 1973 that confirms that this was a general

pattern, and his own detailed study of the Dutch economy over the same time frame yielded similar results as well (Kleinknecht, 1987: Chapter 9).

One hardly needs to be a defender of the 'new economy' thesis to hold that empirical evidence points to an analogous pattern over the last quarter century (Smith, 2000a). Two decades ago Gorden Moore, a founder of the computer chip industry, correctly predicted that computing power would quadruple every 30 months. A similar steep innovation trajectory has characterized computer memory and bandwidth technologies. Further, information technology has diffused rapidly throughout the economy. The available data points to a long-term dynamism in the information technology sector that is not evenly dispersed throughout the economy (Tapscott, 1995: 98). This does not appear to be merely a short-to-medium-term state of affairs.

5. Why Volume III?

One final question remains. If there are good theoretical reasons for asserting that the category 'surplus profits due to innovation' defines a distinct stage in a Marxian reconstruction of capitalism in thought, and if the available empirical evidence confirms that the tendencies derived on this level have force in the social world, where exactly should we place this stage? More specifically, why should it be given a place within the framework of Volume III of *Capital*?

One consideration rests on the fact that a main theme of Volume III is the attempt to articulate the long-run centres of gravity for market prices (Marx, 1894: 279). In Marx's explanation of the production and distribution of surplus-value in any given period prices of production serve as those long-run centres. At the conclusion of this dimension of Marx's theory, however, there is a systematic need to go beyond this relatively abstract standpoint. The very next stage in the systematic ordering should formulate the long-run centres of market prices in a manner that explicitly incorporates the second dimension of Marx's theory, the dynamism of capital from one period to the next. The prices of expanded reproduction derived on the level defined by the category 'surplus profits from innovation' do exactly that. This category thus ought to follow immediately after the discussion of the logical redistribution of surplus-value in a given period concludes in Volume III.

A second reason for assigning this category a systematic place in Volume III brings us to the controversial terrain of Marx's crisis theory in *Capital*. On the one hand, Marx sketches a number of factors that may lead to relatively brief interruptions in capital accumulation, including the need to replace fixed capital, interruptions in trade credits, foolish monetary policies and so on. I believe it is possible to construct at least a rough outline of a theory of short-to-medium-term economic cycles from these scattered remarks. On the other hand, however, I believe that the seeds of a different sort of theory are also found in Volume III, a theory that takes as its object more serious and extended downswings in the rhythm of capital accumulation. Raw materials for this theory are found in Marx's discussion of the tendency for the rate of profit to fall and in the chapters devoted to financial capital. Both of these discussions in Volume III logically presuppose the category 'surplus profits from innovation'. And so in the reconstruction of Marx's theory defended here, the proper systematic place for this category is in Volume III. Unfortunately there is not space here to do more than sketch a brief defence of this reading.

In Part Three of Volume III Marx introduces the so-called law of the tendency of the rate of profit to fall. While various different factors in capitalist crises are explored in different places in Marx's writings, it is beyond dispute that in this crucial text Marx assigns the overwhelming weight to the overaccumulation of fixed capital; the rate of profit tends to fall because C/V increases at a faster rate than S/V (Clarke, 1994). While this law comes into play in short-to-medium-term cyclical downswings, I believe that Marx also meant it to apply to more long-term downturns in capital accumulation.

Critics of this tendency law have complained that Marx fails to provide a plausible explanation why rational agents would invest capital in ways that lowered their profits. As long as differences within sectors are ignored, the complaint holds. But as we have already seen, individual units of capital tend to seek surplus profits through innovation. Geert Reuten has shown that the resulting heterogeneity and differences in fixed capital within sectors allow us to provide the account called for by Marx's critics.

In general, older plants in any given sector have a lower value composition of capital, that is, a smaller ratio between investment in means of production and investment in labour, and a lower level of labour productivity. With output prices assumed uniform in the sector, older firms also appropriate lower profit rates. Suppose an existing stratification extends from plant 1 to plant n, and then assume that some new plant n+1 with a higher value composition and a higher level of labour productivity is added to the sector stratification. It will enjoy lower unit costs, and hence be able to win surplus profits. From the standpoint of this individual unit of capital it will thus be rational to enter the sector in question. As plant n+1 wins market share, it forces some of the oldest units of capital, plants 1 to h, say, to withdraw from the sector. But it is not necessarily rational for all plants to withdraw from a sector when a new, more productive, competitor enters. Nor is it necessarily rational for all the remaining plants to adopt immediately the new technical innovation introduced by plant n+1. Plants h to n have made previous investments in fixed capital that they may not wish to write off. It can be rational for them to remain in operation as long as the prices they receive are sufficient to cover their operating costs, that is, as long as they receive the average rate of profit on their circulating capital. Since the lower unit costs of the leading plant tend to bring down the output prices of the sector as a whole, we may conclude:

> [B]ecause investments and costs are unaffected whilst revenue decreases, the rate of profit of the capital accumulated in the remaining part of the previous stratification (1+h, ..., n) decreases. That of the capital invested in the new plant (n+1) tends at the new price to increase, as compared with the average rate of profit (1, ..., n) at the previous price, or with the rate of profit of the plant just below it in the stratification, n, at the previous price. Since the new plant (n+1) operates at lower production costs than the previous plant (n), then in any case the rate of profit of the new plant capital at the new price is above that of the nth and the average rate of profit. (This is in fact sufficient for the argument.) Because with the additional plant the average VCC [value composition of capital] tends to increase, the average rate of profit tends to decrease.
>
> Reuten, 1991: 87; see Reuten and Williams, 1989: 135–8[12]

This argument, however, only shows that in any given sector there is a tendency for the value composition of capital to increase (due to the entry of a plant with a high value composition and the exit of units with low value compositions) to the point where the surplus-value produced in that sector is not sufficient to valorize the total capital invested in that sector at the previous average rate of profit. There is nothing that suggests that different sectors will necessarily tend to reach this point simultaneously. There is thus nothing in this argument to suggest there is a tendency in capitalism for a general fall in the rate of profit, as opposed

12. This argument assumes a constant rate of surplus-value; on this level of abstraction changes in the rate of surplus-value are due to changes in the ratio of employed workers to the reserve army of the unemployed, and that ratio is unaffected by the above considerations (Reuten, 1991: 88 n.2).

to random declines in particular sectors that may well be compensated by upswings in other sectors. Something more is required.

It is always possible to say that it is sufficient simply to assert a general tendency to overaccumulation crises, leaving an account of the underlying mechanisms to more concrete levels of the theory. It is certainly the case that a full theory of crises in capitalism must take into account the state, foreign exchange and the world market, all of which are outside the scope of Volume III. But ultimately this is true of *all* tendencies derived in *Capital*; they all must take later levels into account if they are to be comprehended fully. That did not stop Marx from attempting to derive, rather than merely assert, other tendencies on the level in which they were introduced. In Volume I, for example, Marx did not simply claim that there is a necessary tendency for innovations that improve labour productivity (increase relative surplus-value), with a promissory note to provide the necessary derivation on a later, more concrete, stage of the theory. He provided an initial derivation at the place in the theory where he introduced the tendency, in the discussion of the capital/wage labour relation on the level of total social capital. Analogously, I would argue, there is a need to provide at least an initial derivation of the general tendency for the rate of profit to fall due to overaccumulation at the place in the theory where this idea is introduced, that is, Volume III.

The notion of individual capitals winning surplus profits within sectors as a result of innovation is not sufficient. We need to introduce differences among sectors based on the appropriation of surplus profits through innovation. The notion of leading sectors in a particular 'long wave' of capital expansion justifies the assumption that the process described by Reuten occurs in the most important sectors of the capitalist economy more or less simultaneously, so that there is a tendency in the economy as a whole for the value composition of capital to increase to the point where the surplus-value produced in the economy is not sufficient to valorize the total social capital at the previous average rate of profit.[13] If this is accepted, it follows that the category 'surplus profits from innovation' logically precedes the category 'overaccumulation crises' within the framework of Volume III.[14]

13. See the attempts to integrate the dynamic of innovation in leading sectors with a long wave theory of overinvestment in van Duijn (1983) and Kleinknecht (1987: 208–9).
14. This is no more than a provisional derivation. One complicating factor here is that process described by Reuten involves a decline in output prices for fixed capital, which in turn implies a decline in input prices for fixed capital,

Marx's remarks on financial capital in Volume III are extremely fragmentary and unpolished. One major theme is that in any given period financial capital benefits from the (logical) redistribution of surplus-value. But there is also at least the broadest outline of a theory relating the financial sector to overaccumulation crises. In the above discussion of the tendency to overaccumulation crises the key to the story is the entry of new units of capital into the leading sectors of the economy. The drive for surplus profits motivated this entry, and we simply presupposed that sufficient investment funds were available. But from where do these investment funds come? We cannot rely on the retained earnings of established firms in this sector. They may not desire the devaluation of previous investments in fixed capital, or they may lack the resources to take full advantage of high potential 'warranted rates of growth'. Financial capital centralizes a pool of investment funds that with relative ease can be shifted to fund new plants in sectors with a reasonable expectation of being able to appropriate surplus profits for an extended period of time (Marx, 1894: 567). With credit money the extension of credit to new plants and sectors can be a multiple of the temporarily idle profits, depreciation funds and precautionary reserves pooled in the finance sector (Mandel, 1972; Bellofiore, 1989). In this manner, finance capital 'appears as the principal lever of overproduction and excessive speculation in commerce' (Marx, 1894: 572).

---

thereby counteracting the increase in the value composition of capital (Reuten, 1991: 88–9). Does this imply that Marx's emphasis on a rising value composition is misplaced? The justification for a negative answer must be postponed until after the state form has been introduced. As the concentration and centralization of capital proceeds, the negative effects of an extensive devaluation of previous investment in fixed capital become more and more serious to the national economy as a whole. At a certain point the state will attempt to avoid devaluation through higher levels of direct and indirect subsidies, lower rates of effective corporate taxation, labour regulations that shift the balance of class forces in favour of capital, deficit spending to prop up growth rates, negotiations regarding currency exchange rates and so on. These sorts of measures aim at socializing the costs of devaluation in order to buy time for established capitals to restructure. But 'restructuring' means adopting yet higher value compositions of capital themselves, that is, introducing some plant n+2. In this manner the process described above begins again on a higher level: while it is rational for plant n+2 to enter the sector, it may also be rational for plants h+y, …, n+1 to remain. The immediate result, once again, is a higher value composition of capital such that the surplus-value produced is not sufficient to valorize the total social capital at the previous rate of profit. The ultimate result is a need for devaluation on a yet more extensive level. This dynamic is crucial for an understanding of turbulence in the global economy in recent decades (Brenner, 1997; Smith, 2000b).

Once an overaccumulation crisis commences, the rate of investment in sectors suffering overcapacity problems slows significantly. A large pool of investment capital is formed once again, now seeking new sectors with a potential for high rates of growth in the future (de Brunhoff, 1978: 47). If the flows of investment capital to these new sectors are high enough, a systematic tendency to capital market inflation results (Toporowski, 1999: 2). The expectations of future earnings – rational or otherwise – eventually become a relatively secondary matter, as financial assets are purchased in the hope of profits from later sales of these assets (Marx, 1894: 615–6, 742). Throughout the course of this speculative bubble, however, it remains the case that financial assets are essentially nothing but claims on the future production of surplus-value. When it becomes overwhelmingly clear that the ever increasing prices of the financial assets are ever less likely to be redeemed by future profits, the speculative bubble collapses and a financial crisis ensues.

This account of financial crises is obviously more a collection of stylized facts than a fully developed theory. It should be sufficient, however, to establish the point at hand. The incipient theory of extended financial crises hinted at in Volume III logically presupposes a theoretical level in which sectors are distinguished according to the above average growth they enjoy in the present, or can be expected to enjoy in the future, and not merely by the use-values they produce or the size of their capital investment. This means that in a reconstruction of Volume III the category 'surplus profits from innovation' as defined above must be assigned a place prior to the category 'financial crises' in a systematic ordering of the essential determinations of the capital form.

Appendix: A proposed reconstruction of Marx's *Capital*

Volume I

The Foundations of Value Theory
(the commodity form, the money form, the capital form)

The Two Dimensions of the Dialectic of the Value Form

The production and distribution of surplus-value	***The dynamism of the capital form***
(the reproduction of total social capital within a given period)	(systematic tendencies underlying transitions between periods)
the theory of surplus-value on the level of total social capital (critique of capital fetishism [1])	innovations that increase relative surplus-value

Volume II

critique of the fetishism of circulation time (time as productive of surplus-value?)	innovations that reduce circulation time

Volume III

critique of capital fetishism (2): constant capital productive of SV?	innovations that reduce constant capital costs
critique of capital fetishism (3): commercial and financial capital productive of SV?	innovations in commercial and financial sectors
critique of land fetishism: land productive of SV?	tendency to the industrialization of agriculture

Surplus Profits from Innovation

Overaccumulation crises
Financial crises

Bibliography

Arrighi, Giovanni (1994), *The Long Twentieth Century* (New York: Verso).

Arthur, Christopher J. (1993), Hegel's *Logic* and Marx's *Capital*, in F. Moseley (ed. 1993a).

— (1997), Against the Logical-Historical Method: Dialectical Derivation versus Linear Logic, in Moseley and Campbell (eds 1997).

Arthur, Christopher J. and Reuten, G. (eds 1998), *The Circulation of Capital: Essays on Volume II of Marx's 'Capital'* (London/New York: Macmillan/St Martin's Press).

Bellofiore, Riccardo (1989), A Monetary Labor Theory of Value, *Review of Radical Political Economics*, 21 (1–2).

Brenner, Robert (1998), The Economics of Global Turbulence, *New Left Review*, 229.

Brunhoff, Suzanne de (1978), *The State, Capital, and Economic Theory* (London: Pluto Press).

Campbell, Martha (1993), Marx's Concept of Economic Relations and the Method of *Capital*, in F. Moseley (ed. 1993a).

Clarke, Simon (1994), *Marx's Theory of Crisis* (London: Macmillan Press).

Dosi, Giovanni and Orsenigo, L. (1988), Coordination and Transformation: An Overview of Structures, Behaviors, and Changes in Evolutionary Environments, in Dosi, *et al.* (eds 1988).

Dosi, Giovanni and Freeman, C., Nelson, R., Silverberg, G. and Soete, L. (eds 1988), *Technical Change and Economic Theory* (London: Pinter).

Duijn, Jacob van (1981), *The Long Wave in Economic Life* (London: George Allen & Unwin).

Foley, Duncan K. (1986), *Understanding Capital* (Cambridge, MA: Harvard University Press).

Freeman, Christopher, Clark, R. and Soete, L. (1982), *Unemployment and Technical Innovation. A Study of Long Waves and Economic Development* (London: Francis Pinter).

Harvey, David (1999), *The Limits to Capital* (London: Verso).

Itoh, Makoto, and Lapavitsas, C. (1999), *Political Economy of Money and Finance* (London: Macmillan).

Kleinknecht, Alfred (1987), *Innovation Patterns in Crisis and Prosperity: Schumpeter's Long Cycle Reconsidered* (New York: St Martin's Press).

Mandel, Ernest (1972), *Late Capitalism* (1st German edn 1972, 1st English edn 1975) (trans. J. De Bres) (London: New Left, 1975).

Marx, Karl (1939), *Grundrisse* (1st Russian edn 1939, 1st English edn 1973) (trans. M. Nicolaus) (New York: Vintage, 1973).

— (1867), *Capital*, Vol. I (1st German edn 1867, 1st English edn 1886) (trans. B. Fowkes) (New York: Penguin, 1976).

— (1894), *Capital*, Vol. III (1st German edn 1894, 1st English edn 1909) (trans. D. Fernbach) (New York: Penguin, 1981).

Mattick, Paul (1991–92), Some Aspects of the Value-Price Problem, *International Journal of Political Economy*, 21/4.

Moseley Fred (ed. 1993a), *Marx's Method in 'Capital': A Reexamination* (Atlantic Highlands, NJ: Humanities Press).

— (1993b), Marx's Logical Method and the 'Transformation Problem', in Moseley (1993a).

— (1995), Capital in General and Marx's Logical Method: A Response to Heinrich's Critique, *Capital and Class*, 56.

Moseley, Fred, and Campbell, M. (eds) (1997), *New Investigations of Marx's Method* (Atlantic Highlands, NJ: Humanities Press).

Murray, Patrick (1993), The Necessity of Money: How Hegel Helped Marx Surplus Ricardo's Theory of Value, in F. Moseley (ed. 1993a).

Reuten, Geert (1991), Accumulation of Capital and the Foundation of the Tendency of the Rate of Profit to Fall, *Cambridge Journal of Economics*, 15.

Reuten, Geert, and Williams, M. (1989), *Value-Form and the State: the tendencies of accumulation and the determination of economic policy in capitalist society* (London/New York: Routledge).

Rosenberg, Nathan, and Frischtak, C.R. (1983), Long Waves and Economic Growth: A Critical Appraisal, *American Economic Association, Papers and Proceedings*, Vol. 73 (2).

Schmookler, Jacob (1966), *Invention and Economic Growth* (Cambridge, MA: Harvard University Press).

Schumpeter, Joseph (1939), *Business Cycles: A Theoretical, Historical, and Statistical Analysis of the Capitalist Process* (2 volumes) (New York: Harper & Row).

Semmler, Willi (1984), *Competition, Monopoly, and Differential Profit Rates* (New York: Columbia University Press).

Smith, Tony (1990), *The Logic of Marx's Capital: Replies to Hegelian Criticisms* (Albany, NY: State University of New York Press).

— (1993), *Dialectical Social Theory and its Critics: From Hegel to Analytical Marxism and Postmodernism* (Albany, NY: State University of New York Press).

— (1997), A Critical Comparison of the Neoclassical and Marxian Theories of Technical Change, *Historical Materialism*, 1.

— (1999), The Relevance of Systematic Dialectics to Marxian Thought: A Reply to Rosenthal, *Historical Materialism*, 4.

— (2000a), *Technology and Capital in the Age of Lean Production: A Marxian Critique of the 'New Economy'* (Albany, NJ: State University of New Press).

— (2000c), Brenner and Crisis Theory: Issues in Systematic and Historical Dialectics, *Historical Materialism*, 5.

Tapscott, Don (1995), *The Digital Economy* (New York: McGraw-Hill).

Toporowski, Jan (1999), Monetary Policy and Capital Market Inflation in Europe, paper presented at Fifth Workshop on Alternative Economic Policy in Europe, Brussels.

Walker, Richard (1988), The Dynamics of Value, Price and Profit, *Capital and Class*, 35.

Webber, Michael, and Rigby, D. (1996), *The Golden Age Illusion: Rethinking Postwar Capitalism* (New York: Guilford Press).

Weeks, John (1981), *Capital and Exploitation* (Princeton, NJ: Princeton University Press).

8
The Rate of Profit Cycle and the Opposition between Managerial and Finance Capital

A discussion of *Capital III*, Parts Three to Five

*Geert Reuten**

Introduction

The third volume of Karl Marx's *Das Kapital* (1894) was edited by Friedrich Engels from Marx's manuscripts dating from 1863–7. In the third part of the book Marx sets out his views on 'The law of the tendency of the rate of profit to fall'. In Marx's day it was taken for granted amongst economists that there is such a law, both on empirical and theoretical grounds. Jevons (1871), for example, writes: 'There are sufficient statistical facts, too, to confirm this conclusion historically. The only question that can arise is as to the actual cause of this tendency' (243–4). In Marx's hands, however, the law gets reshaped into what is more properly a 'theory of the rate of profit *cycle*'. In the first section of this chapter it is argued – based on Marx's manuscripts – that to speak of Marx's 'law of the tendency of the rate of profit to fall' is misleading, and it is shown why this interpretation more likely expresses Engels's view on the matter.

Marx's theory, just referred to, is formulated at the level of 'capital in general', so prior to the differentiation of capital into Industrial Capital,

* I am grateful to Chris Arthur, Riccardo Bellofiore, Martha Campbell, Paul Mattick, Fred Moseley, Patrick Murray and Tony Smith for their comments on an earlier version of this chapter.

Commercial Capital and Finance Capital (the latter treated under different names, mostly Money Capital) which he sets out in Parts Four and Five of the book. In the second and third sections of the chapter I discuss Marx's firmly held view that his theory of the development of the profit rate is 'independent' of that differentiation (cf. Marx 1894F: 320); I conclude that this cannot, in general, be sustained.

In the second section I discuss, in apparent independence of this question, the upshot of Marx's analysis in Parts Four and Five of *Capital III*; namely that he sees capital dominated by Finance Capital.[1] Finance Capital is capital Capital and, as such, unity vis-à-vis labour. I argue that capital is rather to be seen as an internal opposition-in-unity of Finance Capital and Managerial Capital, where the latter is a concretized shape of production capital, as including Industrial Capital. Of course this is a reconstruction, not an interpretation. It might be added that (especially) Part Five must be reconstructed anyway. As Engels remarks in his Preface to *Capital III*: 'It was Part Five that presented the major difficulty [for his editorial work], and this was also the most important subject of the entire book. ... we did not have a finished draft, or even an outline plan to be filled in, but simply the beginning of an elaboration which petered out more than once in a disordered jumble of notes ...' (1894F: 94–5). Engels reports that he himself made 'at least three attempts' at reconstruction but finally gave up. In printed version, many of the sixteen chapters of this part have indeed remained a 'disordered jumble'.

In the third section, I outline elements for a concretization of the Part Three theory in light of the differentiation of capital generally (§3.1) and the opposition between Finance and Managerial Capital specifically (§3.2). I indicate how the relative dominance of one of these factions of capital depends on the particular 'monetary regime' and how this affects the devaluation of capital which is an intimate aspect of the Part Three 'theory of the rate of profit cycle'.

1. Marx's theory of the rate of profit cycle

1.1 General outline

Part Three of *Capital III* sets out Marx's theory of the 'law of the tendency for the rate of profit to fall' (TRPF). This is what Marx names it, and what it is called in much of Marxian theory. Although there is nothing wrong with that terminology – so long as a tendency is conceived of as a force, not a trend – the term has connotations de-emphasizing what is crucial in Marx's presentation, namely the cyclical movement of the rate of

1. Not in the specific meaning of Hilferding (1910).

profit and the dynamics that go along with it. A more accurate label would be the Theory of the Rate of Profit Cycle (TRPC), which is the one I adopt henceforth. In further explaining my terminology and the theory itself I proceed in two stages. In the remainder of this sub-section I provide an outline of the theory, leaving to the next sub-section a more detailed discussion of Marx's text.

Part Three, as edited by Engels, comprises the Chapters 13–15. In Chapter 13 Marx sets out how the compulsion towards profit increase gives rise to the accumulation of capital in the shape of productivity raising techniques of production along with a relative expulsion of labour. We have a tendential rise in the organic composition of capital: the ratio of the value of means of production (K) to the value of labour power (wL, where w is the wage rate and L the amount of labour). Thus:

$$K/wL\ddagger \qquad (1)$$

where ‡ is the sign for tendential rise. Again, a 'tendency' is not a trend in Marx's view, but a force which may get counteracted by other forces.[2]

If we restrict the outlay of total capital to means of production and labour-power, denote the rate of depreciation by δ, represent total surplus-value or total profit by the sign R and gross production by Y, we have:[3]

$$\delta K + wL + R = Y \qquad (2)$$

and for the rate of profit (r):

$$r = R / (K + wL) \qquad (3)$$

Marx does not use this notation, though his own notation gives rise to this. Similar ways of presenting capital outlay and the rate of profit have become usual in Marxian theory, though they are not altogether correct (see §3.1).

From equations (1) and (3) it follows that at any given prevailing distribution between capital and labour (R/wL) – put more succinctly if we keep that ratio of distribution 'momentarily' constant, that is

2. Note that, for example, J.S. Mill adopted a similar view of 'tendency' (cf. my 1996). On the concept of tendency see also Lawson (1998).
3. At this level of abstraction (prior to the differentiation of capital into industrial, commercial and money capital as well as landed capital) total surplus-value and total profit are the same.

$$R/wL = \text{constant} \tag{4a}$$

the rate of profit must tendentially decline. Or more generally, if we consider a force for the rate of surplus-value to be tendentially rising ($R/wL \uparrow$) and if

$$(R/wL) \uparrow < (K/wL) \uparrow \tag{4b}$$

then the rate of profit must tendentially decline, which can be seen from dividing through the right-hand side of representation (3) by wL.

This then is a paramount contradiction of capital accumulation; i.e., that the compulsion for profit increase gives rise to a tendential decrease in the rate of profit.[4]

Chapter 14 of *Capital III* discusses the counteracting tendencies, most importantly the cheapening of the material elements of capital (the prices of wage goods whence w may decline, or those of means of production whence the rise of K may be tempered or nullified) which, of course, affects representation (4b) as a condition.

Chapter 15 discusses the synthesis of the previous two. Crucially, in my view, Marx indicates in this chapter how the tendential drain on the rate of profit is expressed in a cyclical way. Along with the accumulation of capital and the concomitant rise in organic composition of capital, the rate of profit declines. This gives rise to economic crisis in the process of which the rate of profit gets restored, most importantly because of devaluation and destruction (i.e., scrapping) of capital (cf. Section 3 of Chapter 15). Marx then writes: 'The stagnation in production that has intervened prepares the ground for a later expansion of production – within the capitalist limits. And so we go round the whole circle once again' (Marx 1894F: 363–4). Thus it seems that the fall in the profit rate is a periodical matter rather than a trend-like phenomenon, contrary to many interpretations.

1.2 Marx's manuscript and Engels's emphasis

My interpretation of Marx's theory is in some important respects akin to that of Fine and Harris (1976; 1979: Chapter 4); see also Lebowitz (1976).

4. A well-known criticism of this part of Marx's theory is that by Okishio (1961). Reuten and Williams (1989: Chapter 4) and Reuten (1991) indicate how this criticism is based on an equilibrium notion, and that once we take account of heterogeneous units of production in branches of the economy – stratified according technical composition of capital and rates of profit – instead of homogeneous units, it is not difficult to provide the mediations of Marx's theory. (See also §5 of Tony Smith's Chapter 7 in this book.)

Fine and Harris rightly say that 'a more accurate name for Marx's theory is "the law of the tendency of the rate of profit to fall *and* of the counteracting influences to operate"' (1976: 162–3). Certainly, Marx formulates both the tendential fall (Chapter 13) and the counter tendencies (Chapter 14) at the same level of abstraction. But, if this interpretation is correct, then one should at least wonder why Marx called his theory 'tendency of the rate of profit to *fall*', and why so many have read Marx's text as different from the interpretation proposed here. The point is that a careful reading of the text does indeed allow for two interpretations. In the first, dominant weight is given to 'the law as such' (Chapter 13), over its counteractions; Chapter 15 then depicts a 'trend' fall in the rate of profit, even if stretched over a long time. The second reading emphasizes Chapter 15 as a synthesizing and concluding text. Contributing to these different readings are very different notions of 'tendency'. Although I think the 'trend' notion of tendency (the first reading) does not fit Marx's, I will not stress this aspect in what follows.[5]

As far as the text of *Capital III* as edited by Engels is concerned, I think that we should leave the issue here, giving all room for reconstruction and further development of the theory in either way. However, to the extent that one is also interested in Marx's ideas it is useful to turn to Marx's manuscript text from which Engels did his editorial work, and which was published as transcription in German in 1992 (Marx 1894M, manuscripts 1863–67). That is what I will do in the remainder of this section. I will use the following shorthand references:

M	=	Marx 1894M	=	German manuscript [= ms] transcription of 1992 (MEGA II/4)
G	=	Marx 1894G	=	German text of 1894 as edited by Engels (MEW 25)
U	=	Marx 1894U	=	idem in the English Untermann translation of 1909 (Lawrence & Wishart)
F	=	Marx 1894F	=	idem in the English Fernbach translation of 1981 (Penguin)

To begin with my conclusion: it seems that Engels himself had ideas on the issue at hand, which resulted, at least, in a particular emphasis. (I am not saying that Engels was unfaithful to the text, I am saying that his own ideas made him organize the material in the way he did.)

5. See my 1997 for an elaboration of this. The aim of that paper was to inquire into Marx's general notion of 'tendency' – it took the same Chapters 13–15 as a case for that.

The current parts of *Capital III* were devised by Marx as chapters (so the current Part Three corresponds to Chapter 3 of the ms). That is not important. What is important is that Marx's text is not divided into three; there are no section separations; it runs on without *even* blank lines between the current chapters. That already makes a different impression: there is no so-called 'law as such', or at least there is no particular focus on it.

The first pages are similar to the current text (M: 287–301; U: 211–25; F: 317–32). My reading of these is as follows. Marx sets out a hypothetical example of a falling profit rate. Then he writes: (1) this as a tendency is what we perceive in reality (F: 318); (2) it is what the economists perceived and have tried to explain (F: 319). Note that in general – throughout the text – Marx's reference to 'law' (thus also the title of his chapter/part) is rather ambiguous. At least some of the time his 'law' seems to refer to an empirical regularity.

Next Marx moves the emphasis to what he apparently sees as kernel to capitalist development: first, accumulation and concentration of capital go along with rising productivity of labour; and second, a fall in the rate of profit goes along with a rise in the amount of profits. He repeats this over and again (e.g., M: 291, 298, 300). This may seem the law to him: the inverse relation of mass and rate of profit (see also below).

After this Marx – even without one blank line – immediately moves to the counteracting tendencies (the text of Chapter 14). Engels, however, first interpolates a text from much later in the manuscript (F: 332–8; roughly M: 316–20). In G, U and F this is marked by a line or an asterix (e.g., F: 332). This interpolation gives more weight to 'the law as such'. Apart from this, at a crucial point in this text Engels also makes an (unmarked) interpolation of his own. On F: 336–7 (M: 319) Marx writes: 'Viewed abstractly, the rate of profit might remain the same ... The rate of profit could even rise, if ...' After this Engels interpolates: *'Aber in Wirklichkeit wird die Profitrate, wie bereits gesehn, auf die Dauer fallen.'* (G: 240). 'In practice, however, the rate of profit will fall in the long run, as we have already seen' (F: 337; cf. U: 230). In fact we never saw this. Marx did not talk in terms of 'long run'. The problem is that, of all three chapters, this (Engels's) sentence is in fact the strongest statement giving the impression of a 'trend' fall. Moreover it is indeed associated with (Engels's) 'law as such'; if in practice the rate of profit will fall, the 'law as such' might seem dominant.[6]

6. There are several more slight changes in Engels's text, each one of which is perhaps too small to mention. Nevertheless, they contribute to the general emphasis.

The second strongest statement (this time by Marx himself) is at the end of the text/chapter on the counteractions. Note that when Marx sets out the counteracting forces/tendencies he repeatedly indicates that these do 'not annul the general law', but make it operate as a tendency (F: 341). He also says that the latter 'to a greater or lesser degree paralyse' its operation (F: 344; M: 304,306). This is again repeated in a conclusion on page M: 308 (F: 346). The final part may readily give rise to the two rival interpretations of trend versus cycle. In the Fernbach translation we have:

> 'The law operates therefore simply as a tendency, whose effect is decisive only under certain particular circumstances and over long periods' (F:346).

The Marx–Engels text reads:

> 'So wirkt das Gesetz nur als Tendenz, dessen Wirkung nur unter bestimmten Umständen <und im Verlauf langer Perioden> schlagend hervortritt' (G: 249).[7]

Untermann renders (closer to the German; Fernbach's 'decisive' is rather dubious):

> 'Thus, the law acts only as a tendency. And it is only under certain circumstances and only after long periods that its effects become strikingly pronounced' (U: 239).

This can be read in two ways: (1) only in the long run can the rate of profit be perceived to fall; hence 'the law as such' is dominant; (2) the rate of profit falls in particular circumstances; that is, when the forces set out in the tendency-law indeed dominate over the counter-tendencies (my take on the German text is this second one).

After this Marx (M: 309–40) goes into the issues that Engels has placed into Chapter 15, though in different order. Note again that the text is continuous – there are no indications for chapter/section breaks.[8] I select a number of passages from it that seem important. Much emphasis is on an issue introduced at the very beginning of the text; namely that

7. Where the phrase in angle brackets has been replaced for Marx's: 'und auf lange Perioden ausgedehnt' (M: 308). This is not too important.
8. I am not saying that an editor should not try to make a text more readable by structuring it. Marx's text was not ready for publication and Engels did a great job by making it ready. I argue that from the point of view of the two interpretations Marx's original text leans more to a theory of cyclical development, Engels's gives more room to a theory explaining trend.

increases in productivity of labour via increase in the organic composition of capital result in a combined profit increase and rate of profit decrease. He calls this a law: 'The law that a fall in the rate of profit due to the development of productiveness is accompanied by an increase in the mass of profit ...' (U: 225–6).[9] Along this prices fall.

On page M: 322 this is repeated, this time leaning to a possible interpretation of trend: '[We have seen that] as the capitalist mode of production develops, so the rate of profit falls, while the mass of profit rises together with the increasing mass of capital applied' (F: 356). Next Marx amplifies on the depreciation of capital. One page further on, though, he puts this in a different light, first rephrasing the issue in terms of a contradiction, then developing it into periodical crises:

> Simultaneously with the fall in the profit rate, the mass of capital grows, and hand in hand with it goes a depreciation of the existing capital, which checks this fall and gives an accelerating impulse to the accumulation of capital-value. Simultaneously with the development of productivity, the composition of capital becomes higher, there is a relative decline in the variable portion as against the constant. These different influences may at one time operate predominantly side by side spatially, and at other succeed each other in time; periodically [*periodisch*] the conflict of antagonistic agencies finds vent in crises.[10] The crises are always but momentary violent solutions of the existing contradictions – violent eruptions – which restore the disturbed balance.[11]
>
> M: 323; G: 259; F: 357; U: 249; translation amended

Over-production, over-accumulation and devaluation of capital, is the theme of the next pages of Marx's text. An important sentence is: 'Under

9. Engels (G: 236) replaces Marx's term 'herbeigeführte' (M: 316) by 'verursachte' (i.e., caused) which Untermann renders as 'due' and Fernbach as 'occasioned' (F: 332).
10. I don't understand why both Untermann ('from time to time') and Fernbach ('at certain points') do not pick up the periodical here, all the more since one paragraph, further on in the context of depreciation/devaluation of capital, they do translate the German *periodisch* into 'periodical'. *Periodisch* has a connotation of repetition/recurrence.
11. The translations have 'for a time restore' and 'balance for the time being'. Engels has inserted the term 'für den Augenblick'. In this long citation I have, most of the time, mixed the two translations. It is just not the case that the one is generally superior to the other (and this applies not merely to these chapters). I am not complaining; translation is a most difficult task, more difficult than merely writing in a foreign language (which is difficult enough).

all circumstances, however, the balance will be restored by the *destruction of capital* to a greater or lesser extent' (M: 328; cf. G: 264, F: 362, U: 253). The balance will be restored! Note that Engels (thus the translators) takes away Marx's emphasis, though adds: 'durch Brachlegung und selbst Vernichtung' – by capital's laying idle or even by its destruction. (Of course, laying idle implies postponement of a fall in the rate of profit. The 'even' emphasizes the former.)

Next Marx sets out how crisis and its aftermath restores the rate of profit and writes: '*And so we go round the whole circle once again*' (M: 329; G: 265; F: 364; U: 255 – my italics). This is of course strong enough to make the point that we have a cycle of decrease and increase of the rate of profit – along with increase and decrease of the mass of profit etcetera. Two sentences further on Marx makes the point even more strongly by talking of a '*Zirkel vicieux*' (cf. the French: 'cercle vicieux') which Engels renders as 'fehlerhafte Kreislauf' and the translators as 'cycle of errors' (F) and 'vicious circle' (U). Marx – in otherwise fully German texts – apparently feels constrained to make use of the French 'vicieux', since in French 'cercle vicieux' has a double meaning, namely that of 'defeating faulty' (also the one Engels picks up in his German term) and that of an 'endless circle', of lasting recurrence.[12]

Again, one page further on (F: 365), Marx, back to discussing fall in the profit rate, sets out how it is 'accompanied by a temporary rise in wages and a further fall in the profit rate, deriving from this'. Clearly this must be a reference to the boom phase of the cycle and the labour shortage accompanying it.

1.3 Conclusions

In current Marxian theory there are two interpretations of Part Three of *Capital III*: secular trend fall in the rate of profit, versus cyclical development of that rate. The text as edited by Engels allows for either one. I have indicated that the text of Marx's manuscript is much less ambiguous and that it leans more to the cyclical view. I have shown this in particular for some of the phrases in the text that suggest the secular trend interpretation. Therefore, Marx's name 'law of the tendency of the rate of profit to fall' is very misleading. However, his allegiance to that title may well have to do with his general method of 'immanent critique', since indeed 'this' law (not 'his'?) was seen to be a very important empirical law of the Classical Political Economy of his day. Anyway, Marx's text can be consistently read as a theory of parallel increase in

12. Some English dictionaries indicate a similar double meaning for 'vicious'.

the mass and decrease in the rate of profit (upswing of the cycle); turning into a restoring decrease in the mass and increase in the rate (downswing of the cycle); brought about by recurrent 'revolutionizing' of the composition of capital, resulting in increased valorization along with devalorization and in accumulation along with devaluation of capital. *A Zirkel vicieux.*

2. From capital in general to Finance Capital versus Managerial Capital

2.1 Introduction and overview: capital's falling apart

Up to Part Three of *Capital III,* capital was presented as an organic unity in opposition to labour. Even if capitals compete for the highest profit and rate of profit, even if forced to expel competitors from the race, all capital is indifferent or identical in that respect. All capital is (potentially) valorizing capital by subsuming and exploiting labour.[13]

In Parts Four and Five of *Capital III* the organic unity of capital falls apart, apparently without restoration.[14] First, Marx conceptually demarcates 'commercial capital' as an 'independent' offshoot from capital, the latter now termed 'industrial capital'. Commercial capital specializes in the metamorphosis C'–M' (and M–C), and so accomplishes a centralization of the sales process. Second, 'money-capital' is identified as an 'independent' offshoot from industrial capital. Or, as Arthur (2001) highlights, Marx shows how, from the point of view of 'capital in general', capital externalizes in industrial, commercial and money capital.

Banks (or bank-like institutions) specialize in money-dealing activities (related to the circulation of money) and the bringing together of money-capital (M) for either commercial or industrial capital.[15] Their activity and that of money-capital generally, is that of M–M (plus interest). Herein lies the great difference between the first and the second offshoots of industrial capital: whereas the first engages in a particular *metamorphosis* within the circuit of industrial capital, the second does not. Money-capital merely engages in a uniform transfer, turning money into money – or, as we will see later, money into money-capital.

Thus we see, at one and the same time, a falling apart of the general *individual* circuit of capital (Volume II, Part One) and a particular social synthesis in the shape of a recomposition of constituent parts of capital.

13. On the concept of subsumption in *Capital,* see Murray (1998) and (2001).
14. Not quite so for Marx, as we will see in §2.5 and §2.8.
15. Fine (1985) argues that money-dealing is an aspect of commercial capital. Nevertheless, it becomes subsumed under Banking Capital.

In Part Four, Marx merely posits this recomposition (as 'functional', but also 'conceptual' in the sense of particularization) without explicitly showing the conflicts to which this might give rise. For example, he explicitly states that both commercial and industrial capital normally share *equally* in the general rate of profit as per their respective capital investment (U: 395). For money-capital, this is less obvious; indeed, while industrial capital and commercial capital are organically unified by the, tendential, 'one for all, and all for one' general rate of profit, money capital seems to *separate* itself off in this respect. In this sense, capital seems to fall apart. Or is this a mere appearance, and can capital hope for restoration of unity (as Marx seems to suggest)? If capital does fall apart, it is no longer clear what capital is, or perhaps what strives to be Capital (i.e., capital Capital).

Whereas commercial capital is not returned to in Volume III, money-capital and its relation to industrial capital receives thorough (though I think incomplete) treatment in the sixteen chapters of Part Five. Besides, Marx shows how the relation of separation between these two capital constituents, as based on the fact that they do *not* each specialize in a phase of metamorphosis of the circuit – as is the case of commercial capital – impacts on crises and cycles of production.

The object of this section is to extract out of Part Five of *Capital III* how Marx posits the interconnection of industrial capital and money-capital. Is this interconnection one of inherent unity, one of separation-in-unity (as Hilferding conceived it), or one of opposition-in-unity and so conflict? Or can we perhaps lay bare epochal conditions for unity or conflict; that is, conditions implied by, or grounding, a particular regime of accumulation? (cf. §3.2). My aim will be a further articulation of the connection between these two constituents of capital as set out by Marx.

The text of Part Five, especially, – as edited by Engels from Marx's notebooks – is in the shape of a phenomenal analysis rather than that of a systematic dialectical presentation.[16] Even bare elements of the latter are missing. I will not endeavour any reconstruction of the dialectic, but rather bring out the conceptual analysis that Marx seems to develop. I will not go into Marx's analysis of credit and credit money, as set out in the same Part Five (on this see Campbell, 2001).

Marx's analysis of 'money-capital' may be seen to be developed in three phases – as summarized and commented upon in §2.2–§2.6 below: (1) the

16. Some chapters do not even reach a phenomenal analysis, as they are rather comments on, especially, parliamentary investigations, e.g., on England's Bank Act of 1844.

development of industrial capital's money-dealing into an autonomous *money-dealing capital* (§2.2); (2) the development of *interest-bearing capital* as a separate entity which has 'functioning capital' in the shape of the enterprise as its counterpart (§2.3); (3) the development of interest-bearing capital into interest-bearing capital and *joint stock capital*, hence the development of enterprise into the management of 'functioning capital' (§2.5). At this stage we will see capital completely sublimated as M–M'.

In §2.8 I will indicate that Marx's analysis of joint stock capital is deficient and come up with elements for a reconstruction, which initiates oppositions within capital, particularly between Finance Capital (interest-bearing capital and joint stock capital) and Managerial Capital as set out in the concluding §2.9.

2.2 From industrial capital (IC) to: IC and ***Money-dealing Capital***

Given the turnover time of capital (developed in *Capital II*, Part Two) a part of capital must always exist as a hoard, repeatedly dissolved into means of circulation and means of payment. This is what Marx calls 'money capital in the process of [its] *technical functions*', that is the functions of money arising from monetary circulation associated with commodity circulation. It 'acquires autonomy as the function of a special capital', that is '*money-dealing capital*' (III–Four–19, F: 431–2, 438).[17] Note that Marx (F: 435) casts this 'intermediary function' of money-dealing capital (MDC) in terms of an institutional separation indicating, in my view, not a *necessary* separation (i.e., doubling or bifurcation), but 'merely' functional separating out of money-capital from industrial and commercial capital. (In fact big industrial and commercial companies may adopt money-dealing roles themselves during the course of development of capitalism.)

It should also be noted that Marx considers money-dealing in what he calls its 'pure form', that is, separate from the credit system (and particularly from credit money).[18] Further, at this stage MDC is treated in abstraction from the functions of lending and borrowing money-capital

17. III–Four–19, F: 431–2 refers to Capital III, Part Four, Chapter 19 in the Fernbach translation: 431–2. (Alternatively reference to the Untermann translation is indicated as U: xxx; reference to the German original as G: xxx.) From now on, I will use this short-hand reference, using only chapter and page references when volume and part are clear from the context.
18. Marx's proceeding in this respect, as initiated in Volume II, has been set out in careful detail by Martha Campbell (1998 and 2001). In earlier work I neglected this and I thank her for pointing this out.

(to be treated in Part Five). Thus MDC 'pure' bears only on the technical functions mentioned. This by itself, Marx writes, 'distinguishes money-dealing quite fundamentally from dealing in commodities, which mediates a metamorphosis' within the circuit of capital, i.e., M–C–M'–C' etc. However, with money-dealing too we have:

> the general form of capital *M–M'*. The advance of M means that the person advancing it receives $M + \Delta M$. But the mediation between *M* and *M'* involves only the technical aspects of the metamorphosis, and not its material [*sachlichen*] aspects. ... It is equally clear that their profit is simply a deduction from surplus-value, since they are dealing only with values already realized ...
>
> III–Four–19, F: 437–8; G: 333–4

Contrary to commercial capital in this respect (III–Four–17, F: 395), Marx does not say that money-dealing capital must yield the average rate of profit, though both of these capital factions share in surplus-value.

2.3 From money to: ***Interest-bearing Capital*** *(IBC); and from industrial capital to: functioning capital in the shape of the enterprise*

In Chapter 21 (Part Five) Marx introduces 'Interest-bearing Capital' (IBC). It is not developed from money-dealing capital but rather from the general commodity form and the conversion of money into capital, whence money's 'use-value' consists in 'the profit it produces when converted into capital. In this capacity of potential capital, as means of producing profit, it becomes a commodity, but a commodity *sui generis*. Or, what amounts to the same, capital as capital becomes a commodity' (III–Five–21, U: 338–9). Because of this apparent capacity for potentially producing profit, a 'price' is offered for commanding it, that is, extra money above its value, or an interest.[19]

19. Marx indicates that the term 'price' for this, is irrational (21, U: 353 ff); on this see also Schefold (1998: 135–6). In their 1999 book, Itoh and Lapavitsas comment on interest and the 'capacity of potential capital, as means of producing profit' and complain that this classical approach is problematic since 'seen broadly, interest is not only a portion of the surplus value generated in accumulation, but also part of the money income accruing to borrowers across society' (61). They seem to confuse money and money-capital. Lending out money (including putting money in the bank, or lending it to a friend) is *not* the same as lending *money-capital* (which the bank might do by lending that money to a company; or an individual directly so). Surely not all interest is paid out of surplus-value (when workers amongst themselves, or mediated by a bank, lend and borrow money against interest

> [B]eing loaned out as capital, money is loaned as just the sum of money which preserves and expands itself ... This relation to itself, in which capital presents itself when the capitalist production process is viewed as a whole and as a single unity, and in which capital appears as money that begets money, is here imparted to it as its character, its designation, without any intermediary movement. And it is relinquished with this designation when loaned out as money-capital.
>
> III–Five–21, U: 345

This then is the ultimate sublimation of capital in the form of money-capital: to acquire the character of begetting money as an external thing, without the requirement of any intermediary movement. 'The characteristic movement of capital in general, the return of money to the capitalist, ... assumes in the case of interest-bearing capital a wholly external appearance, separated from the actual movement of which it is a form' (21, U: 348). Whereas from the point of view of IBC, capital may have the character of 'money that begets money', to the 'functioning capitalist' or the entrepreneur (industrialist or merchant) the interest on loan capital represents nevertheless a share in the gross profit of their enterprise, leaving for them what Marx calls the (net) *'profit of enterprise'* (23, U: 373). 'It is indeed only the separation of capitalists into money-capitalists and industrial capitalists that transforms a portion of the profit into interest, [and] that generally creates the category of interest; and it is only the competition between these two kinds of capitalists which creates the rate of interest' (23, U: 370).[20] Here we see indeed the intro-

no surplus-value comes in). But it is a fallacy to turn this around so as to conclude: 'Interest ... simply reflects the general possibility of augmenting a sum of money through lending' (Itoh and Lapavitsas 1999: 65), which is rather tautologous, and not explanatory. (Fine [1985: 398] is to the point here: 'it is not the payment of interest as such which characterises IBC, but the use to which the loan is put.') 'Worker' in my example above is a character mask appropriate to the current level of abstraction (but the issue cannot be treated at this level). Generally, and more concretely, individuals as consumers may want to save for future *consumption* (e.g., at old age). That might involve a positive interest rate, but depending on intertemporal preferences, might equally well involve a negative rate: I want to be able to consume at the age of 70 even if I have to pay a 'price' for that. But again this cannot be turned around (in the fashion of Marshall or Böhm-Bawerk): saving is not by definition 'waiting'. Robinson (1953: 54–5) is superb on this.

20. If this creation of the category is read as a historical treatment, instead of a (nascent) systematic, this would of course be wrong as Marx was well aware. Still, one might wonder why Marx for such a crucial category did not differentiate a general and a determinate concept (on the latter terms see Murray, 1988).

duction of *two* competing points of view of capital; in the one money-capital and interest is the starting point, in the other entrepreneurial capital and profit.[21]

From all of Part Five (recall that for Marx the material was largely in notebook form) one gets the impression that whereas Marx struggles with the question of what point of view should be given priority in his analysis of Capital, he decides for the priority of IBC. This is most clear for the determination of the rate of interest. Whereas in the first chapter of the part (21) he states that there is no law of interest, 'no law of division except that enforced by competition' (21, U: 356), the next chapters are in many respects a qualification of that view.[22] Early on in Chapter 23, for example, he firmly states that given the processes related to the general rate of profit (i.e., the gross profit of enterprise as set out in Parts One to Three of *Capital III*), 'the size of the [net] profit of enterprise is determined exclusively by the rate of interest' (23, U: 373). Here IBC is clearly given the dominant weight in the balance of competitive power.

The quantitative aspect of the rate of interest in connection to the business cycle will be briefly expanded upon in the next sub-section. In the rest of the current sub-section I will be concerned with the qualitative separation between interest and profit of enterprise. Given the theme of this paper, it is important that the existence of interest *in the eye of the entrepreneur* is not merely the consequence of the brute power of one faction of capital (the moneyed) over other; but is rather seen as both the legal and due reward for a function of capital (cf. §2.8–§2.9).

> The interest he [the entrepreneur] pays to the latter [the owner of money-capital] thus appears as that portion of gross profit which is due to the ownership of capital as such. As distinct from this, that portion of profit which falls to the active capitalist appears now as profit of enterprise, deriving solely from the operations, or functions, which he performs with the capital in the process of reproduction, hence particularly those functions which he performs as entrepreneur in industry or commerce. In relation to him interest appears therefore as the mere fruit of owning capital, of capital as such abstracted from

21. We see these also represented in the orthodox economics literature from Böhm-Bawerk till today: in one view, interest reigns supreme (with any remaining net profit being just a disequilibrium residue), in the other it is rather profit that matters – interest can be done away with (in extremo, Keynes's 1936 view).
22. See also Schefold (1998: 136–7) on the order of presentation of these chapters.

> the reproduction process of capital ... as though they originated from two essentially different sources.
>
> 23, U: 374–5

(Marx points out that whereas an individual money-capitalist may have the choice of lending out capital or using it as productive capital himself, this cannot be applied to 'the total capital of society'. It would be absurd, he writes, 'to presume that capital would yield interest on the basis of capitalist production without performing any productive function, i.e., without creating surplus-value' (U: 377–8).)

The separation of capital into IBC and functioning capital indeed shapes the sublimation of capital referred to. Interest-bearing capital as mere ownership of capital, which begets money, does not even confront labour: '[the] antithesis to wage-labour is obliterated in the form of interest, because interest-bearing capital as such has not wage-labour, but productive capital for its opposite' (23, U: 379). The entrepreneur, the functioning capitalist, on the other hand steps down to perform a labouring function himself, so mediating between Capital and labour:

> his profit of enterprise appears to him as distinct from interest, as independent of the ownership of capital, but rather as the result of his function as a non-proprietor – a *labourer*.
>
> He necessarily conceives the idea for this reason that his profit of enterprise, far from being counterposed to wage-labour and far from being the unpaid labour of others, is itself a *wage* or wages of super-intendence of labour, higher than a common labourer's ... because the work is far more complicated.
>
> 23, U: 380[23]

This view represents till today one important strand for the explanation of profits within the Neoclassical economics literature (see the analysis of current textbooks on this issue by Naples and Aslanbeigui, 1996).

2.4 Interest and profit of enterprise: fluctuation over the cycle of production

In Chapter 21, as I indicated in §2.3, Marx states that there is no law of interest. Again in Chapter 22 he writes that the 'circuit described by the rate of interests during the industrial cycle' falls outside the scope of his

23. Marx comments: 'So that the labour of exploiting and the exploited labour both appear identical as labour' (U: 383).

inquiry, since that 'requires for its presentation the analysis of the cycle itself ... which cannot be given here' (22, U: 358). Chapter 30 nevertheless describes at least elements of the fluctuation of the interest rate during the cycle, though indeed in the absence of an analysis of the cycle itself. At least it is not a complete analysis, but rather one from only one aspect, that is the general expansion of Industrial Capital (again revealing the notebook character of the text: industrial capital instead of enterprise is a conceptual retreat; the same goes for 'money-capital'). Figure 8.1 provides a schematic excerpt of Marx's findings (cf. 30, U: 488–90). He lets the cycle start at the end of the crisis period.

Phase of cycle of industrial capital (IC)	**Interest rate** (Inverse of relative abundance of loan capital)
End of crisis	
1. *Slack* Contraction of IC	At minimum
2. *Improvement in prosperity* 'The middle period': expansion of IC	Between minimum and average
3. *Over-exertion* Expansion of IC: over-production (inflation of prices)	At average
4. *Crisis* Superabundance of idle IC	At maximum

Figure 8.1 The cycle of the interest rate over the industrial cycle (Marx)

In Chapter 31, Marx indicates that in the prosperity phase 'the industrial and commercial capitalists now prescribe terms to the money-capitalist' (U: 495). That is, the relative abundance of loan capital (which of course also existed in the slack, but without effect) provides a power base to IC. The expansion of accumulation in this phase, writes Marx, 'is promoted by the fact that the low interest – which coincides ... with low ... and ... slowly rising prices – increases that portion of the profit which is transformed into profit of enterprise' (495). That is, the low interest functions as leverage to the profit of enterprise. In contrast, during overexertion and especially crisis, 'the rate of interest may rise so high that it temporarily consumes the whole profit of some lines of business' (502).[24]

These passages bring out the conflict of 'interest' within factions of capital. This will be the theme for the remainder of this chapter.

24. See also U: 361–2, 365, 366, 499 on the long-term development of the rate of interest.

2.5 From IBC and the enterprise to: IBC and ***joint stock capital*** *in the form of IBC and the management of functioning capital*

Capital's division between IBC and the enterprise is highlighted in the institutional existence of the joint stock company and joint stock capital (JSC). Marx initiates this movement at the end of Chapter 23 (U: 387 ff) and further expands on it in Chapter 27.[25] With astonishing foresight Marx does not view the JSC as essentially different from IBC, but rather as a *developed form* of it. This is key to the rest of the current chapter. Joint stock companies entail the

> transformation of the actually functioning capitalist into a mere manager, administrator of other people's capital, and of the owner of capital into a mere owner, a mere money-capitalist. Even if the dividends which they receive include the interest and the profit of enterprise, i.e., the total profit (for the salary of the manager is, or should be, simply the wage of a specific type of skilled labour, whose price is regulated in the labour-market like that of any other labour), this total profit is henceforth received only in *the form of interest*, i.e., as mere compensation for owning capital that is now entirely divorced from the function in the actual process of reproduction, just as this function in the person of the manager is divorced from ownership of capital. *Profit thus appears* [*stellt sich so dar*] ... *as a mere appropriation of the surplus-labour of others*, arising from the conversion of means of production into capital ...
>
> 27, U: 436–7, emphases added

This quotation brings out two important issues. First, dividends take the *form* of interest, and share capital takes the form of interest-bearing capital (external capital). (Note that this is much the way joint stock capital has further developed in the twentieth century: for the investor shares are just a portfolio alternative to bonds and other fixed interest-bearing investments; they differ merely on a scale of risk – as is also the case for varieties of IBC proper.)[26]

25. Although Marx does not say this, in exactly these words, the JSC is, in fact, the abolition of the entrepreneur. We no longer have the risk-taking individual, but merely the manager/management of joint stock who risk not their own capital, but the capital of others and hence, like labourers, risk 'no more' ultimately than the loss of their jobs. Accordingly, 'entrepreneur' becomes a rather empty term; the conceptual stretching to 'institutionalized innovation' does not do this away.
26. For a portfolio holder investment in shares is decided upon in comparison with the going interest rate (and expectations about that rate). At any state

Second, and related, we seem to have a complete separation of ownership of capital and the management of the process of reproduction of capital. All distributed profits (interest plus dividends) take the form of interest and are lapsed into one category. (We see this reflected in twentieth-century Neoclassical economic equilibrium theory in which interest and profit are treated as identical.)

Here then we see the complete sublimation of capital: all capital takes the form of interest-bearing capital (M) → (M + ΔM).

Along with this complete sublimation, we see capital in one of its roles, the entrepreneurial, stepping down to adopt a labouring role, so seemingly forming an alliance with labour, in opposition to interest-bearing money-capital.

It is tempting, following one of Hegel's favourite metaphors, to cast this in terms of the Trinity. God the Son steps down to mediate between God the Father and human beings, apparently becoming one of them. The all time question being of course: is he human being or God? Or perhaps both? The entrepreneurial mediator between Capital and labour, where does he stand? We return to this question in §2.8.

2.6 Ideas of profit

In the differentiation of capital shown by Marx, we discern the following succession in ideas of profit:

1. From the standpoint of *naive capital* (manufacturing capital), profit is produced by labour through surplus-labour but it 'naturally' accrues as a just reward to the owners of means of production (functioning capitalists). (This is also the point of departure of Classical Political Economy, for which profit is at once produced by labour and a 'just reward' of ownership in work.)[27]
2. From the standpoint of (sophisticated) *undifferentiated industrial capital*, profit is seen as springing from capital – i.e., the undifferentiated ownership of capital together with capital in process. (This is the focus of twentieth-century mainstream Neoclassical Economics, though with 'interest' substituted for profit.)

---

of expectations about future dividends and future changes in share prices, the current price of shares varies inversely with the current rate of interest. (See also Itoh and Lapavitsas, 1999: 111–14, who after bringing this out, bluntly state that the rate of interest is determined in the market (113). Yes, but that is no explanation. Of course for the individual portfolio investor the rate of interest can be treated as a given.)

27. See Reuten (1999: 96–7) for quotations from Smith's *Wealth of Nations*.

3. From the standpoint of capital *differentiated into IC and IBC* (i.e, industrial capital, or enterprise, and interest-bearing capital), profit is differentiated into profit of enterprise as springing from the labour of the functioning capitalist (the entrepreneur) and into interest as springing from the ownership of money-capital. (This is the point of view of Institutional as well as Management Economics.)
4. From the standpoint of capital *completely differentiated* into ownership and management, profit=interest springs from 'the surplus-labour of others' but accrues as sublimated to the ownership of money-capital. Thus we have the developed state of the point of departure.

2.7 Money capital and finance capital

Marx, we have seen, calls the guises of capital in its circuit (M–C ... P ... C'–M') production capital, commodity capital and money capital. For the capital externalization (Arthur) he has the names industrial capital, commercial capital and – again – money capital (sometimes also loan capital and credit capital, with somewhat different connotations and meanings). Although for the first two we have different names for different aspects, this is (mostly) not the case for money-capital.

So far in this section I have followed Marx's terminology current in his day, but in what follows I will generally adopt the term *finance capital* for the meaning of externalization (that is, *finance* capital for financing proper, and *financial* capital for financing including money-dealing).[28] The term finance capital also has the advantage of connecting to contemporary everyday usage of the term.

In terms of the previous discussion we thus have Finance Capital (FC) which consists of two factions, IBC and JSC. These differ, first, in degree of risk bearing and consequent degree of reward. Second, JSC has at least the formal ownership of the company. FC is alike in that it is an interest-bearing capital (in the case of IBC) or takes the form of interest-bearing capital (in the case of JSC).

Institutionally financial capital includes: (1) banks; (2) insurance companies; (3) pension funds; (4) investment companies; and (5) individual investors. They all make portfolio decisions concerning their investments and cannot be categorized institutionally into either IBC or JSC. They all invest money as capital. The first four, each for different purposes, also collect money from companies and individuals (including

28. Note that the term 'finance capital' is used in a general sense and not in the particular sense of Hilferding's (1910) *Finance Capital*, that is a particular connection of banks and industry under the hegemony of the former.

labour) so as to invest this either as *capital* or as *money* (see footnote 19).[29] In this particular sense they are money-dealers or rather financial intermediaries. The role of money-dealing in the technical sense of §2.2, however, is predominantly the domain of banks (though, as mentioned, other companies can also adopt this role). The crucial *differentia specifica* of banks is that they are legally granted to create credit money (that is, under authority and the umbrella of a central bank). This vests in them a financial power beyond the mere money collecting activity of the rest of FC.

2.8 Finance Capital and ***Managerial Capital***

Marx does not develop the issue of ownership of capital versus management (§2.5) any further. With JSC, apparently, interest-bearing capital is the standpoint of Capital. The category of capital management is underdeveloped within Marx's analysis. In this sub-section I briefly set out a further conceptualization as relevant for the theme of this chapter.

In view of the separation between ownership and management that he outlines, Marx consistently amplifies on the JSC from the point of view of the capitalist mode of production generally, in particular the potential consequences of joint stock companies for social transition. He sees, with rare overoptimism, the JSC as a prefiguration of associated production:

> This result [the complete divorce of ownership of means of production and labour] of the ultimate development of capitalist production is a necessarily transitional phase towards the reconversion of capital into the property of producers ... of associated producers, as outright social property.
>
> 27, U: 437

Indeed this is one way a system contradiction can get resolved. The other is a system internal transcendence. What Marx could not see, at a time when the joint stock company was still in its infancy, was the emergence and development of *managerial capital* as a separate category of capital.

Remarkably, managerial capital stems precisely from joint stock capital as a highlighted *form* of interest-bearing capital – that is, just the point

29. Evidently *non olet*: financial institutions may not care whether money collected is invested as capital or as money (e.g., mortgage loans). The point is the different use: investment or consumption. In the books of these institutions this difference is generally crystal clear (though individuals might use mortgage loans for portfolio investment and, in the short run, firms might use business loans for consumption purposes).

so accurately emphasized by Marx. But whereas shareholders, as against loaners of capital, are the *legal* (juridical) owners of the company's capital, they are not necessarily the *economic* owners. The management not only commands share capital and loan capital (together, in the current finance jargon, 'external capital') but notably also the capital grown out of *retained profits*. This latter category may usefully be called *managerial capital*.[30] (In the current finance jargon it is called 'internal capital'.)

As long as the management satisfies the shareholders with an as-if-interest dividend, the growth of managerial capital may continue (to the extent that it drives up the price of their shares so that shareholders perceive it as being in their own interest). Although managers, as Marx emphasizes, indeed view their work as the result of labour, this managerial capital grants managers an actual stake in capital. As long as they serve the company they are the holders of this capital, and they may acquire a legal ownership in it through (combinations of): bonuses and share options; buying up shares and balance sheet reorganizations, so manipulating share prices and the exhibited rate of profit. On top, to the extent that the managerial capital is relatively large, there is no need for new share capital. Thus there is (at least) a potential conflict of interest between shareholders (JSC) and these holders of management capital, not because they are labourers – though they conceive of what they do as work – but because they *are* functioning capitalists, rather than 'mere manager, administrator of other people's capital' (cf. the quote in §2.5).[31]

Thus the mature JSC involves the movement of a separation between legal and economic ownership, whence the management of functioning capital develops into the separate category of 'functioning managerial capital'.

This obviously complicates the picture of capital. JSC seems indeed, as Marx emphasizes, the most developed form of capital. Legally we indeed have a complete separation between capital ownership and capital in process – labour in process of production of surplus-value. Indeed as the mere ownership of money-capital can be shown to breed no extra money, surplus-value must flow from capital in process, that is, the labour of management and the labour of the workers. Thus for Marx the

30. In practice, it has grown from both a mere reserve to secure dividends in bad times, and a vehicle for extended investment.
31. For an opposite view see Pinto (1998: 224, 228) who downplays a potential conflict between financial capital and management. For him financial capitalists are 'the' capitalists. Note that in my view *capital* does not escape capitalist control (as Pinto suggests, referring to Berle and his followers: 224); it is in the firm control of managerial capitalists.

JSC, as we have seen, seems to lance the ideology of the productivity of (money-)capital.[32]

As indicated, however, there is no complete economic separation between ownership and process. If for managers, managerial capital is the heart of the matter – and finance capital just an external bother of nuisance – we seem to have landed in a reworked *third* stage of the idea of profit, described in §2.6: in ideology part of gross profit springs from capital in process. Hence the term 'economic profits' in some of the neoclassical textbooks (see Naples and Aslanbeigui 1996). With it the ideology of the productivity of capital seems in part restored, to be effective both in theory and practice.

In this perspective we have a complex multitude of oppositions and alliances within and between capital and labour.

2.9 Summary and conclusions: Finance Capital and Managerial Capital – unity or opposition?

In Marx's incomplete drafts for Part Five of *Capital III*, discussed in this section, an opposition between money-capital (loan and credit capital) and industrial capital is mainly addressed in his treatment of the industrial cycle, when the interest rate, and consequently the remaining net profit rate, rises and falls according to the shortage or abundance of money-capital vis-à-vis the needs of industrial capital.[33]

In Marx's presentation (or rather mere analysis) this is an opposition between the entrepreneurial industrial capital on the one hand, versus the interest-bearing capital (IBC) on the other. However, that opposition gets (or should get) superseded when Joint Stock Capital (JSC) enters and when therefore (in Marx's view) we have a complete legal and *economic* separation between ownership and management; that is, when all capital is furnished by IBC and JSC. In this constellation all gross profit goes to the financiers anyway – thus there is no conflict over the cycle. (From Marx's own point of view, therefore, Chapter 27 on JSC is probably ill placed by Engels – or another new chapter should have followed.)

32. Hence, presumably, Marx's euphoria about the emergence of JSC – see the previous citation.
33. With respect to IBC particularly, Marx brings out in a discussion of parliamentary reports concerning England's Bank Act of 1844 how this act was aimed at safeguarding 'the value of money' as against the value of commodities, and how raising the rate of interest is used as an instrument for that (32, U: 514–16). We see here continuity in the policy of central banks till today.

In Marx's view of complete separation there is no conflict within capital over the division of the general rate of profit. The only conflict is that between labour and *'Capital = finance capital'*, since the management of capital in process is the work of labour. The interesting upshot of this is that the initial externalizations of capital get, so to say, reinternalized into capital in general.

For finance capital (in the absence of managerial capital), we indeed have the complete sublimation of capital as M–M' on the one hand and the transparency of 'interest=profit' being the product of labour. In this perspective Marx's euphoria about the transitional potentiality of JSC is understandable.

Indeed this completely sublimated fourth stage of the idea of profit (§2.6) seems ideologically untenable, in as much as the first was.

From this point of view (Marx's) there is not much reason to reconsider the TRPC (Part Three) in the light of any oppositions within capital: with a fully developed JSC there is no conflict over the division of the profit governed by the, one for all, general rate of profit.

However, with the opposition between Finance capital and Managerial capital as set out in the previous sub-section, there is ample room for such conflict within capital, which also complicates the capital–labour relation generally.[34] Capital, the amalgamate of Finance capital (FC) and Managerial capital (MC), is first of all a unity-in-opposition to labour, representing the (economic) ownership of the means of production in the form of capital. It is an indirect opposition for FC and a direct one for MC (as emphasised by Marx in the context of the entrepreneur and profit of enterprise).

Second, not only is capital a unity-in-opposition to labour, it also is an internal opposition-in-unity which goes beyond and deeper than any normal conflict among capitals. With 'competition in general' all capital is in principle *alike* – even if relative power positions are in movement all the time (cf. capital's stratification). With the separations set out, however, capital is rather internally in opposition since capital factions are *not alike*: i.e., finance capital versus managerial capital. Whereas 'capital in general' is *indifferent* to branches of production – and can in principle flow from the one to the other and back – and whereas, within finance capital, it can flow to become either IBC (in strict sense) or JSC and back, with FC versus MC this is distinct. Although the management of enterprises can strategically manage the proportions between MC and FC (and within the latter IBC and JSC), MC *cannot* flow to become FC

34. This last complication is amplified upon in Reuten (1998b).

unless it abolishes itself. FC equally *cannot* flow to become MC, or it would equally abolish itself.[35]

The conflict between FC and MC comes to the fore first of all in the context of the cycle of production generally – Marx's analysis in this respect (§2.4) so regains relevance.[36] Second, and more important, amongst capital there is also a triangulated complex opposition-in-unity concerning the general monetary state of the economy: between MC and FC, within the latter between JSC and IBC, and again between IBC and MC.

In this light Marx's TRPC will briefly be reconsidered in the remaining part of this chapter.

3. Outline of a concretization of the TRPC in light of capital's internal opposition-in-unity

In this section I set out elements for a concretization of Marx's Theory of the Rate of Profit Cycle (TRPC) (*Capital III*, Part Three). I proceed in two steps. First the TRPC is reconsidered in light of the externalizations set out in Part Four, focusing on the components of capital (§3.1). Next I connect with the TRPC the conflicts between capital factions alluded to in the conclusions of the previous section (cf. Part Five), focusing on the finance of capital (§3.2).

3.1 The concretization of MDC and CC considered as capital in general

In Part Four, we have seen, Marx introduces Money-Dealing Capital and Commercial Capital as offshoots from what he then calls Industrial Capital. Here he also makes *explicit* that part of 'capital in general' is accumulated in money-dealing and commodity dealing. In discussions of the TRPC this is usually neglected.[37]

In the first section of this chapter we saw that, at the level of capital in general, the capital accumulated is usually presented as $(K + wL)$ in this or a similar notation (e.g., Marx's $C + V$; cf. equations 2 and 3 in §2). However, once capital's dealing in money and commodities has been

35. This applies to categories (individuals could flow). Space does not allow us to go into the further complication that within the institutions of financial capital, there is a similar opposition between management and their financiers. This, though, is less relevant for what follows.
36. A rising interest rate during the later phases of the cycle (overexertion and crisis) will normally not so much affect JSC's dividend, but rather the managerial profit (or retained profits).
37. I have myself made this mistake (or grandiose simplification) even in writings where I explicitly considered the TRPC and finance capital at a more concrete level.

made explicit, this is no longer adequate, since part of capital is accumulated in those dealings. In addition to accumulation in means of production (K) we have the following three capital items:

1. Part of capital is accumulated in a hoard of currency money (M_{ch}).[38]
2. Part of capital is accumulated in commodities. Although commodities as raw materials and commodities in process may be considered to have been included in K, this is not at all obvious for commodities as ready product (C). Anyway the latter have a different status from K especially when we consider technical change.
3. Money-dealing involves credit – even if this function is not adopted by a special category of capital.[39] At the level of capital in general the credit between capitals may be considered to cancel out. However, this is not so for the credit between capital and labour.[40]

On the other hand, even if the presentation of capital as ($K + wL$) or as ($C + V$) has the obvious advantage of bringing out labour's organic part in the production of capital, capital is in fact never invested or accumulated in a wage fund (though the amalgamate of money hoarded serves *for* that). Labour is always a service in flow; in the balance sheets its production result can only appear in commodity form or money form.

Total (active) capital accumulated ($\check{C}$),therefore is to be represented as:

$$\check{C} = K + C + M_{ch} + O \tag{5}$$

where:

$\check{C}$ = total capital

38. Campbell (1998) stresses this, at the level of *Capital II*.
39. Note that in *Capital* (III–Four–19) Marx considers 'money-dealing capital' in what he calls its 'pure form', that is 'separate from the credit system', and only later, in Part Five, 'fully develops' it: that is, including the credit system (U: 436–8).
40. At the finance side of capital, even at the level of capital in general, part of capital is brought together by way of (as Marx indicates) the conversion of money into capital. In a developed monetary system this involves the conversion of bank money of account into capital. At the macroeconomic level the money of account of capitalists themselves may be considered to cancel out against their current accounts with banks. But not so for labour. In a developed monetary system, money in circulation chiefly takes the form of accounting money. Both the current accounts of and the deposits by labour are converted into either capital or consumer loans. O in equation (5) below must then taken to be net loans (positive or negative).

K = value of stock of means of production
C = value of stock of commodities
M_{ch} = money: currency hoard (of banks)
O = *net* credit between capital and labour (at the active side: consumer loans [to labour], including long term loans on mortgage basis; at the passive side: current accounts of and the deposits [by labour] converted into either capital or consumer loans).

For the rate of profit on 'capital in general' (with these modifications preferably called the macroeconomic rate of profit) we have:

$$r = R / [K + C + M_{ch} + O] \tag{6}$$

Dividing this expression through by wL we have:[41]

$$r = [R/wL] / [K/wL + C/wL + M_{ch}/wL + O/wL] \tag{7}$$

In the light of §1 the components *R/wL* and *K/wL* need no further comment. Suffice it to say that, as before, *K/wL* is a measure for the technique in use, or a measure for the relative expulsion of labour, and that it develops roughly in line with the cycle of the rate of growth of production, i.e., pro-cyclical. For the newly added components I restrict to the following notes, each time taking the cycle of production as reference point.

1. *C/wL*. Generally the ratio of commodity stock to wages moves counter-cyclically (though with changes in commodity stocks ahead of changes in wages). Thus the C-ratio has always exerted some counteraction to the K-ratio. Apart from that there is always *structural* pressure for a relative decline of commodity stocks *(C)* which is not particularly affected by the cyclical development. This is highlighted in 'just-in-time-production' (Smith 2000). With just-in-time-production we seem to have reached a limit for a *structural* decline of *C/wL*. Along with it goes a dampening of the cyclical counteraction of the C-ratio to the K-ratio.

41. In earlier work I considered that this *wL* ought to be prefixed by some turnover coefficient. This is redundant as long as *wL* is consistently measured. As the rate of profit is usually measured on a year base, one might *for example* take the wage bill for the year.

2. M_{ch}/wL. Similarly the ratio of currency hoards to wages moves countercyclically, so exerting some counteraction to the K-ratio. Along with it there is a structural pressure for decline of the M_{ch}-ratio (which gained new momentum with the cutting loose from precious metal standards).[42] Its limit will of course be reached when all 'world money' has become money of account. So here too the cyclical counteraction dampens.
3. *O/wL*. In the numerator we have *net* credit between capital and labour. Cyclically this credit to wages ratio seems approximately constant. (So we can neglect any structural trends – that is, in reference to the *K/wL* ratio; generally these loans (*O*) will contribute to the rate of profit.)

Two conclusions can be drawn from this short discussion. First, capital's dealing in commodities and money has exerted important influences on the development of the general rate of profit. The three factors discussed cannot be neglected in historical or contemporary empirical studies. Second, we have also seen that in a developed capitalist system the counteracting effects of these factors on that of the *K/wL* ratio gradually fade away. This might seem to underline the force of Marx's abstraction in his presentation of the cyclical development of the general profit rate.

3.2 Finance Capital versus Managerial Capital in context of the TRPC

The theory of the rate of profit cycle (TRPC), we have seen in §1, is formulated at the level of capital in general. In §2, I discussed Marx's view of the concretization of capital-in-general into, on the one hand, the ownership of finance capital, as interest-bearing capital (IBC) or in its form (joint stock capital – JSC), and on the other the labour of management of functioning capital. If this view is correct, a further development of the TRPC, at the more concrete level of the externalization of capital (beyond §3.1), is not very pressing: forces acting on the profit rate are, before and after the externalization, at the fore of the sharp opposition between capital and labour. Marx's capital differentiations do not affect this, which was indeed Marx's view (III–Three–12, F: 320).

However, in §2.8 and §2.9 when setting out the category of managerial *capital* (MC), we have seen that capital is an internal opposition-in-unity. How is the TRPC concretized in this perspective?

42. First by cutting loose money circulation from gold reserves. In the fourth quarter of the twentieth century even existing precious metal hoards were increasingly sold on the market.

Let us start with recapitulating the abstract determinants that are not modified by the internal separation of capital. First we have the requirement for production of surplus-value, hence the capital to labour opposition generally.[43] Second, the forces giving rise to pro-cyclical change in the organic composition of *capital* are not affected. Third, we have the contradiction that the drive for a higher rate of profit generates a pro-cyclical decline of that rate; it is restored through the cyclical restructuring of capital whence part of capital gets destroyed, and '*we go round the whole circle once again*' (Marx, as quoted in §1.2).

For Marx an intimate part of the cyclical development of the profit rate is the devaluation/depreciation of capital that goes along with (a) the cost decrease related to the rise in the composition of capital, and (b) the restructuring of capital. At the same time, however, processes of general price change – say price deflation and inflation – are bracketed by Marx. He can do this due to the fact that in his hands the labour theory of value operates – at least also – as an *analytical* measuring device.[44] The point is that bracketing processes of price change is a useful abstraction *both* when considering capital in general *and* when the externalization of capital is played out in the way Marx sets it out (as indicated in the first paragraph of this sub-section). However, if capital operates as an internal opposition-in-unity with Finance Capital and Managerial Capital as poles, this bracketing will not suffice. In the remainder of this section we will see how the playing out of this opposition depends on the *monetary regime* in operation. I will broadly distinguish two such regimes, a deflationary and an inflationary monetary regime, though without going into their institutional determinants.

Before setting these out let us first recall the profit rate decrease captured by the TRPC. The upturn processes associated with the TRPC result in the *newly* accumulated capitals – i.e., those with relatively high *K/wL* ratio and low unit costs – to realize relatively more profit in comparison with previously accumulated capital – i.e., those with

43. The moments of concretization, though, may affect the *process* of production of surplus-value, to the extent that the dynamics of production undergo change. This applies both qualitatively and quantitatively.

44. This is not the place to expand on this. Suffice to say that a labour theory of value can be adopted in three different ways: (1) because labour is considered the source of value; (2) because labour is seen to be an actual (less or more complicated) determinant of price; and (3) because labour can (to some degree) function as an *analytical* measure. In my view Marx adopts (1) and (3), stressing that the monetary value-form is the *actual* measure. (Abstract-) labour-embodied theoreticians usually adopt all three. (For amplification see my 1999.)

relatively low *K/wL* ratio and high unit costs. For the latter the actual labour productivity of profit decreases, and they are confronted with an intertemporal *devalorization*: they realize less value-added than before since prices have been driven down. Thus we have a 'redistribution' of value-added from old to newly accumulated capital (at an, on average, higher *K/wL* ratio).

(A) Managerial versus Finance Capital in a deflationary monetary regime

Along with this, however, we have a process affecting the *capital* accumulated rather than the production and distribution of (*surplus-*) *value*. Next to the *devalorization*, we 'normally' also have a *devaluation of capital*. Since generally more efficient production results in general price decrease, this also affects the value of the capital previously accumulated in means of production and commodity stocks (active capital). The point is that 'today's' price decrease of means of production, affects 'today's' new investments in means of production. Therefore, and *quite apart* from any new productivity rise (and along with it new price decrease) of today's investment, today's means of production can be bought more cheaply.

This affects all capitals previously accumulated (yesterday's stratification of capital). There are now two possibilities. One is that they see their profit rate (further) falling (in case of historical cost accounting). Another is that they devalue their capital according to the price decrease of means of production (in case of current cost accounting).[45] Note that this is a pure balance sheet operation, which has the effect that (from this part) any decline in the rate of profit is no longer visible, i.e., after this operation.[46]

What we would 'normally' see, therefore, is that along with the upturn process associated with the TRPC, i.e., productivity increase and *devalorization*, we see prices decline, or price 'deflation', resulting in *devaluation of capital*.[47]

So far we have, like Marx, only been looking at the 'active side' of capital (assets), and not at how it is being financed, i.e., its 'passive side' (liabilities). Clearly, at the level of capital in general 'finance' for any one capital is simply and merely the reinvestment of the surplus-value

45. For the devalorization they might have done the same.
46. Note that with the restructuring of capital in a later phase of the cycle, we see the same *and* of course also a devaluation of capital due to *material* destruction of capital which we see equally reflected in the value of capital on the balance sheet.
47. I put price 'deflation' in inverted commas since price deflation (as opposed to general price decrease) is *also* the result of a particular monetary regime. Its proper presentation falls outside the scope of this chapter.

produced for that capital.[48] Also, we have thus far not differentiated between financial capital and what I shall call *business capital*, that is all capital of the nonfinancial sector. From now on I adopt both of these differentiations.

Business capital is most vulnerable for the devaluation of capital along with general price decline to the extent that it is financed by loan capital (*LC*). This can readily be seen if we compare the active side of business capital ($B\check{C}^b$), the left-hand side in equation (8) below, with the passive side, i.e., the way business capital is financed, the right-hand side of (8):

$$K^b + C^b + M_a{}^b = B\check{C}^b = (SC^b + LC^b) + MC^b \quad (8a)$$
$$K^b + C^b + M_a{}^b = B\check{C}^b = (FC) + MC^b \quad (8b)$$

where:

all superscripts b refer to business capital;
K^b = the investment in means of production (plant);
C^b = the investment in commodities; note that C^b is equal to the macro C in equations (5)–(7);
$M_a{}^b$ = the accounting money of business held with banks;
$B\check{C}^b$ = business capital of (non-financial) companies;
SC^b = share capital: invested in business companies by the financial sector;
LC^b = loan capital: loaned to business companies by the financial sector, both long term (bonds, etc.) and short term (call money, etc.);
MC^b = managerial capital of the business sector (nonfinancial companies);
FC = finance capital, i.e., $FC = SC^b + LC^b$.

Equation (8) represents, in fact, a short-hand balance sheet of business companies. In comparison with the macro equation (5) we have on the active side instead of the hoards of currency money (M_{ch}) and consumer loans (*O*) – taken on by financial companies – the accounting money of business held with banks ($M_a{}^b$).

Of course, not only means of production (K^b) but also the stock of commodities (C^b) are affected by devaluation of capital. Whereas these

48. If we consider the passive side at the level of capital in general, then we see what happens at the active side directly translated at the passive side. Any devaluation of active capital is also a devaluation of passive capital. That looks ugly (and may be psychologically deceptive) but a general price decrease implies also that the purchasing power of the devalued passive capital has increased in parallel.

two components get devalued, the borrowed capital on the right-hand side (LC^b) remains the nominal sum of its initial value. The same applies to the share capital as quoted in nominal value.[49] Thus to the extent that the active capital is financed with loan capital, devaluation of capital is more than a nominal burden. It will outrun reserves built up as MC, and in its absence the burden falls on share capital's now shrinking value. (The counterpart is that financiers having lent Loan Capital (LC) equally profit from the devaluation, as the purchasing power of their loan capital, when matured, has increased.)

'Normally' then, the enforced productivity increase captured by the TRPC, and the price decrease associated with it, not only operates on the production of surplus-value or business profit (devalorization) but also on the value of the stock of capital (devaluation). Loan capital operates 'normally' as a burden on the net results of business. From their perspective financiers will be eager to provide Loan rather than Share Capital (SC). Together this puts finance capital in a relative power position. As long as the process keeps going, even sitting on their money breeds extra purchasing power.[50] Nevertheless when the long-run average rate of profit is (expected to be) larger than the long-run average price decrease financiers will invest capital (in mixtures of LC and SC).

The depression effects that usually go along with price 'deflation' of course also affect employment and should affect the wage rate. But as the great theoretician of deflation, Keynes (1936), indicates, nominal wage rate decreases are usually difficult to exert. The 'normal' situation of productivity increase and tantamount price decrease, then, is highly problematical for capital.

It may well be the case that Marx when composing his TRPC had a similar 'regime' in mind. What is more, his presentation of complete legal and *economic* separation between ownership and management, where the only conflict is that between labour and 'C̲apital = finance capital' is consistent with this. Whence the so-called Managerial Capital, if a category at all, is negligible. Marx's abstract presentation of the TRPC seems appropriate. Nevertheless, an opposition between capital factions seems implicit when taking into account the devaluation of capital.

49. To polish up the balance sheet, share capital may get devalued along with the active capital side. The alternative is to keep on showing the loss on the balance sheet (negative reserves).
50. In this perspective Keynes (1936) could make explicit that, at the supply side of loaning, interest is 'the price for parting with liquidity', whereas he could on the other hand hold on to the view that labour is 'the sole factor of production' (213–14).

(B) Managerial versus Finance Capital in an inflationary monetary regime

We now turn to the 'abnormal' situation of productivity increase together with generalized price increase. In the context of this chapter I cannot go into the processes producing inflation. I merely indicate that any price inflation (in fact prices increasing beyond the decrease implied by productivity increase) is the outcome of a particular monetary regime.[51] (Note that the term 'normal' merely serves as a reference point: the 'abnormal' was the 'normal' situation of at least the second half of the twentieth century.)

Along with the *devalorization* captured by the TRPC (the Engels–Marx 'law as such') we see then, instead of devaluation of capital, a continuous *revaluation of capital*. From the point of view of business companies this revaluation may compensate or overcompensate the devalorization. An overcompensating revaluation of capital (assets/active side) is of course equally shown on the passive side (liabilities). Since both loan capital and share capital are stated in nominal value, this will be shown in business company reserves – what was called MC in §2. Thus beyond any customary retention of *profits* as reserves, *capital* revaluation boosts MC.

This makes explicit the tripartite opposition-in-unity of capital. Let us first take SC and MC together (assuming no conflict between them) and counterpose these to LC. With revaluation of capital, the more loan capital business uses for its finance the more it gains in this respect. Thus both in a deflationary and in an inflationary monetary regime we see the conflict revealed though with reversed power positions.

It could be argued that in such an inflationary situation loan capital requires an inflation premium on top of the normal interest rate. However, in an inflationary situation we also have a complete shift in the power relations between loan capital and managerial (cum share) capital. Whereas in a deflationary situation loan capital can afford to 'sit' on its money (price decrease increases the purchasing power automatically), inflation compels lending out money capital at any price (loan capital is forced to 'part with liquidity' – a negative 'real' interest rate is better than none).[52] Inflation then puts managerial (cum share) capital in a power position.[53]

51. See Reuten and Williams (1989: 147–57) and Reuten (1998a, 1998b).
52. The empirical figures of the second half of the twentieth century confirm this (see Reuten, 1998b; Reuten and Went, 1999).
53. Note that this applies to some lesser extent to the banking section of finance capital, depending on the size of their own managerial finance capital – to the extent that their managerial finance capital is invested in business loans they do suffer. Note also, it is not just loan capital that suffers but also labour, to the extent that their money reserves are put on accounts with banks to be converted into capital.

Second, a relative defeat of Loan Capital (LC) also affects the power structure between Managerial Capital (MC) and Share Capital (SC). To the extent that company reserves have grown, MC gains a relative independence from SC: there will usually be no need for new additional share capital, and the old share capital is stuck 'forever' in the company (even if its holders may change). MC can then actually treat SC as a flexible interest-bearing-capital (cf. Marx). What is more, to the extent that LC due to the monetary regime is on the defensive – with relatively low real rates of interest – 'rates of dividend' can decrease. The working out of this potential conflict is highly dependent on regional business and fiscal law, as well as on the structure of financial institutions (banks, pension and insurance funds – including the latter's MC). Their description is beyond the scope of this chapter.

If the monetary regime is crucial to the relative power structure of capital's opposition-in-unity, the question is, of course, whether especially an inflationary monetary regime can last in capitalism. Three factors are of importance here.

First, such a regime boosts managerial business profits, hence general economic growth. A first limit approaches when full employment is reached; therefore, labour can seek higher wages, putting a drain on business profits.

Second, continuing inflation is constrained by the very functions of money (especially money as a store of value) and so the monetary system generally. Loan capital will increasingly take flight into investment in commodities (including precious metals and real estate). Ultimately this will have the effect that loan capital is converted into money of account, and so ends up with banks.[54] Increasingly then the conflict is not between managerial capital and finance capital generally, but between managerial capital and *banks* especially.[55]

In the context of the current chapter, however, a third factor is of primary interest: the contradiction of the opposition between finance and managerial capital. To the extent that managerial capital increasingly extends the reach of its power over finance capital, business managerial profits increase and *hence* business managerial capital (MC^b). However, when managerial capital outgrows finance capital (see equation 8) or, in the limit, gets rid of finance capital – for share capital

54. That is, if financiers *net* invest in commodities it must end up as money of account.
55. In my 1998b I indicated that this gets translated in a change of policy by central banks, i.e., a general change of the monetary regime.

by buying up shares – the full burden of the cyclical *devalorization* as captured by the TRPC falls on managerial capital. This is so since revaluation of capital can no longer provide compensation for the devalorization of capital (we merely have an inflation of both sides of the business balance sheet).[56]

Interestingly this limit case would take us back again to Marx's presentation of the TRPC for capital in general.

(C) Balance of power: moderate inflation

The fact that managerial capital in the limiting case of an inflationary regime bears the full burden of TRPC's devalorization, does not mean that MC has an interest in deflation; indeed we saw in sub-section (A) that with continuous deflation MC vanishes. Only with inflation, MC enters the arena. The contradiction is rather that MC is in opposition to FC over the distribution of profit, but ultimately loses when it ultimately wins.[57] The joint interest of MC and FC is to maintain a regime of moderate inflation, so pressing down 'real' wages automatically; that is, a regime under which MC and FC can coexist in moderate harmony.[58]

Summing up. Marx in his exposition of the TRPC brackets general price change – hence generalized devaluation or revaluation of capital. Deflation and devaluation of capital seem to fit his view of the dominance of finance capital. Only with inflation and revaluation of capital does it become explicit that capital is an opposition-in-unity. Moderate inflation, thus also moderate revaluation of capital – along with the devalorization and restructuring of capital as captured by the TRPC – seems to provide a *modus vivendi* for both factions of capital.

4. Conclusions: FC's and MC's shifting opposition-in-unity in face of the rate of profit cycle

In the first section of this chapter, we saw that the *Capital III* theory of the development of a general rate of profit has a misleading name: Tendency of the Rate of Profit to Fall (TRPF). An alternative reading of the theory as one of cyclical development of the rate of profit (TRPC) is

56. That is of K^b and C^b on the left-hand side of equation 8, and of MC^b on the right-hand side.
57. In this context it is interesting to note that, in the still moderately inflationary circumstances of 1999, a large multinational company such as Unilever paid its shareholders an amount of cash above normal dividend of $8 billion instead of cancelling loan capital.
58. Consider also that central banks, especially the ECB, now regard a price inflation of 2 per cent as the 'price stability' target.

supported by Marx's manuscript text for Part Three. Marx seems to posit the contradiction that forces generating an increase of profits also result in a decrease in the rate of profit (upswing of the cycle) which – along with restructuring of capital – generates a decrease of profits and an increase in the rate of profit (downswing of the cycle). 'And so we go round the whole circle once again.' It is a silly cycle of valorization and construction then devalorization and destruction, as based on the rationality of money. It is not a mighty God's punishment, as in the case of Sisiphus perpetually rolling his stone uphill never arriving at the top, but the fetish of Money that engenders the *Zirkel vicieux*.

In the second section, when discussing Parts Four and Five of *Capital III*, we have seen how Marx aptly conceives of joint stock capital or share capital (JSC) as a *form* of interest-bearing capital. He also envisioned the appearance of JSCs as pointing to a complete separation of capital ownership and capital in process, or between capital ownership and labour as including managerial labour. Finally then, for Marx, Finance Capital shining as C̲apital, operates as a *unity* vis-à-vis labour (§2.1–§2.6).

I have argued that this view neglects the difference between legal ownership and economic ownership. In fact managers of JSCs command their company's capital and have economic ownership of what I have called *managerial capital*, as grown out of retained profits (and especially – as we saw later – out of revaluation of capital). So management has, at least potentially, a firm stake in capital generally. In this way I posited the developed form of capital, contrary to Marx, as an 'internal opposition-in-unity', where factions of capital are in conflict over the distribution of profit (§2.7–§2.9).

In the third section we saw how this opposition is played out in the context of the TRPC, especially relating to the devaluation of capital. This opposition does not do away with devaluation – paradoxically, not even when we have an inflationary revaluation of capital! The conflict is over what faction of capital bears it, which depends on the monetary regime. First, in a deflationary regime Finance Capital will exert hegemony (similar to Marx's view), though, because of the depressive effects that go along with it, such a regime means a Pyrrhic victory for Finance Capital. Second, a full inflationary regime means a self-defeating hegemony for Managerial Capital – on the one hand because it bears the full burden of the effects implied by the TRPC, including capital 'devaluation'; on the other hand because such a regime undermines the pragmatic functions of money. Third, a regime of moderate inflation (what central banks nowadays call 'price stability') provides a *modus vivendi* for both of the capital factions, operating in relative harmony in opposition to labour – without, though, doing away the *Zirkel vicieux*.

Bibliography

All years in brackets are the original dates of publication as referred to in the text; editions quoted from may differ and are provided where appropriate.

Arthur, Christopher J. (2001), Capital in General and Marx's *Capital* (this volume).

Arthur, Christopher and Geert Reuten (eds) (1998), *The Circulation of Capital: Essays on Volume II of Marx's 'Capital'* (London/New York: Macmillan/St Martin's Press).

Bellofiore, Riccardo (ed.) (1998), Marxian Economics: A Reappraisal (2 volumes) (London/New York: Macmillan/St Martin's Press).

Campbell, Martha (1998), Money in the circulation of capital, in C.J. Arthur and G. Reuten (eds 1998): 129–58.

— (2001), The Credit System (this volume).

Fine, Ben (1985), Banking capital and the theory of interest, *Science and Society*, XLIX/4: 387–413.

Fine, Ben and Harris, Laurence (1976), Controversial issues in Marxist economic theory, in R. Miliband and J. Saville (eds), *Socialist Register 1976* (London: Merlin Press).

— (1979), *Rereading Capital* (London: Macmillan).

Hilferding, Rudolf (1910), *Finance Capital; A Study of the Latest Phase of Capitalist Development* (London: Routledge & Kegan Paul, 1981).

Itoh, Makoto and Lapavitsas, Costas (1999), *Political Economy of Money and Finance* (London: Macmillan).

Jevons, W. Stanley (1871^1, 1879^2), *The Theory of Political Economy* (Harmondsworth: Penguin, 1970).

Keynes, J. Maynard (1936), *The General Theory of Employment Interest and Money* (London: Macmillan).

Lawson, Tony (1998), Tendencies, in J. Davis, W. Hands and U. Mäki (eds), *The Handbook of Economic Methodology* (Cheltenham/Northampton: Edward Elgar): 493–8.

Lebowitz, Michael A. (1976), Marx's falling rate of profit: a dialectical view, *Canadian Journal of Economics*, 9/2: 232–54.

Marx, Karl (1894G), ed. F. Engels, *Das Kapital, Kritik der Politischen Ökonomie, Band III, Der Gesamtprozesz der kapitalistischen Produktion* (MEW) 25 (Berlin: Dietz Verlag, 1972).

— (1894U), *Capital, A Critique of Political Economy, Volume III, The Process of Capitalist Production as a Whole* trans. of 1894G (Ernest Untermann, 1909) (London, Lawrence & Wishart, 1974).

— (1894F), *Capital, A Critique of Political Economy, Volume III*, trans. of 1894G (David Fernbach, 1981) (Harmondsworth: Penguin, 1981).

— (1894M), eds M. Müller, J. Jungnickel, B. Lietz, C. Sander und A. Schnickmann, Karl Marx, *Ökonomische Manuskripte 1863–1867*, Text Teil 2.

Marx, Karl and Engels, Friedrich *Gesamtausgabe* (MEGA), Zweite Abteilung, Band 4, Teil 2: 285–340 (Berlin/Amsterdam: Dietz Verlag/Internationales Institut für Sozialgeschichte Amsterdam, 1992).

— (CW 33), *Economic Manuscript of 1861–1863* (Continuation), *Collected Works* Vol. 33 (New York: International Publishers, 1991).

Murray, Patrick (1988), *Marx's Theory of Scientific Knowledge* (Atlantic Highlands, NJ: Humanities Press, 1990).
— (1998), Beyond the 'commerce and industry' picture of Capital, in C.J. Arthur and G. Reuten (eds 1998): 33–66.
— (2001) Marx's 'Truly Social' labor theory of value: abstract labor in Marxian value theory, Part II, *Historical Materialism*, 7 (2000): 99–136.
Naples, Michele and Nahid Aslanbeigui (1996), What does determine the profit rate? The neoclassical theories presented in introductory textbooks, *Cambridge Journal of Economics*, Vol. 20: 53–71.
Okishio, Nobio (1961), Technical changes and the rate of profit, *Kobe University Economic Review*, 7: 85–99.
Pinto, Nelson Prado Alves (1998), Finance Capital Revisited, in Bellofiore (ed. 1998a): 216–32.
Reuten, Geert (1991), Accumulation of Capital and the Foundation of the Tendency of the Rate of Profit to Fall, *Cambridge Journal of Economics*, 15/1: 79–93.
— (1996), A revision of the neoclassical economics methodology; Appraising Hausman's Mill-twist, Robbins-gist, and Popper-whist, *Journal of Economic Methodology*, 3/1: 39–67.
— (1997), The notion of tendency in Marx's 1894 law of profit, in F. Moseley and M. Campbell (eds 1998): 150–75.
— (1998a), Destructive creativity; institutional arrangements of banking and the logic of capitalist technical change, in Bellofiore (ed 1998, Vol. 2): 177–93.
— (1998b), The European Monetary Union: a nest for Finance Capital, paper for the International Symposium of Marxian Theory VIII, Bergamo, 7–11 June 1998 (revised version 2001).
— (1999), The Source versus Measure obstacle in value theory, *Rivista di Politica Economica*, 89/4–5: 87–115.
Reuten, Geert and Went, Robert (1999), Monetarismus als politische Doktrin; Kritik des institutionalisierten Monetarismus der Europäischen Wirtschafts- und Währungsunion, Supplement der Zeitschrift Sozialismus, 3/99: 12–38.
Reuten, Geert and Williams, Michael (1989), *Value-Form and the State; the tendencies of accumulation and the determination of economic policy in capitalist society* (London/New York: Routledge).
Robinson, Joan (1953), The production function and the theory of capital, *Review of Economic Studies*, Vol. 21: 81–106; reprinted in G. Harcourt and L. Laing, *Capital and Growth*.
Schefold, Bertram (1998), The relationship between the rate of profit and the rate of interest: a reassessment after the publication of Marx's manuscript of the Third Volume of Das Kapital, in Bellofiore (ed. 1998, Vol. 1): 127–44.
Smith, Tony (2000), *Technology and Capital in the Age of Lean Production: A Marxian Critique of the 'New Economy'* (New York: State University of New York Press).

9
The Credit System

Martha Campbell

In describing the objective of Part 5 of *Capital*, Vol. III, Marx states that he is considering the credit system only to the extent 'necessary to characterize the capitalist mode of production in general' (1894: 525). As this indicates, the credit system is, in Marx's view, so essential that no presentation of capital would be complete without it. It points also to a distinctive feature of Marx's account, namely, that he derives the credit system from capital, which he initially presents as industrial capital by itself. That is, he appeals to the requirements and inherent tendencies of industrial capital to explain why the credit system evolves.[1]

Starting from industrial capital, however, poses a problem for Marx. To show that capital creates the credit system requires an understanding of what capital is and how it operates. But capital, being what it is, cannot be conceived at all without money. Marx handles this problem by starting with commodity money (giving rise to much criticism and bafflement).

If, as will be argued here, Marx demonstrates that capital creates the credit system, then he never meant to leave money as commodity money, that is, to suggest that capitalism operates with commodity money. This is simply the form of money capital does not create but inherits from previous society. Since, according to Marx, any form of money is a universal equivalent, characteristics of the universal equivalent (identified in *Capital*, Vol. I) are preserved in bank money. In

1. This isolation of industrial from commercial and interest-bearing capital is not meant to be historically realistic. Marx emphasizes that the two other forms precede industrial capital. The latter is the 'basic form' within capitalism since, when capital encompasses production, it encompasses all economic activity.

particular, the indirectly social character of capitalist production and the objectivity of value, which results from it, figure prominently in Marx's argument in *Capital*, Volume III. One consequence of this argument is that bank money emerges as the form of money specific to capitalism replacing the troublesome commodity money of Volume I.

The first section of this chapter examines the reasons Marx gives to explain why capitalism produces the credit system. The second section considers the effects of the credit system on the functioning of capital; chief among which are its collapse or financial crises. Since Marx refers again to metallic money in connection with crises, the third section examines what he means by the collapse of the credit system.

1. The evolution of the credit system

In *Capital*, Volume 1, before Marx takes the credit system into account, he treats money as given by the original accumulation.[2] Together with the other prerequisites for production, it is presented as the property of capitalists; it constitutes the fund capital needs to begin its circuit. When Marx returns to money in *Capital*, Volume III, he revises this first account. Here the credit system, consisting of the banking system, and the bond and stock markets, takes the place of the original accumulation. It supplies all forms of capital (including capitals within the credit system itself or interest-bearing capital) with advances of money and of money-capital. Marx supplies the basis for this switch (between his Volume I and Volume III accounts) by his argument that the credit system evolves of its own accord within capitalism, because it removes barriers to the expansion of capital. This section considers the reasons he gives for its evolution.

Marx presents two complementary lines of argument to explain why the credit system develops. Along one, he argues that the banking system develops to overcome the limits of trade or commercial credit. This type of credit arises when one capitalist sells commodities to another in exchange for a bill of exchange – a promise to pay by a certain date – rather than for money. Trade credit can be extended beyond two capitalists to the group of capitalists that is linked by regular transactions because the different individual capitals in it carry out different stages of the circuit of one product. Within such a group, the bill arising in one transaction can, in turn, be used by the creditor to buy on credit.[3]

2. Both the supply and the form of money are given.
3. For example, A buys on credit from B, issuing a bill to B. B, in turn, uses A's bill to buy on credit from C. C completes the circle by using the bill to buy from A, which cancels out A's debt. Each accepts the bill because they know they can use it as means of purchase.

Marx includes the development of clearing houses for bills within the limits of trade credit. These enhance the circulation of bills because they allow reciprocal debts to cancel out each other.

The reason to replace money with credit is that this reduces both the total capital and the amount of capital in money (i.e., idle) form that each capitalist needs in order to function. Commercial credit, however, can only replace money to a limited extent. Capitalists must still use money in transactions with non-capitalists, principally workers (but also, the state).[4] They also cannot use credit whenever the seller's commodity belongs to a different nexus of transactions than the buyer's; the seller cannot use the buyer's bill as a means of purchase and so will not accept it. The most important limitation, however, is that with commercial credit by itself, capitalists are dependent on the timing of sales and must hold money reserves to meet their debts in case sales returns are delayed (see 1894: 611). According to Marx, the banking system represents an advance over commercial credit because it eliminates this last reason for holding money.

The distinctive characteristic of the banking system is that it concentrates the total money reserves in society into one pool for use by all individual capitals. This 'socialization' of money for capital is the hallmark of the credit system; because it is missing from commercial credit, the latter, as De Brunhoff says, 'is on the borderline between the monetary and credit system'.[5] Banks lend from this fund by issuing their own promises to pay – either as banknotes or as bank deposits – and these are credit money.[6] The existence of banks allows commercial credit to be transformed into credit money by the practice of discounting. This

4. Marx is well aware that capitalists must use money to buy wage labour (see Marx, 1885: 140–1, 490 and also Campbell, 1998: 138–9). He regards this as one of many reasons why capital needs money (he presents these reasons in *Capital*, Vol. II, see Campbell, 1998). Hence he does not attribute the development of the credit system (therefore, money's form as bank money) to the fact that wages must be paid in money.
5. De Brunhoff, 1973: 81. Commercial credit, unlike the elements of the credit system proper, is always connected to the reproduction of real capital. As a result, it serves methodologically as an anchor, a way of making visible the ties between real reproduction and credit, when these become more tenuous in the credit system.
6. Marx describes banknotes as 'credit money proper' and notes of the central bank as 'more or less legal tender' (1894: 525, 529). Unlike bills of exchange, which are due to be paid at a definite time, bank debt is 'payable at any time', meaning on demand (*ibid.*). Hence this is at least one of the key differences between credit and money.

is the purchase by a bank of bills of exchange with banknotes. Since bank debt, unlike bills, does not have a payment due date, discounting is an advance of money.[7] Once nonfinancial capitalists can have bills discounted, they can accept bills from a wider range of other capitalists and are freed from the necessity of holding money reserves against delays in sales returns.

Marx's second line of explanation is that the credit system develops from the hoards required for the circulation of capital. With the concentration of all hoards in the banking system, banks become the 'general managers of money capital' in charge of the system of payment and of lending (Marx, 1894: 528). This is the 'socialization' of money for capital, which evolves because of the advantages it entails for capital. The amount of money required to support any given level of economic activity is reduced not only because all capitalists share the hoard, but also because banks need to hold as money only the fraction of their debts that they are, on average, asked to redeem.[8]

The point of both lines of argument is that the credit system is the specific product of capitalism because, in numerous ways, it overcomes barriers to the expansion of capital.[9] With the credit system, first, both money lending and the source of money become internal to the capitalist economy. Banks as intermediaries are links between capitalist lenders and capitalist borrowers robbing 'usurer's capital of its monopoly' (Marx, 1894: 738).[10] Likewise, the creation of credit money by the banking system restricts 'the monopoly of the precious metals' (*ibid.*). Second, the credit system liberates capital's expansion by reducing the quantity and costs of capital in money form. The substitution of credit between capitalists for money, functioning as means of circulation, is essential given that capitalism produces for sale and on a massive scale. Without credit 'the nation's capital [would have] to double, so that commerce

7. The discounting of bills is simply a short-term bank loan. The reason to pose the argument, as Marx does, in terms of the discounting of bills is that this reveals the connection between commercial credit and bank credit.
8. In modern terms, this is the money multiplier, meaning that bank deposits are a multiple of bank reserves.
9. See also De Brunhoff (1998: 184) who states that Marx presents the credit system as 'an institution peculiar to the capitalist mode of production'.
10. Marx emphasizes the character of banks as intermediaries, in part, because, historically, this is the way commercial and industrial capital liberate themselves from independent usurers. Originally, this subordinates interest bearing capital to industrial capital (see also De Brunhoff, 1998: 184). In addition, it places all money reserves, even of noncapitalists such as landlords, at the service of capital (see Marx 1894: 741).

would purchase the entire national product with its own capital before selling it again' (Marx, 1894: 612). The availability of the banking system to individual capitalists eliminates the need for them to hold reserves for the circulation of capital; the near monies that take the place of reserves (loans to banks and holdings of securities) collect surplus-value; fractional bank reserves mean that 'the reserve fund of the business community is reduced to a necessary minimum' (*ibid.*: 528). Further, the cost to capital of borrowing money is reduced since bankers lend at lower interest rates because they specialize in evaluating borrowers.[11] Third, the socialization of capital through the securities markets and the banking system liberates capital's inherent impulse to expand from the limits of previously accumulated capital, allowing a 'tremendous expansion in the scale of production, and enterprises that would be impossible for individual capitals' (*ibid.*: 567).[12]

Last, the credit system distributes capital over the economy as a whole and, in this way, unifies all individual capitals into one total social capital. It is, therefore, the means for equalizing the rate of profit on different capitals. This equalization (or the movement towards it) is the law 'on which the whole of capitalist production depends' (*ibid.*: 566).

In all the foregoing respects, the evolution of the credit system embodies the 'free development' of capital, positing 'itself in the forms adequate to it' (Marx, 1973: 650). Marx, it should be noted, is not particularly interested in giving a full account of credit money; he specifically states this is beyond the scope of his plan (1894: 525). It seems likely that the integrating aspect of the credit system (referred to last) is the most significant point for Marx. As will be argued in the next section, the interconnection established by the credit system among all individual capitals is a precondition for crisis.

2. Consequences of the credit system

While, on the one hand, the credit system evolves because it overcomes barriers to the expansion of capital, it also allows real capital to expand,

11. Marx quotes this point from a follower of Saint Simon: bankers lend at lower interest 'than the landlords and capitalists could do, as these could more easily be mistaken in their choice of borrower' (1894: 741).
12. For this reason, Marx argues that 'the development of the credit system ... necessarily runs parallel with the development of large scale production' (1885: 261). Also, that projects that require large start-up outlays of capital (such as railways) can only be conducted on a capitalist basis because of the formation of joint stock companies and prior to this can only be undertaken by governments (see 1894: 567).

at least temporarily, past barriers that are still in force. In addition, it takes off on its own, independently of the reproduction of real capital. On the other hand, because the credit system overcomes barriers by the socialization of capital, it increases the interconnections among individual capitals, which increases the complexity of the capitalist economy. Socialization also reduces the total reserve, which increases the fragility of the system. These two characteristic features of the credit system taken together mean that when the delayed barriers assert their existence, the result is a crisis that is generalized to all capitals.[13]

To elaborate the first point, the independence of the credit system is inherent in interest-bearing capital. As emerges most starkly from Marx's account of interest-bearing capital apart from the institutional forms of the credit system (Chapters 21–24 of *Capital*, Vol. III), the circuit of interest-bearing capital is completely external to the reproduction of real capital (meaning industrial and commercial capital). This separateness, in turn, is the reason for the doubling of claims that pervades all aspects of the credit system (i.e., one by real capital, or, in fact, by any borrower, the other associated with a financial asset, or any lender).[14] It is also the reason why the rate of interest is arbitrary: since interest-bearing capital does not carry out any part of the reproduction of real capital, there is no value basis for the division between interest and profit of enterprise.[15] Last, it is the reason why the credit system is the source of illusions.

With commercial credit by itself, credit is given to a buyer only to accomplish the sale of commodities. Even if bills embody prices that ultimately cannot be realized, they are inextricably tied to the circulation of real capital. When bills are discounted by the banking system (when they join the credit system proper), however, they can become detached from the circuit of the real capital to which they correspond and appropriate other capital. This does not occur with the discount of a

13. Thus Marx argues that 'the form of crisis belongs to periods with developed credit systems' (1894: 682). This attributes crisis to the characteristics just listed that are introduced by the credit system. If the crisis were purely monetary, it would occur with any form of money, including commodity money.
14. As Marx states (1894: 601): 'With the development of interest bearing capital and the credit system, all capital seems to be duplicated.'
15. Schefold (1998: 138–9) proposes the interesting hypothesis that Marx treats the controversy over the 1844 Bank Act at such length to illustrate his case that there is no natural rate of interest; that the interest rate is instead determined by such accidental factors as banking legislation. This controversy also shows that society (as represented by government) is not controlling the economy (i.e., eliminating crises).

normal bill, which simply involves an advance of money. The bill corresponds to some intermediate stage of the value of commodities, which are in process towards their final form, and will be paid by the revenue from their final sale. By discounting the bill, the banker anticipates this final sale or 'prevalidates' it. In an expansion, normal bills may be discounted so that the reproduction of capital can speed up or proceed on a larger scale. By contrast, the discount of accommodation bills, meaning bills that 'do not represent any real transactions' masquerades as an exchange of money now for money later but involves an advance of money-capital (because the bill is fictitious or represents no real value, but its seller receives value in money form from the bank when it is discounted) (Marx, 1894: 674).[16] Since Marx regards banks as intermediaries, in his words, the seller of an accommodation bill 'gets his hands on other people's capital' (*ibid.*: 555). Because normal bills may turn into accommodation bills with a decline in prices or a halt in sales, the two are often indistinguishable in practice.[17] Once an advance is made, it is unclear whether it was an advance of liquidity or of capital. That is, whether the advance is repaid by the sale of commodities corresponding to the bill, meaning that the sale just required extra time, or whether it is repaid out of the circuit of a new capital.

The transformation of normal into accommodation bills is virtually inevitable, since it occurs on a regular basis at the end of economic expansions. Credit, which in the expansion corresponds to an increase in the speed and scale of the circulation of real capital, turns into credit that merely allows production to continue past the time when final sales have slowed.[18] In this way, the credit system allows industrial and

16. Engels states that 'there can only be a capital advance with the discount of a bill if the bill is an accommodation bill' (Marx, 1894: 559). Marx seems to be absolutely intrigued by accommodation bills and to revel in their myriad forms. These range from situations in which commodities are purchased just to discount the bills drawn against their final sale (1894: 536), to paying off a previous bill by issuing another (*ibid.*: 526), to duplication of bills on the same commodities (*ibid.*: 540). In essence, these are all forms of adding to an existing loan to prevent the bankruptcy of the borrower.
17. Engels states that 'no banker will accept an [accommodation bill] if he recognizes it for what it is' (Marx, 1894: 559), but Marx cites testimony of bankers indicating that they cannot tell whether a bill is 'drawn for produce or for wind' (*ibid.*: 541). Evaluating a bill's quality is made more difficult because bills are bought and sold by different kinds of intermediaries (e.g., billbrokers as well as banks).
18. 'Markets are overstocked and the apparent prosperity is maintained only by credit' (Marx, 1894: 705).

commercial capital to outstrip realization, as De Brunhoff says, deferring 'the limits of money circulation' (1998: 184). The impulse for expansion lies in 'the tremendous elasticity of the reproduction process' (Marx, 1894: 419). Capital is, by nature, always ready 'to pursue the production process past its capitalist barriers' (*ibid.*: 640) since the scale of production is determined more by the quantity of capital and the need of the capitalist 'production process for continuity and extension' (Marx, 1885: 221). By anticipating value realization (e.g., by prevalidating bills) the credit system gives capital's impulse to expand freer reign.

The other credit system duplicates of real capital, such as bonds and stocks, are from the outset less connected to the circulation of their corresponding real capital than commercial credit. As interest-bearing capital, their circuit is external to that of real capital to begin with. They become further detached from real capital in a variety of ways. Most straightforwardly, their value is determined by capitalization, independently of the value of real capital, and varies with the interest rate and supply and demand. Detachment from real capital is carried further when financial assets are issued by parties other than commercial and industrial capitalists. Marx's statement (1894: 735) that interest-bearing capital (within capitalism) is distinguished from usurer's capital (before capitalism) by the 'transformed figure of the borrower' as an industrialist or merchant is, in fact, an idealization. With capitalization, any regular revenue seems to arise from a capital value, which 'capital' then seems to be the revenue's source. Because the credit system inverts shares into sources of surplus-value, anyone with a regular revenue may borrow by issuing financial assets. Besides borrowing by real capital, interest-bearing capital may lend to itself, landowners may obtain mortgages and governments issue securities. The final, and most striking, step in detachment is speculation in financial assets based on their expected future price rather than their more distant connection to surplus-value.[19]

The second aspect, the increased complexity and fragility of the reproduction of capital, is introduced by commercial credit. This enhances fragility because it imposes a time constraint on the final sale of commodities. It adds to complexity because all capitals participating in the reproduction of one commodity are linked by the circulation of the same bill. All are therefore dependent on the sale of that commodity at its expected price. Failure to sell in the specified time or at the expected price leads to forced sales to meet debt commitments and therefore to

19. This is the form of detachment that Keynes laments (1936: Chapter 12).

deflation.[20] The pressure to sell may be alleviated temporarily by discounting bills. Ultimately, however, the credit system reproduces these same characteristics on a larger scale.

The range of interconnections among individual capitals is extended as 'advances among industrialists and merchants fuse' in the banking system (Marx, 1894: 614). Credit money enters circulation through discounting bills. As Marx emphasizes, the circulation of credit money is determined by the circulation of bills, rather than by simple monetary circulation (see *ibid.*: 525). This means that it involves the same interconnections as bills, that like bills it is associated with forced sales, and also that it functions as means of payment rather than as means of purchase.[21] Reliance on interest-bearing capital imposes narrower limits on the acceptable rate of gross profit, raising its lower limit to the rate of interest. Because the reserve of money is reduced to the minimum reserve required on average, it is insufficient for the exceptional circumstances that always arise.[22]

The really crucial aspect of fragility, however, is that all credit shares the same fate. When the collapse comes, good credit (that would have been socially validated) is devalued along with bad credit (issued in connection with speculation and fraud).[23] Marx describes the crisis as an attempt to transform all credit into money. Since money is only a fraction of credit, this transformation cannot be accomplished. Because individual capitals have replaced money reserves with bank deposits and securities, when they are unable to meet debt commitments, the commodity price deflation that would have occurred without the credit system is replaced by bank runs and securities market crashes.

In summary, with the credit system, capitalism creates its own form of money, its own more liberal method of financing capital's expansion,

20. If the commodity cannot be sold at its expected price, a 'whole series of transactions which retrogressively depend on this one transaction, cannot be settled' (Marx 1904/10: 514).
21. Part of Marx's reason for emphasizing that the circulation of credit money (banknotes) is based on the circulation of bills is that this makes the quantity theory completely absurd. By the time money as means of payment enters circulation, the commodities corresponding to it have already left it (see Marx, 1867: 234). Hence 'the quantity of money in circulation no longer corresponds with the mass of commodities in circulation during a given period' (*ibid.*: 237).
22. This is the reserve that banks would hold of their own accord in the absence of legal regulations on reserves.
23. See Marx, 1894: 621. Most bills represent actual purchases and sales (but on too large a scale). Added to these is speculation on borrowed capital and fraud.

and, with financial assets, a completely novel kind of asset that, by its detachment from real capital, involves its own principle of pricing. The overextension of reproduction relative to final realization, together with increased fragility, means that any restriction on credit 'acts as the feather which, added to the weight already on the scales, is enough to tip the balance' (Marx, 1894: 705).[24] Complexity insures that all capitals are caught in the same net. *All* commodities and *all* financial assets have to prove their value by being transformed into money. This 'collapse of credit into the monetary system', as Marx calls it, involves the discredit of all credit (banks runs and the devaluation of financial assets).

3. The collapse of the credit system

The credit system promotes the expansion of capital, but financial crises are evidence that the reproduction of capital is still subject to constraints. The assertion of these constraints is merely delayed by the operation of the credit system; as De Brunhoff says, 'the credit system defers limits of money circulation, but does not suppress them' (1998: 184). A problem arises in connection with Marx's account in *Capital*, Volume III, regarding how far the collapse of the credit system proceeds. If the credit system is created by capital, as Marx maintains, then once it is developed it should remain a permanent part of capitalism. In other words, the assertion in a crisis of the constraints on capital's reproduction should not abolish the credit system itself. Marx's references to gold money, however, could be taken to suggest precisely this: that the credit system is eliminated by its collapse so that capitalism reverts back to the pre-capitalist form of money. To resolve this problem, this section examines what Marx means by the collapse of the credit system.

Regarding the constraints on the reproduction of capital, two points should be noted. First, Marx discusses the credit system entirely within the context of the distribution of surplus-value among capitals. The credit system introduces a new principle of profit and loss for individual capitals. As Marx observes, within the credit system 'gambling ... now appears in place of labour as the original source of capital ownership' (1894: 609). The gambling he has in mind involves transactions in

24. This is overextension of both industrial and merchant capital, as well as speculation and debts associated with it; as Marx says: 'too much trade, too much production, too much credit' (1894: 640). The restriction Marx refers to is the limit imposed by the 1844 Bank Act, which stipulates that the central bank can only create notes (lend to private banks) in accordance with its gold reserve. The crises Marx discusses are all created by the central bank refusing to expand its note issue (or loans).

securities (that is, in fictitious capital) by which winners 'get their hands on other people's capital' or expropriate capital and surplus-value from each other. While this really is a source of capital for individuals, both Marx's reference to 'other people's capital' and the context in which he discusses the credit system suggest that gambling cannot add to the total value of capital. By contrast, when Marx presents the exploitation of labour as the source of surplus-value in *Capital*, Volume I, the case he makes is that this is the only possible source of a net increase in surplus-value for capital as a whole. Thus the idea that gambling is a source of capital must be one of the illusions generated by the credit system.[25]

Second, the particular way the credit system defers constraints is that credit of all kinds (commercial, banking, the securities market) is based on expected prices; in Marx's terminology, on ideal rather than realized value.[26] Lender and borrower share 'confidence in the social character of production' and this confidence 'makes the money form of products appear as something evanescent and ideal', that is, as superfluous and a mere formality (Marx, 1894: 707–8). It is a matter of 'confidence' rather than objective evidence because the 'society' of two, lender and borrower, cannot impose their evaluation on society at large. In other words, the credit system inherently operates on the pretence that indirectly social (private and independent) production is directly social. Credit versus money merely repeats the opposition between private and social that obtains between value in commodity form (ideal) and value in money form (realized). Marx indicates early in *Capital*, Volume I, that this is the opposition that becomes plain in a crisis: 'the antithesis between commodities and their value form, money' appears as an 'absolute contradiction' (Marx, 1867: 236). This opposition is fundamental to capitalism (Marx first presents it in terms of simple circulation, but it is preserved throughout as he develops the more complex aspects of capitalism).[27] It is not overcome simply by the change in money's form from precious metal to bank money. Hence Marx adds that in a crisis 'the monetary

25. The reference is to Chapter 5 of *Capital*, Volume I. Compare Ganssmann's (1998: 154) more ambiguous statement: 'In juxtaposing … labour and the "game" of speculation as principal modes of appropriation, Marx himself indicated that it is necessary to step away from his value theory in order to analyse the realm of money as a symbol of self-expanding wealth.'
26. Because the credit system operates on this principle it can disguise disproportionalities and delay the manifestation of the reduction in surplus-value that occurs with technical change. Thus the credit system promotes expansion in the sense that it allows expansion to proceed even though the conditions for the reproduction of capital are not met.
27. See also De Brunhoff, 1998: 179, 182.

famine remains whether payments have to be made in gold or in credit-money' (*ibid.*: 237).[28]

Thus one meaning of Marx's claim that the credit system is not 'emancipated from the monetary system' is that ideal values, provisionally validated by credit, must ultimately be realized (1894: 727). This is the original and most basic monetary constraint; it has nothing to do with the metallic form of money. While in *Capital*, Volume I, Marx suggests that credit money still functions as money in a crisis (so that at least this part of the credit system is preserved), in *Capital*, Volume III, he states that 'precious metal remains the foundation from which the credit system can *never* break free' (1894: 741).

In part, statements to this effect refer to the regulations established by the Bank Act of 1844, which make the creation of central bank money conditional on a gold reserve. This regulation forces the central bank to cease acting as a lender of last resort whenever the gold reserve is reduced. Private banks, in turn, must refuse to discount bills because they would lack sufficient reserves to meet their own liabilities. Commercial credit is thereby detached from the banking system. The credit system is eliminated in the sense that credit reverts to commercial credit by itself, outside the credit system (i.e., with no access to the pool of funds the credit system creates). The restriction of loans by the central bank would have this same effect no matter why the central bank imposes the restriction. The quantity of gold just happens to occasion this restriction in the institutional framework established by the Bank Act.[29]

Since, for Marx, the definitive characteristic of the credit system is the creation of a pool of funds accessible to all capitalists, in part also, the 'collapse of the credit system,' just means the denial of access to the pool. Marx speaks of this as 'hoarding', but by this he means the refusal of banks to discount bills (that is, to lend).[30] Keynes's comment on hoarding is perfectly compatible with Marx's argument. As Keynes notes since 'it is impossible for the actual amount of hoarding to change as a result of decisions on the part of the public', hoarding cannot mean 'the actual

28. This passage also indicates that Marx knows that money is credit money and, as Ganssmann says, that 'Marx did not claim that gold as the money commodity cannot be replaced by a "representative" even in such an extreme situation' (1998: 150).
29. For example, the same effect results when the central bank attempts to control inflation by refusing to accommodate demand for money. As Wolfson (1994) shows, the pursuit of this policy by the US Federal Reserve from 1966 to 1979 produced a series of 'credit crunches'.
30. See Marx, 1894: 546, 661, 674–5. He also means the sale of securities, principally by banks, but also by others, in order to meet liabilities (see *ibid.*: 669).

holding of cash' (1936: 174). Keynes, therefore, substitutes 'propensity to hoard' for 'hoarding', an increase in the propensity to hoard resulting in an increase in the rate of interest rather than an increase in the quantity of cash held. This same substitution can be made in Marx's account; it implies only that a spike in the rate of interest is one of the manifestations of hoarding.

These meanings of the collapse of the credit system do not entail a reversion to gold money. Moreover, Marx knows that the tie between credit money and gold exists only because it is established by the Bank Act. It would be strange if he considered this tie to be necessary since he regards the Bank Act as foolish. In opposition to it, he argues that no tie between credit money and gold is necessary domestically (see 1984: 649, 674). This leaves gold as world money.[31] Marx emphasizes, however, that capital transcends national boundaries. Since he argues that capital creates credit money as its own form of money, it would be inconsistent to maintain that it is necessarily tied to precapitalist money at the international level.

Even if we suppose that Marx is deceived by the institutions of his day, however, his references to gold make a point that still applies to credit money. This is that capitalism is intrinsically uncontrollable: it is a system of production that is socially determined to the core except in the respect that it is not subject to social control. For this reason, value – the social character of products – appears as an objective property of products (as Marx emphasizes, it seems to be *their* property not *ours*).

The objectivity of value stems from the indirectly social (in other words, simultaneously private and social) character of production. The entire significance of money as universal equivalent is that it mediates (allows the existence of) this contradiction but does not remove it.[32] Money accomplishes this mediation by being the thing, external to the commodity that stands for the commodity's social character or value. Since this same opposition between commodity and money is repeated in the opposition between credit and money, in discussing the credit system and its collapse Marx speaks again of money as a 'thing'. By this he means, not that money is gold, but that money is the social character of production, which must take the form of a thing because production

31. Thus, as Ganssmann argues, reserves for international trade 'appear as the last anchor of an otherwise free-floating credit system' (1998: 152). This Ganssmann calls Marx's 'strong argument', but he points out that Marx is entertaining alternatives to it (*ibid.*: 186).
32. See Marx 1867: 198.

is indirectly rather than directly social. That this is Marx's meaning is shown by his constant association between money as a 'thing' and the contradiction between private and social: money 'is in actual fact nothing but a special expression of the social character of labour and its products, which however, as antithetical to the basis of private production, must always present itself in the last instance as a thing' (1894: 742–3)

> This social existence that it [money or gold as money] has thus appears as something beyond, as a thing, object or commodity outside and alongside the real elements of social wealth.
>
> *ibid*:. 707

> [the collapse of the credit system][33] shows strikingly by its effects that production is not really subjected to social control, as social production, and that the social form of wealth exists alongside wealth itself as a *thing*.
>
> *ibid*.: 708

> As long as the *social* character of labour appears as the *monetary existence* of the commodity and hence as a *thing* outside actual production, monetary crises ... are unavoidable.
>
> *ibid*.: 649[34]

It is methodologically simpler to express the objectivity of value in gold money because credit money, and the bank regulations associated with it, create the appearance of government control of the economy.[35] The Bank Act of 1844 is one attempt at monetary policy intended both to regulate the value of money and to make 'crises ... impossible once and for all' (Engels in Marx, 1894: 688). That the Bank Act actually brings about and intensifies crises does not say much for social planning. The deliberations of Parliament, which Marx cites so extensively, do not inspire confidence either. From Marx's perspective, it is ridiculous to

33. Marx actually says 'a drain of gold' but he is referring to the institutional arrangements of the 1844 Bank Act, under which a drain of gold necessitates a reduction in lending by the central bank which brings about a collapse of the credit system. To make his statement more general, I have referred to this collapse.
34. That money is a thing 'outside actual production' or 'outside the real elements of wealth' shows that Marx is not speaking of money as a commodity.
35. Alternatively, they create the appearance (emphasized by the monetarists), that all crises are attributable to the government.

suppose that these 'experts', who have no idea what capital is, will devise a means of overcoming the crises inherent in capitalism.[36]

Even if the central bank can learn to act so that it is not itself the source of financial crises, it does not have a free hand. The arbitrariness of the interest rate allows some leeway for institutional determination but this only favours financial capital at the expense of industrial and commercial capital (or vice versa). The central bank cannot create value by increasing credit money. If its prevalidation of credit is not confirmed by value realization, it only engages in a pseudo-social validation, which benefits some factions of society at others' expense (that is, it redistributes value).[37] In Marx's view at least, as long as production 'decisions' are left to the market, money, since it realizes value, is the thing by which social conflict (among capitalists and between capitalists and workers) is managed. In this sense, credit money is just as much a thing as gold money.

4. Conclusion

This chapter has focused on Marx's case that capital creates the credit system. By his account, the credit system emerges because it allows capital to internalize money and finance and to overcome, as well as disregard, factors that would otherwise constrain expansion. As has been argued also, Marx's descriptions of the collapse of the credit system do not imply the abolition of the credit system itself. His references to gold are instead appeals to the objectivity of value.

For these reasons, Marx's presentation of the credit system in *Capital*, Volume III, should be taken as a revision of his presentation of money in Volume I. It is one of the intentional revisions entailed by his method. In this instance, Marx needed the results established in both Volumes I and II to show why the credit system emerges from capital.[38] On this interpretation, Marx not only recognizes that the modern form of money is bank money but he shows why money in capitalism necessarily takes this form.

Bibliography

Bellofiore, Riccardo (ed.) (1998), *Marxian Economics – A Reappraisal*, Vol. 1 (London/New York: Macmillan/St Martin's Press).

36. In particular, they argue endlessly over whether capital is money or commodities, a point Marx addresses in *Capital*, Vol. I (1867: 255).
37. See Reuten and Williams (1989: 86–7) and De Vroey (1984) who calls pseudo-social validation 'extra money'.
38. For a discussion of the aspects of the credit system that emerge in *Capital*, Vol. II see Campbell (1998).

Brunhoff, Suzanne de (1998), Money, interest and finance in Marx's *Capital*, in Bellofiore (ed. 1998): 176–88.

— (1973), *Marx on Money* (English trans. Maurice Goldbloom) (New York: Urizen, (1976).

Campbell, Martha (1998), Money in the circulation of capital, in C.J. Arthur and G. Reuten (eds), *The Circulation of Capital: Essays on Volume II of Marx's 'Capital'* (London/New York: Macmillan/St Martin's Press, 1998).

Ganssmann, Heiner (1998), The emergence of credit money, in Bellofiore (ed. 1998): 145–56.

Keynes, John Maynard (1936), *The General Theory of Employment, Interest, and Money* (New York/London: Harcourt Brace Jovanovich).

Marx, Karl (1867), *Capital, Volume I* (English trans. Ben Fowkes) (Harmondsworth: Penguin, 1976).

—(1885), *Capital, Volume II* (English trans. David Fernbach) (Harmondsworth: Penguin, 1978).

— (1894), *Capital, Volume III* (English trans. David Fernbach) (Harmondsworth: Penguin, 1981).

— (1904/10), *Theories of Surplus-value, Part II* (ed. and trans. by S. Ryanzanskaya, 1968) (Moscow: Progress Publishers).

— (1973), *Grundrisse* (English trans. Martin Nicolaus) (Harmondsworth: Penguin).

Reuten, Geert and Williams, Michael (1989), *Value-Form and the State; the tendencies of accumulation and the determination of economic policy in capitalist society* (London/New York: Routledge).

Schefold, Bertram (1998), The relationship between the rate of profit and the rate of interest: A reassessment after the publication of Marx's manuscript of the third volume of *Das Kapital*, in Bellofiore (ed. 1998): 127–44.

Vroey, Michel de (1984), Inflation: a non-monetarist monetary interpretation, *Cambridge Journal of Economics*, 8: 381–99.

Wofson, Martin (1994), *Financial Crises* (2nd edn) (Armonk, NY: M.E. Sharpe).

10
Rent and Landed Property

Martha Campbell

For Marx of the *Contribution*, the theory of rent is to resolve the apparent contradiction between the labour theory of value and the existence of prices for commodities that are not products (Marx, 1859: 63). When Marx considers rent in Part Six of *Capital*, Volume III, he does explain how the price of land is derived, but he defines his overall purpose in other terms. His aim is to spell out 'the specific relationships of production and exchange that arise from the investment of capital on land' (these being part of the analysis of capital), and, more narrowly, to consider these 'only in so far as a portion of the surplus-value that capital produces falls to the share of the landowner' (1894: 752, 751). There is a shift in emphasis between these two accounts. In the *Contribution*, Marx is occupied with correcting a problem in the classical theory of value. In *Capital* by contrast he underscores his principal difference from classical theory: the idea of capitalism as constituted by specific social relations of production and of these as the source of economic 'laws'.

This difference is central to Part Six. In Ricardo's account, the natural characteristics of land ('the original and indestructible powers of the soil' as he calls them) are the ultimate determinants of rent. Together with the 'natural law of population', they determine the long-term course of rent and so of profit and of accumulation. In Marx's alternative, the source of rent is instead the economic power that ownership of noncapital can exert against capital. The 'powers of the soil' influence the extent of this power, but they are largely not original and are significant not by themselves but relative to techniques of production. In place of population growth, the process of technological innovation inherent in capital, and so capital's nature, determines the course of rent over time. As the power of ownership is to occupy centre stage, the proper point of entry into Marx's theory of rent is with landed property.

1. Landed property in the context of capitalism

By landed property, Marx means specifically the individual private ownership of land such that land is accorded all the characteristics of a commodity (it is alienable and has a price). Historically, landed property emerges from the original accumulation as the counterpart of wage labour, the demise of traditional modes of land use and their replacement by private ownership 'freeing' one segment of society from the possession of any objective means of production. Thus landed property guarantees that labour-power will be available for capital to purchase, and as a result is essential both for the historical emergence and perpetuation of capitalism (1894: 754).[1]

Apart from this, the characteristic feature of landed property is that it does nothing; Marx describes it as superfluous and completely passive (1894: 760, 908). By this he means that landowners do not participate in or contribute to the development of capitalist production but merely seize part of the resulting surplus. This differentiates landed property both from the other classes in capitalism and from its own place prior to capitalism. Landed property becomes passive with the transition to capitalism since surplus is then based on the relation of capital to wage labour instead of the control of land, and profit is then the normal (or dominant) form of surplus instead of rent. By the claim that rent presupposes profit, therefore, Marx means both that the subordinate status of rent is distinctive of capitalism and also that 'rent in the modern sense [is] an excess over and above the average profit'.[2]

Although Marx speaks of landed property as one of the three great classes of modern society, it seems odd that a class that is characterized by inaction could be necessary. Hence Marx entertains the suggestion made by James Mill that capitalism could function just as well with state

1. In developed capitalism as Guidi (1998: 89) notes, 'capital produces labour power as its own presupposition'. Guidi and Harvey both maintain (although for different but complementary reasons) that landed property is nevertheless still necessary. Guidi argues that the monopoly in land hinders 'access to the capitalist class or to self-employment'. Harvey (1999: 371) argues that rent and private land ownership are 'necessary to the perpetuation of capitalism ... as basic coordination devices in the allocation of land to uses'.
2. Marx, 1894: 918. Marx will derive the quantitative determination of rent from the second point. It also makes sense of his claim that average profit is formed in 'the non-agricultural spheres of production' (*ibid.*: 936, see also 783, 874).

as with individual ownership of land (1904/10: 152). The state, Marx agrees, could take over landed property's sole essential function of keeping land from common use (see *ibid.*: 44). This could raise awkward questions about the private ownership of other means of production. Further, since land is, in fact, privately owned, it is bought as an 'investment' or regarded as capital by its owners; as Marx says, 'the bourgeois himself has become the owner of land' (*ibid.*: 45). It follows that landowners could come to regard themselves simply as capitalists and cease to act as a distinct class as a result.[3] Even if they do, however, their perception does not abolish the difference between land and the other means of production or between land and interest-bearing capital (anymore than the idea of human capital makes workers into capitalists). While other means of production can be produced by capital and money is a form of capital, land remains external to capital.[4] Setting aside the question whether private land ownership is necessary and proceeding on the assumption that it exists, Marx's rent theory is intended to specify the portion of surplus-value that landowners can seize.

Landowners seize surplus-value merely by withholding land from use unless rent is paid; this withholding is their sole 'action'. This is a permanent means of capturing surplus-value from capital because capital must use but cannot produce land.[5] It is true that the barrier established

3. Marx implies that landed property could cease to be a separate class, for example, by the claim that under capitalism 'landed property ... receives its purely economic form by the stripping away of all its former political and social embellishments' (1894: 755). Taking the point further, Harvey argues that land ownership in capitalism necessarily 'treats the land as a pure financial asset' meaning that 'land is bought and sold according to the rent it yields' or that land is used to 'acquire money' (Harvey, 1999: 371, 347, 366). From this it follows that landed property is not a separate class with its own interest but becomes assimilated into interest-bearing capital (see *ibid.*: 346). It should be noted, however, that this view of land by its owners does not obliterate the difference between the determination of interest by the supply and demand for money capital and the determination of rent by the monopoly over land. Marx emphasizes the difference between them (see, for example, 1894: 911 and 1904/10: 33–4).
4. On the otherness of land relative to capital, see Guidi (1998: 81–5). Since land is not capital, the lease contract, like the wage contract, involves a conflict between capital and noncapital (Marx draws attention to the parallel, see 1894: 949–50). This may be why Marx presents landed property as a separate class.
5. Marx's best discussions of the principle that land cannot be produced appear in connection with differences in the quality of land or differential rent (see especially, Marx, 1894: 784–5). The principle applies, however, to land as such and is the basis for Marx's case for the impossibility of zero rent land (which, as will be argued below, is the real point of his theory of absolute rent).

by landed property can be partially circumvented in various ways. The effectiveness of a given land area can be increased, in agriculture, by more productive methods of cultivation, for natural resource extraction, by the development of synthetics, and in building, by high-rise construction.[6] As Marx argues in connection with absolute rent, these alternatives to increasing the extent of land use affect how much surplus-value landed property can capture. Still, capital must use some land, and, since landowners can prevent this use, they have no reason to allow it without receiving some payment. It follows that all land in use commands some rent. In other words, zero rent land, on which Ricardo's rent theory is based, is incompatible with the private ownership of land. In addition, the quantity of land, in the sense that matters for economics, is not the quantity given by nature, but the supply of land on the market. This quantity is restricted so that every parcel in use exacts rent. In other words, land is scarce or as Ricardo says 'not unlimited in quantity' because it is privately owned.[7]

Ruling out the possibility of zero rent land opens the way, in turn, to Marx's explanation for the price of land. This is based on the same principle as the explanation, earlier in *Capital*, Volume III, of the price of financial assets. Land and financial assets are both claims to future incomes. The prices of both are derived backwards from these incomes by capitalization. That is, they correspond to the amount of 'capital' that would yield the given amount of income, at the prevailing rate of interest (see e.g., Marx 1894: 944). Since both kinds of income, interest and rent, result from the division of surplus-value, or surplus-value captured from true capitals, Marx's explanation for these prices is consistent with his theory of value.[8]

6. The point on synthetics is made by Mandel (1981: 60) and suggests a reason for their development in capitalism.
7. Ricardo (1817: 70). As Marx states, landowners cannot affect the 'absolute quantity' of land but 'can affect the quantity of it on the market ... in all civilized countries a relatively significant portion of the land always remains uncultivated' (Marx, 1894: 891). By contrast, by positing zero rent land 'Ricardo does not credit the ownership of land with any economic effect' (1904/10: 94).
8. With this Marx fulfils his promise of *Capital*, Vol. I, to show how the price of land can be explained within the framework of value theory. According to Böhm-Bawerk's famous critique, all versions of the labour theory of value are demonstrably inadequate because they are necessarily unable to explain the price of commodities, such as land, that are not products (see Böhm-Bawerk, 1884: 387). Böhm-Bawerk makes this case before the publication of *Capital*, Vol. III, but is not dissuaded by its argument. In his view, 'Marx's third volume contradicts the first' since Marx starts from the assumption 'that commodities

There remains a problem regarding unused land. It plays an essential role since withholding some land from use may be the precondition for extracting rent on the rest. Unused land commands no rent but, to keep up the appearance of land as a commodity, must have a price nevertheless. In accordance with the principle of uniform price, Marx argues that land with the same characteristics has the same price whether or not it is rented out.[9] With a price assigned to all land, the landowner appears as an investor (or capitalist) rather than as a passive bystander, and rent appears as the 'return for his equivalent' rather than as tribute ('something obtained for nothing' Marx, 1894: 911).

Under capitalist conditions, the landowner rents to a capitalist producer (for example, to a capitalist farmer). One of Marx's chief concerns is to identify the particular form of conflict that the lease relationship entails, given that it involves the capitalist use of another's private property in land.[10] As he argues, two factors make the length of the lease a focus of conflict. The first has to do with permanent improvements in land, 'permanent' meaning that capital is incorporated with the land and cannot be detached from it at the end of the lease.[11] The capitalist, as the overseer of production and owner of capital, is the one to make improvements. In some cases, these are unavoidably associated with the use of land. Marx claims, for example, that cultivation by itself constitutes an improvement, transforming 'the earth from a mere raw material into earth capital'.[12] Once made, permanent improvements are

exchange according to their values' and later 'simply drops' that assumption (Böhm-Bawerk, 1894: 30, 21). Böhm-Bawerk explains the price of land in exactly the same way as Marx ('the sale price of land is a multiple of its rent calculated on an interest usual in the country' *ibid.*: 71) but would presumably consider this to violate Marx's value theory. This claim concerns the meaning of value in Marx's theory and the interpretation of the 'transformation', not the theory of rent.

9. See Marx (1894: 807) 'as soon as land is sold, it is sold as rent bearing and the prospective character of the rent ... does not distinguish the uncultivated land from the cultivated'.
10. It is worth emphasizing that land is 'another's' from the standpoint of capital not just in the sense that it belongs to another owner but in the sense that it is not capital.
11. The phrase 'permanent improvements to land' is somewhat misleading since it suggests that the land is permanently changed (see Marx, 1894: 844). Improvements are permanent from the standpoint of capital since capital is permanently sunk in the land.
12. Marx (1894: 757). He confines this claim to cultivation 'conducted in any kind of rational way' and specifically excludes the 'brutal exhaustion of the soil' exemplified by cotton growing in the antebellum Southern USA (*ibid.*: 756). Other improvements include drainage, levelling and irrigation.

characteristics of the land (its 'new natural fertility') because they are inseparable from it (Marx, 1894: 813). As such they belong to the landowner at the end of the lease. Worse yet for the capitalist, since the land has been improved, its owner can command a higher rent in the next lease. For Marx, this is 'one of the greatest obstacles to a rational agriculture' created by landed property (1894: 755). It induces the capitalist to keep permanent improvements to a minimum, the more so the shorter the lease. The length of the lease matters in this connection because, by the end of a long lease, the capital spent on improvements may be fully depreciated and recovered by the capitalist.

The second reason for conflict over the length of the lease has to do with the process of innovation. As in industry proper, agricultural methods of production change constantly as capital searches for lower-cost techniques that will add to profits.[13] In industry, the innovating capitalist captures surplus profit until the new technique is generalized. In agriculture, the capitalist innovator captures surplus profits only until the end of the current lease. In the next lease, all surplus profit (whatever its source) is transformed into differential rent and captured by the landowner. If the lease expires before a new technique is generalized, the agricultural innovator forgoes surplus profits that an industrial innovator would have kept. The agricultural capitalist, therefore, must divide the spoils of innovation with the landlord, the terms of this division depending on the length of the lease. The longer the lease, the greater the share captured by the capitalist.

The foregoing expands on Marx's characterization of landed property: landowners are passive beneficiaries of the development of production because they capture the surplus-value resulting from permanent improvements and technological change. Capital investment for either purpose creates a tendency for rent to rise, which if realized, leads in turn to an increase in the price of land.[14] By this account, the pressure for rent to rise comes from both (1) the technological change inherent in capital and (2) how closely rent adjustments keep pace with this

13. Capital's own contribution to the irrationality of capitalist agriculture consists in its orientation 'towards the most immediate monetary profit'. As this exploits the land for the 'most rapid possible enrichment' of both capitalist and landowner, it conflicts with the fact that land is the condition for human life (1894: 754, n.27; 949).
14. That rent increases are caused by investment of capital is one of Marx's principal themes throughout Part six (see for example, 1894: 757, 822, 830–1, 846). Whether capital investment actually translates into an increase in rent depends on a variety of other factors, principally, what happens to the price of agricultural output (see Engels's addition *ibid.*: 859).

change, as determined by the standard length of the lease. As with the length of the working day, Marx argues that the length of the lease depends on the relative power of the landowner and the agricultural capitalist (see 1894: 813). The amount of rent, as will be shown below, is determined in principle by the extra surplus-value generated by agricultural production at the time a new lease is negotiated.

2. The formation of extra surplus-value and its transformation into rent

Landed property cannot, in principle, withhold normal profits from the agricultural capitalist without driving capital out of the agricultural sector. Further, since landed property is not engaged in value creation, it can only withhold extra surplus-value that capital generates of its own accord. By this reasoning, Marx confines rent to the two 'pockets' of extra surplus-value that result from competition among capitals. First, extra surplus-value exists within one industry because firms differ in productivity while competition establishes one price for their product. Second, it exists, before it is redistributed by the formation of the general rate of profit, in those industries whose composition of capital is relatively low and whose product, therefore, has a value greater than its price of production. As these are the only sources of extra surplus-value delimited by Marx's value schema, he treats them as the origin of the only normal forms of rent. The first is the source of differential rent (which, as we will see, has two forms) and the second, of absolute rent.[15] The transformation of extra surplus-value into rent only involves its seizure from capitalists by landlords. This would be simple if extra surplus-value could be easily identified and were fixed, independently of the landlord's intervention; as will emerge, however, this is true only in the case of the first form of differential rent.

Before turning to the forms of rent, a comment is in order about the problems posed by this aspect of Marx's argument and how they will be handled. Reflecting the unfinished state of *Capital*, Volume III, Marx explains the quantitative determination of rent entirely by way of examples (the rent tables). Further, these yield conclusions only if they are bolstered by a host of assumptions (e.g., about the price of agricultural output, the length of the lease, the proportion of total output produced with each type of soil). Throughout this mass of cases and conditions, Ricardo is the ever-present adversary. The attraction of Ricardo's account for Marx (which makes it worth opposing) is that it

15. As Marx states 'These two forms of rent are the only normal ones' (1894: 898).

incorporates rent into value theory. Everything else from Ricardo, Marx discards as either (1) arbitrary, because based on false natural determinacy or (2) inconsistent with the private ownership of land (Marx's alternative to Ricardo's explanation of differential rent is meant to correct the first defect and his theory of absolute rent, to correct the second). In keeping with Marx's guiding purpose, the focus here will be on the conceptual revisions he introduces to correct these errors in Ricardo.

2.1 Differential rent

The place to begin is with the theory of differential rent, since it will supply a way of determining the amount of absolute rent.[16] As already noted, differential rent arises from productivity differences among firms. In agriculture these arise from two sources: from the characteristics of land, fertility and location, and from differences in production technique, as in industry proper. Classifying differential rent by these sources, Marx calls the first, differential rent I (DI), and the second, differential rent II (DII).

Only the first form of differential rent, therefore, depends on features of production that are unique to agriculture, characteristics of land. To isolate the value consequences of these characteristics, Marx starts with the same assumption as Ricardo, that all agricultural capitalists use the same quantity of capital.[17] It is not until Marx considers differences in production technique, in connection with differential rent II, that he realizes that this assumption has a different meaning in his framework than in Ricardo's. As he comes to see, by 'the same quantity of capital' Marx really means the 'normal average amount' of capital that is characteristic of the industry and that corresponds to the dominant technique of production.[18] This means that the theory of differential rent I, abstracts from differences in technique to assume that all firms are using the technique that is normal at any given time.

16. Marx indicates in his outline (1894: 860) that differential rent should be treated before absolute rent (although this is not the sequence in which he wrote Part Six). His reason seems to be that, since the two forms of rent are independent of each other, differential rent can be explained more easily on the assumption that zero rent land is the bottom of the differential rent hierarchy (see *ibid.*: 883). This is different from the reason given here.
17. See Marx, 1894: 788, 789. Marx adds that this is the same quantity of capital per acre, but otherwise takes over Ricardo's assumption unmodified.
18. The normal technique in turn implies a normal organic composition of capital. This is a point of dispute between Ball and Fine. Ball argues that because of differences between individual farms (e.g., distance from markets, land type) 'normal technical composition of capital ... whilst valid for manufacturing

Marx's reformulation of Ricardo's assumption is crucial as it holds the key to refuting Ricardo's natural 'laws'. Whereas Ricardo conceives of fertility as natural (as he says, 'the original and indestructible powers of the soil'), Marx maintains throughout (even before he explicitly reformulates Ricardo's assumption) that fertility 'always involves an economic relation, a relation to the given ... level of agricultural development' (1894: 790). The 'level of development', in the meaning Marx eventually gives it, is the composition of capital corresponding to the normal technique.[19] Marx's insight is that fertility – in the sense that is relevant to agriculture at least – is not the objective characteristics of the soil but the consequences of these characteristics for agricultural productivity. Since 'no land yields any product without a capital investment' land can only be ranked as more or less productive (or fertile) relative to some technique of production; the technique that sets the standard is the one that is normal at any given time.[20] Moreover, as Marx emphasizes, in the context of developed capitalism, even the objective properties of the soil are not natural but the result of permanent improvements (see 1894: 813). Since fertility both depends on the technique of production and is created by permanent improvements, it is socially created like location, land's other objective property.[21] If, as Marx maintains, permanent

industries has ... no meaning in agriculture' and that Fine mistakenly transposes this concept from one to the other. Harvey (1999: 356) appears to support Ball: 'the normal capital must also vary according to the nature of the soil.' Fine concedes the point, but he is correct as a reading of Marx (1986b: 177). Marx's references to the normal technique are so numerous that his intention is unmistakable (see 1894: 815, 843, 844, 861, 876). Moreover, the normal technique assumption is not only present but necessary to Marx's argument. Marx's most important point is that the classification of land as more or less fertile is relative to some particular technique.

19. Marx explicitly bases his discussion of differential rent I on the assumption that some level of development is given (see 1894: 791, 797). He also identifies the level of development with the organic composition of capital ('we can measure the course of development by the relative growth in constant capital compared with variable' *ibid.*: 894).
20. Marx, 1894: 843. 'When it is said that 1 acre of A, the land that governs the production price, yields such and such a product ... and that the better types of land ... yield so and so much differential product ... this always assumes that a definite capital is applied, i.e., that considered normal under the given conditions of production' (*ibid.*).
21. As Harvey (1999: 356) puts it, 'fertility is ... a social product'. Because permanent improvements involve increased investment of capital, Harvey appears to classify them as DII (their effect is that 'D–2 is converted directly into DR–1' *ibid.*). Marx, however, separates permanent improvements from changes in the normal technique (see 1894: 844). Further, in the interpretation here,

improvements make land more uniform, then development should have the same levelling effect on fertility as it has on location.[22]

Revising the concept of fertility supplies Marx with his first case against Ricardo's 'law' of declining agricultural productivity, rising rents and falling profits. If fertility is not fixed once and for all by nature but is relative to a standard production technique, then fertility changes as production techniques change. As Marx demonstrates by citing actual instances, new technologies need not have the same effect on different soil types. Technical change does not just improve fertility but rearranges the fertility hierarchy that determines differential rent. With a new technique, soil types may change both their position in the fertility hierarchy and their degree of difference within that hierarchy. In particular, a new technique may transform soil that was previously not arable into the best type of land.[23] Hence the progress of cultivation towards ever worse soil is not a law as Ricardo maintains. Nor is there any foundation for his inverse relation between rent and profit. For example, according to Marx, the case that is shown by experience to be the 'general rule' is that new technology has the greatest effect on better land types (increasing their degree of difference from inferior soil, 1894: 795). Under these conditions, rent would increase without a rise in the price of agricultural output (which is still determined by cost of production on the worst soil). If the price of agricultural output remains the same (or even falls if inferior land is taken out of cultivation), wages do not rise, therefore, profit does not fall.

Since capitalism abandons traditional methods of production and constantly revises production techniques, rearrangements of the soil hierarchy are not accidental or exceptional. Thus the rankings of different soil types and differentials between them are not fixed over time. This means that no law follows from differential rent I (and so from characteristics of land) dictating the course of rent over time. Further, as the

DI may already be the result of permanent improvements (and even when it is not, cannot be defined apart from the use of capital, i.e., some technique of production). Hence Marx's conception of DI challenges Ricardo's notion of fertility in terms of nature by itself.

22. Marx suggests that capitalist agricultural production involves the same tendency towards standardization as manufacturing. He maintains, for example, that almost all permanent improvements are undertaken to make a particular piece of land the same as land elsewhere (see 1894: 879).
23. 'With the development of natural science and agronomy, the fertility of the land itself changes' (Marx, 1894: 904). Here Marx cites a case in which a particular soil type switches from worst to best with the change in technique. (See also *ibid.*: 798.)

example just given illustrates, the course of rent has no direct impact on the course of profits. All that remains from Ricardo is that at any given moment, there is a fertility hierarchy, which shows differences in productivity and in surplus-value per acre of land.[24] Because these differences are associated with distinct pieces of land, the formation of extra surplus-value and its transformation into rent (seizure by the landlord) are identical (see Marx 1894: 861). This simple principle does not apply to the other forms of rent.

With the second form of differential rent, Marx is concerned with productivity differences between 'successive investments of capital on the same land'.[25] Whereas with the first form of differential rent, one technique is taken as normal across all land types, with the second form, what is at issue is the transformation from one normal technique to another, as successive innovations are introduced, generalized and supplanted. Although Marx superimposes technical change on the hierarchy of soil types, differential rent II has to do with the accumulation process of capital, not with the characteristics of land. Since, as in industry proper, the prospect of higher profits drives the accumulation process, technical change moves towards increased labour productivity (lower labour cost) and a rising organic composition of capital.[26] As technological innovation proceeds, the effects of capital investment overwhelm differences in natural characteristics of land: 'capital, which in this sense is synonymous with the means of production already produced, becomes the decisive element in cultivation' (1894: 814). With this, the only difference between capitalist agriculture and capitalist industry is that the landowner stands ready to capture any excess profits.

The chapters on the second form of differential rent are the most convoluted in all of Part Six, but some key points do emerge. One of the main principles Marx wants to establish is that rent per acre increases (and so also the price of land) with the investment of capital.[27] His case

24. Marx suggests that Ricardo arrives at his law of rising rents because, once it is established, a fertility hierarchy appears to have arisen by movement from best to worst land (see 1894: 796).
25. Marx, 1894: 861. Distinguishing the two forms of rent, Marx states: 'In both cases [DI and DII] the land shows differing fertility for the same capital investment, but now [DII] the same land does for a capital invested successively in different portions what in differential rent I is done by different kinds of land for different capitals of equal size ...' (1894: 816).
26. Marx refers to the rising organic composition of capital throughout his discussion of DII; for some instances see 1894: 828–9, 901.
27. Marx evidently considers the point important as he repeatedly states that it is the distinguishing principle to emerge with DII (see 1894: 821–2, 830–31, 846, 880, 912–13).

for this principle seems to be that, as in industry, the accumulation of capital is the driving force underlying increased productivity; in agriculture, the accumulation process would involve an increased 'concentration of capital on the same area' of land, and so a rise in rent per acre (1894: 830). It seems also that Marx wants to establish this principle because it would put the final flourish on his critique of Ricardo. Beyond his negative case that rent does not rise because of Ricardo's 'original powers of the soil', Marx would establish that it rises instead because of the action of capital. Differential rent, however, does not depend just on productivity but on a multiplicity of factors. As a result, Marx can demonstrate that rent rises with the intensity of capital only under specific conditions, but not as a general rule. To take a simple case: if additional capital is invested on every land type (e.g., because the normal technique has changed), rent would increase because output per acre has increased *provided that* the price of output remains the same and the productivity differentials between land types are preserved (see 1894: 830, 912). Marx can argue that Ricardo's 'law' requires even more restrictive conditions and that these conditions are empirically unlikely, but he cannot free his own principle from qualifications.[28] Moreover, he does not need to. His fundamental point is that rent depends on capital (not that it rises as capital investment increases). He has already established several senses in which this is true. As extra surplus-value, rent results from competition (since it presupposes a rate of profit) and so from the interaction of capitals. Differential rent I depends on fertility, which is a relation that involves the technique of production (and so capital) as one of its elements. The new meaning to emerge with differential rent II, is that rent depends on the innovation process inherent in capital. Since this perpetually increases the organic composition of capital, its result is that capital becomes ever more dominant.

While this appears to be Marx's main point, several other principles emerge in connection with differential rent II. First, the extra product resulting from successive investments of capital (i.e., marginal products) 'are blurred' and 'can no longer be recognized or distinguished' (Marx, 1894: 842, 843). This is because the capitalist producer is concerned with the total output produced with the total capital investment (i.e., with the average product of capital).[29] It follows that the differentials arising

28. For the conditions required for Ricardo's law see Marx, 1894: 818–19.
29. Marx disposes of marginal productivity theory with the comment that 'it would be nonsense to say that a third of the capital had produced 1 qr, and the remaining two-thirds had produced 4 qrs' (1894: 876, see also 842, 843, 861). His 'successive investments of capital' are changes in the normal

from successive investments of capital are hard to identify. As a result, the transformation of extra surplus-value into rent becomes a matter of chance (for example, whether the timing of the lease enables the landowner to capture the surplus profits generated with one technique before techniques change again [see Marx, 1894: 878, 844]).

Second, already existing rents may limit the extent to which the intensity of capital per acre can be increased. For example, if average productivity decreases with successive investments of capital, in the absence of rent, capital intensity could be increased on better lands until the cost of production rose (i.e., productivity fell) to the same level as that on the worst land, which sets the market price. Once a particular productivity differential on better land is captured in rents, however, it cannot be reduced by further investments of capital, since rents will not be rolled back. Under these conditions, already established rents block increased intensity of capital (a point Fine emphasizes and that will come up again in connection with absolute rent).[30] If the limitation this places on the output of better lands keeps worse lands under cultivation to fill the total demand, it keeps the price of agricultural output high. Rent would then be responsible for the high price of agricultural output (contrary to Ricardo). In addition (and more important than scoring another point against Ricardo), landed property intervenes in and modifies the innovation process of capital.[31]

Third (and also relevant to absolute rent), the interaction between the two forms of differential rent may give rise to differential rent on the worst land. This is the case, for example, if in the face of increased demand for output, productivity on the worst land is higher than the productivity resulting from the use of additional capital on better land. Because the latter sets the market price, the former yields surplus profit; with this 'all cultivated land would bear rent in the sense of simple differential rent' (Marx, 1894: 873).

---

production technique, i.e., qualitative rather than purely quantitative transformations of production. Fine also interprets DII in this way. As he explains, he emphasized the 'increasing size of capital as opposed to infinitesimally small increments of capital' to counter 'the whole recent tradition of Marxist rent theory [which] has treated DRII as comparable to the Ricardian intensive margin' (1986b: 176).

30. Thus Marx argues that capital 'comes up against a more or less artificial barrier [as] a result of the merely formal transformation of surplus profit into ground rent which is the consequence of landed property' (1894: 870, see also 862–71, 877).

31. See Harvey (199: 357) who emphasizes this point and argues that it undermines 'the neutral posture of the landowner with respect to accumulation'.

2.2. Absolute rent

Marx is originally convinced of the necessity for absolute rent by the mistakes that follow from Ricardo's exclusion of it. To establish that rent does not affect the price of output, Ricardo argues that all rent is differential and that price is set by zero rent land. In the context of capitalism, however, rent presupposes landed property and it, in turn, precludes the free use of land. To avoid this logical impossibility in Ricardo's theory, Marx incorporates absolute rent into his own, attributing it to the only remaining potential source of extra surplus-value: that which agriculture would generate if the composition of capital were lower in agriculture than in industry. Marx's case that privately owned land cannot be used for free implies that rent must be paid regardless of the organic composition of capital (just as it must be paid regardless of productivity differences, as Marx argues against Ricardo). Marx allows that rent could be based on a pure monopoly price, meaning an output price greater than both price of production and value. He rejects this option, though, because it implies that rent enters the price of agricultural output 'as an element independent of its value' (1894: 892). Alternatively, he excludes monopoly price from *Capital*, Volume III because it 'belongs to the theory of competition' (*ibid.*: 898).[32] While Marx's critique of Ricardo is valid, his theory of absolute rent is questionable.

Most obviously, Marx's absolute rent depends on whether the organic composition of capital is in fact lower in agriculture than in industry. Marx argues that this is historically true because of 'the earlier and more rapid development of the mechanical sciences', but a later start does not mean permanent backwardness (1894: 894). In his effort to save this aspect of Marx's theory, Fine emphasizes Marx's case (in connection with DII) that landed property may block the use of additional capital (thereby preventing an increase in organic composition) by refusing to lower already established differential rents.[33] Marx has proposed other, more straightforward, impediments to capital investment in agriculture: that permanent improvements both become the landowner's property and

32. Apparently, Marx wants to avoid the monopoly price explanation because he thinks it would amount to abandoning the theory of value (monopoly price is 'arbitrary' [1904/10: 332] or determined simply by supply and demand – 1894: 910). The pitfalls of monopoly price explanations are amply exemplified by the errors of Physiocracy, Malthus and Anderson (who posits diminishing returns in agriculture) (see 1904/10: 162–3).
33. For Fine 'perhaps the most important conclusion to be drawn from Marx's theory of DRII [is] its preoccupation with obstacles to the development of capital accumulation' (1986: 126).

raise rent, and that innovation generates less extra profit for the agricultural than for the industrial capitalist. Still, as Marx acknowledges, none of these guarantee that agriculture will be forever relatively backward.[34] Further, since the requirement to pay rent does not vanish with a rise in the agricultural organic composition of capital, there is nothing to guarantee that absolute rent will remain within the limits Marx sets.

A second, and simpler, issue is that Marx gains nothing by positing a relatively low agricultural organic composition of capital. If the price of agricultural output is above the price of production, whether it is below or above value makes no difference. In either case, it is a price established against and in spite of the competitive pressure to equalize the rate of profit. In both cases also, price is 'independent of value' in the sense that Marx does not avoid having to appeal to supply and demand to explain it. He grants that a price below or equal to value but above price of production is a 'monopoly price' but distinguishes this from a 'genuine monopoly price', one that is above value as well as price of production (1894: 897, 898). From the standpoint of the forces that establish price, however, this is a distinction without a difference. The whole problem – of the organic composition of capital and of different kinds of monopoly price – arises because Marx wants to keep rent from being 'an element independent of its [the commodity's] value' (1894: 892). This, however, is Ricardo's problem. It is a condition imposed on the explanation of rent by Ricardo's theory of value; it should never have become an issue for Marx. Maintaining that the price exceeds the value of agricultural output would not undermine Marx's version of the theory of value (although it would undermine Ricardo's); it would just mean that the agricultural sector withdraws from rather than contributes to the pool of surplus-value that all capital shares. Appealing to supply and demand does not contradict value theory either. Marx is not bothered by

34. As he says 'this is a historical difference and can therefore disappear' (1904/10: 244). In *Capital*, Vol. III, Marx indicates that he is just assuming a relatively low agricultural organic composition of capital (1894: 896). As he also reiterates, all that would happen if the difference in organic composition disappeared is that nondifferential rent would result from a pure monopoly price. Thus Marx's theory does not involve the 'strange implication' Blaug sees in it 'that absolute rent is negative if the agricultural sector is more capital intensive than the rest of the economy' (1997: 273). This is because absolute rent is not, as Blaug thinks, 'owing to the fact that agriculture operates with an organic composition of capital below the average' but to the private ownership of land (*ibid.*).

it when he explains the division of surplus-value between interest and profit of enterprise by the supply and demand for money-capital.

Finally, Marx does present another solution to the determination of absolute rent. In a second line of argument he maintains that 'absolute rent can only be small in normal conditions' (1894: 906). (Marx adds 'whatever the excess value of the product over its price of production'. He means that rent may not capture the entire excess, but the point applies even if there is no excess, i.e., regardless of the composition of capital.) The reason is that the rent on any given piece of land is limited by the costs associated with the other ways of producing agricultural output that would remain if that piece of land were to be withdrawn from cultivation. For example, rent on a given piece of land cannot exceed the cost of producing more output by using more capital intensive methods on the other lands under cultivation. If it did, capitalists would adopt such methods and refuse to rent the piece of land in question. Marx reasons that since unrented land is 'economically worthless', owners will be willing to allow land to be used for a small rent (meaning the price of agricultural output need only rise slightly above the price of production [1894: 891]).

This fulfils the purpose Marx intended for the theory of absolute rent, namely, to establish the impossibility of zero rent land. The 'small' rent is based on the principle of differential cost and Marx's argument for it is exactly the same as his case for differential rent on the worst land. While this leaves no separate quantitative principle determining absolute rent, the valid point in Marx's argument for absolute rent is that ownership must have economic significance. In the case of land, this significance is enforced against capital by keeping land 'scarce' – withholding its use.[35]

On this interpretation, Marx's argument for absolute rent is strikingly similar to Keynes's explanation for the yield on capital: 'the only reason why an asset offers a prospect of yielding during its life services having an aggregate value greater than its initial supply price is because it is *scarce*; and it is kept scarce because of the competition of the rate of interest on money' (1936: 213). Thus ultimately, for Keynes, capital has a yield because the special properties of money prevent the rate of interest from falling to zero. The parallel case in Marx is that the private

35. Because the 'supply' of land is the amount owners make available for use, not the amount of land in existence, it is never the case that 'if land were in super-abundant supply competition among landlords would drive rent on the margins of cultivation to zero' (Scott, cited by Evans, 1999: 2113).

ownership of land makes land scarce and so prevents rent from falling to zero.

3. Conclusion

It has been argued that Marx's chief objective in the theory of rent is to identify the relations of production associated with the use of land in capitalism and to establish these, in place of Ricardo's original powers of the soil, as the determinants of rent. This chapter has focused on the principal ways in which Marx achieves this objective. Regarding the relations themselves, he argues that the dominance of capital assigns a 'purely economic form' to land ownership. Echoing his description of the wage contract, he examines how the conflict between capital and landed property plays out in the lease contract. In connection with the first form of differential rent, Marx redefines fertility as the relation between the objective characteristics of land and the normal technique of production. In connection with the second, he examines the implications for rent of capital's process of technological innovation. While his argument on absolute rent is flawed, its flaws do not affect Marx's chief point. This is that the meaning of capitalist private property is the command over value.

Bibliography

Ball, Michael (1986), On Marx's theory of agricultural rent: a reply to Ben Fine, in B. Fine (ed. 1986), *The Value Dimension* (London: Routledge Kegan Paul): 152–174.

Blaug, Mark (1997), *Economic Theory in Retrospect* (5th edn) (Cambridge: Cambridge University Press).

Böhm-Bawerk, Eugen von (1884), *Capital and Interest* (English trans. W. Smart, 1890) (New York: Kelley & Millman, 1957).

— (1894), Karl Marx and the close of his system, in *Karl Marx and the Close of His System* (Introduction and ed. P.M. Sweezy) (New York: Augustus M. Kelley, 1966).

Evans, Alan W. (1999), On Minimum Rents: Part 1, Marx and Absolute Rent, *Urban Studies*, Vol. 36, 12: 2111–20.

Fine, Ben (1986a), On Marx's theory of agricultural rent, in B. Fine (ed. 1986), *The Value Dimension* (London: Routledge Kegan Paul).

— (1986b) On Marx's theory of agricultural rent: a rejoinder, in B. Fine (ed. 1986) *The Value Dimension* (London: Routledge Kegan Paul).

Guidi, Marco E.L. (1998), Land rent and the logic of *Capital*, in R. Bellofiore (ed. 1998), *Marxian Economics: A Reappraisal*, Vol. 1 (London/New York Macmillan/St Martin's Press).

Harvey, David (1999), *The Limits to Capital* (2nd edn) (London/New York: Verso).

Mandel, Ernest (1981), Introduction to Marx (1894/1981).

Marx, Karl (1859), *A Contribution to the Critique of Political Economy* (English trans. S. Ryanzanskaya and ed. Maurice Dobb) (New York: International Publishers, 1970).

— (1894), *Capital, Volume III* (English trans. David Fernbach) (Harmondsworth: Penguin, 1981).

— (1904/10) [written 1861–63] *Theories of Surplus Value, Part II* (ed. and English trans. S. Ryanzanskaya, 1968) (Moscow: Progress Publishers).

Ricardo, David (1817, 1819, 1821) *On the Principles of Political Economy and Taxation, Volume I, The Works and Correspondence of David Ricardo*, Piero Sraffa (ed.) (Cambridge: Cambridge University Press, 1970).

11
The Illusion of the Economic
The Trinity Formula and the 'religion of everyday life'

Patrick Murray

> 'Capital-profit (profit of enterprise plus interest), land-ground-rent, labour-wages, this trinity form holds in itself all the mysteries of the social production process.'
>
> Marx, 1894: 953

> 'The forms of revenue and the sources of revenue are the *most fetishistic* expression of the relations of capitalist production. ... The distorted form in which the real inversion is expressed is naturally reproduced in the views of the agents of this mode of production. It is a kind of fiction without fantasy, a religion of the vulgar.'
>
> Marx, 1971: 453

Capital reaches its consummation in 'The Trinity Formula', the chapter that opens the seventh, and concluding, part of Volume III.[1] This unfinished chapter rounds out Marx's six-fold project in *Capital*:

1. In speaking of consummations in Volume III, we should not forget that what we know as the three volumes of *Capital* are far from fulfilling Marx's plan for a comprehensive critical investigation into capital. On some of the issues involved with the incompleteness of Marx's work, see Shortall, 1994; Rosdolsky, 1968; Rubel, 1981; Oakley, 1983; Lebowitz, 1992; and Chris Arthur's chapters in this volume.

1. to present and examine in the form of a systematic dialectic the social forms constitutive of the capitalist order, beginning with the (generalized) commodity;
2. to expose capitalist society, in its enlightened secularism, to be idolatrous and fetishistic;
3. to reveal that the social egalitarianism of capitalist society harbours class domination;
4. to examine and critically evaluate representations and theories of capitalism;
5. to show how capitalist social forms naturally exude ideological representations; and
6. to reveal capitalism to be a historically specific mode of production whose contradictory dynamics point towards its eventually giving way to a historically new mode of production.

As such, the chapter sheds a great deal of light on Marx's purposes and accomplishments in *Capital* and on the structure of his exposition. The title 'The Trinity Formula' drives home Marx's master theme that capitalism is the secular epitome of Christianity's 'cult of man in the abstract' (Marx, 1967: 172).[2]

According to Engels, the manuscript of the chapter on the Trinity Formula begins as follows:

> We have seen how the capitalist process of production is a historically specific form of the social production process in general. This last is both a production process of the material conditions of existence for human life, and a process, proceeding in specific economic and historical relations of production, that produces and reproduces these relations of production themselves, and with them the bearers of this process, their material conditions of existence, and their mutual relationships, i.e. the specific economic form of their society.
>
> Marx, 1894: 957

2. The idea that secular capitalist society is the fulfilment of Christianity goes back to Marx's essay 'On the Jewish Question'. For Marx, 'criticism of religion is the premise of all criticism' (Marx, 1843: 175). Since Volume III, Part Seven, concludes with a brief, unfinished chapter on classes, we may wonder if the theme that, for all the egalitarianism radiated by the forms of simple commodity circulation, capitalism as a class society deserves pride of place. Perhaps it is best to see the 'master theme' as the congruity of these two seemingly incongruous ideas: *capitalism is an egalitarian society and capitalism is a class society*. See Marx, 1845: 78; Marx, 1939: 248–9; and Marx, 1867: 164, 280.

This is an apt beginning to the conclusion of *Capital*, for those opening sentences express the most fundamental, if widely overlooked, point of the book: *capitalism is not 'the economy in general'*. That there is no economy in general follows from the complex statement that expresses perhaps Marx's most seminal insight: 'All production is appropriation of nature on the part of an individual within and through a specific form of society' (Marx, 1939: 87). The chapter's two opening sentences remind us of the *double character* of the capitalist mode of *production*. It is a particular instance of the human provisioning process and as such shares several features with all human modes of provisioning, features that Marx describes in treating of 'the labour process in general' back in the first part of Chapter 7 of Volume I. At the same time, the capitalist production process is a 'valorization process' with many socially distinctive features that Marx conceives of as the various *value forms*, e.g., the (generalized) commodity, exchange-value, money, capital, wages, profit, interest, rent.

Marx's task in *Capital* is to stick with this original insight and to think through the capitalist production process (at a certain level of abstraction) in its *actuality*, that is, in its double character, its *use-value* and *value* dimensions. Among the chief results of this investigation is that the social forms determining the capitalist provisioning process (the value forms) have the power to reproduce and extend themselves, continually reweaving and widening the net of capitalist relations. In this, Marx returns to the point he made in a more preliminary way in *Results of the Immediate Production Process*, the manuscript apparently intended as the transition from the first to the second volume of *Capital*, 'This form of mediation is intrinsic to this [the capitalist] mode of production. It perpetuates the relation between capital as the buyer and the worker as the seller of labour' (Marx, 1867: 1063). Similarly, the purpose of the reproduction schemes at the conclusion of Volume II is to respect the double character of capitalist production and show how, in its circulation process, capital can, simultaneously, reproduce and expand itself *both materially and formally*.[3] 'It is precisely here that the principal difficulty lies, in the analysis of reproduction and the relationship of its various components, both in their material character and in their value' (Marx, 1894: 983). It's not simply *resources* in: *more resources* out; it's *capital* in: *more capital* out.[4] The complex task of *Capital* is one that economists

3. See Moseley, 1998.
4. See Marx, 1971: 514. To find out how prevalent this obliviousness to social form remains today, ask someone what capital is or look up the 'answer' in an introductory economics textbook.

before, during, and after Marx's lifetime not only have not undertaken; they have failed even to recognize. The failure to grasp the theoretical need to sort general features of the provisioning process out from socially specific ones reaches gigantic proportions in the vulgar economists' 'Trinity Formula', but Marx is quick to remind us that, for all their insights into errors collected in the Trinity Formula, the classical political economists 'remained more or less trapped in the world of illusion their criticism had dissolved, and nothing else is possible from the bourgeois standpoint' (Marx, 1894: 969).

The first six parts of Volume III complete the systematic dialectic of capitalist social forms (at least for a certain level of abstraction) by working through the dialectical development of the *necessary forms of appearance* of surplus-value. Surplus-value, which Marx introduced in Chapter 4 of Volume I, necessarily appears as something other than itself, namely profit, interest (and its counterpart, profit of enterprise) and rent. Volume III's lengthy exposition of the necessary forms of surplus-value's appearance builds up to Part Seven as the capstone to all three volumes.

I will argue that this exposition of the necessary forms of appearance of surplus-value closes the second, and much much longer, of two circuits of thought that comprise *Capital*. Each circuit is organized around a fetish. The first explains how and why the *product* of the capitalist mode of production is a fetish. This circuit investigates the commodity and its twin fetish, money. 'Commodities and Money', Part One of Volume I, makes up the first circuit. Part Two, 'The Transformation of Money into Capital', provides the needed transition from the first to the second circuit, from the sphere of circulation to the sphere of production. The second explains how and why the *three factors of the labour process in general* (raw materials, produced means of production and living labour) become fetishes inasmuch as each of the three appears to be an independent source of value and therewith of revenue (rent, interest and profit of enterprise and wages, respectively). This second circuit begins with the first chapter of Part Three of Volume I, 'The Labour Process and the Valorization Process', and culminates in the first chapter of Part Seven of Volume III, 'The Trinity Formula', which could well bear the sub-title, 'The Fetishism of the Factors of Production'.

Marx's probing of the variants of the Trinity Formula, a doctrine of vulgar political economy, discloses it to be a compendium of errors and ideological misrepresentations propagated by the capitalist mode of production. The most basic and pervasive of these is the history-stopping idea that capitalism is not a *particular* historical mode of production but *the economy in general.*[5] I will call this 'the illusion of the economic'; it is the basis of everyday, pseudo-scientific (as in the case of vulgar political economy) and even scientific misconceptions of the capitalist mode of production.

How can the vulgar representations of the capitalist mode of production, which Marx calls the 'religion of everyday life' (Marx, 1894: 969), and even widely shared scientific ideas, such as those of Classical Political Economy, be so riddled with half-truth and total miscomprehension? Marx addresses this problem in his characteristic, historical materialist way. That is, he explains which features of the society under consideration give rise to them. In this chapter, we will pay close attention to those aspects of capitalism that engender 'the illusion of the economic'.

A stubborn obstacle to reading *Capital*, 'The Trinity Formula' in particular, is the common, but mistaken, idea that Marx adopts the Classical (Ricardian) labour theory of value and then drives it to radical conclusions in the theory of surplus-value. The thought comes to this: Marx was a Left Ricardian. Removing this roadblock is exceedingly difficult. To state the difference between Marx and Ricardo bluntly, Marx's theory of value is his theory of *the specific social form of* labour under capitalism; Ricardo's labour theory of value is oblivious to the elusive problematic of social form. The gulf between the two is wide, and the consequences of not recognizing it are grave. Unfortunately, the usual interpretation of 'The Trinity Formula' reinforces the misjudgement that Marx was a Left Ricardian.

On the Left Ricardian reading of *Capital*, the critique of 'The Trinity Formula' packs quite a wallop. It is a résumé of what is taken to be the book's central achievement, the demonstration that capitalism is a system of class exploitation wherein control of land and the produced means of production by landowners and capitalists enables them to expropriate surplus-value from the class of wage-labourers. The classical labour theory of value seems to serve this argument well. In fact, the leading Left Ricardian idea is that Marx's theory of exploitation is the logical outcome of classical value theory – its 'truth', as Hegel would say. The conventional reading of 'The Trinity Formula' has Marx teaming up with *Classical* Political Economy – once Marx has straightened out its kinks – to smash the idols of *vulgar* economics. There is truth in this standard reading, but not nearly enough.

5. Expressing the standpoint of Classical Political Economy, Marx writes in the *Poverty of Philosophy*, 'Thus there has been history, but there is no longer any' (Marx, 1847: 121).

Ricardian value theory, when properly developed, seems to pull the rug out from under the vulgar economic ideas expressed in the Trinity Formula. If labour is the source of all value, then the class of wage-labourers creates all value. This suggests two things: (1) since neither capitalists nor landowners add value, neither class deserves any revenue; and (2) the revenues they do get, rent and profit (interest and profit of enterprise), must be siphoned off from the class of wage-labourers. Consequently, each of the Trinity Formula's three propositions governing the forms of revenue, namely: (1) rents compensate the contribution of land (the proprietor of land); (2) interest compensates the contribution of capital (the capitalist); and (3) wages compensate the contribution of labour (the wage-labourer) appear to be false. In the first two cases, neither party adds value, so no compensation appears justified. The problem in the case of wage labour is the reverse; since it adds more value than it receives, wages appear to shortchange workers. Such apparent injustices call for redress. But of what sort?

Left Ricardians answer this question variously. But they have two things in common: (1) being inattentive to matters of form, they slur the difference between *wealth* and *value*; and (2) they recommend some form of the redistribution of 'wealth'. Let me venture a rough typology of variants of Left Ricardianism. A *reformist*, social democratic sort of Left Ricardianism calls for the use of state power, usually the powers of selective and progressive taxation, to shift 'wealth' from landlords and capitalists to wage labourers. A more *radical* Left Ricardianism can take different forms. One involves the transfer of all surplus-value into worker-run banks; another would involve the conversion of all firms into worker-owned cooperatives. Yet another recommends replacing money with 'time-chits', a move intended to smother surplus-value. A *revolutionary* type of Left Ricardianism has more in common with a Marxian approach; it calls for a redistribution not of revenues but of land and the means of production.[6] This form of Left Ricardianism rightly despairs of creating a just society without overturning the property relations on which capitalism rests. Yet, even the revolutionary Ricardian project remains centred on remedying or eliminating exploitation, that is, the apparently unjust appropriation of surplus-value from workers by capitalists.

Ironically, the basic Left Ricardian conception of justice is the standard commercial one: equal value for equal value. Because Ricardian theory

6. Marx makes much of this difference in the penultimate chapter of *Capital*; see Marx, 1894: 1019.

is oblivious to the problematic of the social form of wealth; because, consequently, Ricardian theory cannot help but run 'wealth' and 'value' together, it is the *surplus*, not the *value*, in surplus-value that troubles the Left Ricardian. *Value* is not a problem; only its (mal)distribution is. But for Marx, value *is* a problem, a monster of a problem.[7]

Understanding Marx to be a radical Ricardian, while it coheres with some important aspects of Marx's criticism of the vulgar economists' Trinity Formula, aborts Marx's deepest ideas. This is to be expected, for those ideas reject Ricardian value theory on account of its bourgeois inattention to *social form*. Questions shunted away by Ricardian theory make up Marx's subject matter. Ricardian theory worries about whether 'wealth' is being *distributed* fairly. It does not trouble itself, however, about the social form of this wealth or the multiple implications of that social form. Economics of all varieties is terribly hard of hearing when it comes to the questions that preoccupy Marx. Questions such as: what does it mean for a society that, generally, it produces wealth in the social form of the commodity? My objective in this chapter, then, is to offer an alternative exposition of 'The Trinity Formula', working from the assumption that Marx's own theory of value is a theory of capitalist social forms. Marx offers not a new improved version of the classical labour theory of value but a radical break with it. By examining the roots of 'the illusion of the economic', I hope to expose the sources of the plausibility of Ricardian ideas. Hopefully that will make them less believable.

1. Organizing *Capital* around two fetishes: the product and the labour process

Here is my hypothesis regarding the structure of *Capital*: it can be broken down into two 'from–to' movements of greatly different lengths. Each reveals a strand of the fetishism characteristic of the capitalist mode of production. The first movement shows how *commodities*, the *products* of the capitalist mode of production, are mysteriously possessed of social powers that appear to be natural properties. As value, the commodity has clout. Belonging to the same movement, *money* arises alongside the world of commodities. With its social power of immediate exchangeability seeming to spring right out of the earth, money is a yet more blinding fetish than the commodity. The first movement starts *from* the double character of *products* in the characteristically capitalist form, that

7. This is not to suggest that Marx is not concerned about exploitation, the *surplus* in surplus-value. On the contrary, the upshot of *Capital* is that, since generalized commodity circulation is inseparable from the circulation and accumulation of capital, the two are inseparable: *no surplus-value, no value*.

is, *from* the *use-value* and *exchange-value* of the commodity, *to* the necessity for one commodity's value to appear in the body of another commodity (exchange-value as the necessary form of appearance of value), *to* the 'fetishism of the commodity', and *to* the money fetish.

The second movement tracks the fetishism caused by the social form of the *labour process* under capitalism. This extends *from* the double character of the capitalist labour process – *labour process in general* and *valorization process* – *to* the necessary forms of appearance of surplus-value (profit of enterprise, interest and rent) and *to* the Trinity Formula, which expresses the fetishism of the three *factors of the labour process* under capitalism. My claim is that, just as Marx's exposition of the double character of the *product* of the capitalist production process, the commodity, sets up the treatment of the fetishisms of the commodity and money, with the exposition of the double character of the capitalist *labour process* itself (in the first chapter of *Capital* devoted to capital proper, Chapter 7), Marx intentionally sets up 'The Trinity Formula'.[8] It parallels Chapter 1's section on the fetishism of the commodity in providing a retrospective and commentary on the results of the ponderous task of thinking through the double character of the labour process under capitalism. If the first movement penetrates the mystery whereby products, mere things, are possessed of social power, the clout of purchasing power, the second movement explains how the three personifications of the factors of the labour process taken in general (produced means of production, raw materials of production and labour), respectively, the capitalist, the landowner and the wage-labourer, draw revenues in the forms of interest, rent and wages. For Marx it is to be expected that a fetish-ridden labour *process* will result in a fetishistic *product*.[9]

These parallel developments expose twin tendencies of capitalism: (1) to slur, in the minds of its participants, *general* features of both wealth and the production of wealth with historically *determinate* forms that both wealth and the production of wealth take – *wealth* with *value*; *production* with *valorization* – and (2) to make a fetish of wealth and of the three factors involved in the production of wealth.[10] These two tendencies are actually two aspects of the same reality, capitalism's oddly

8. Volume III was drafted in 1864–65, a couple of years before Volume I was published (1867).
9. In these respects, *Capital* echoes the Paris manuscript 'Estranged Labour'; see Marx, 1844: 279.
10. On the distinction between general and determinate abstractions, see Chapter 10 of Murray, 1988.

asocial type of sociality.[11] Thus, in the first development, the commodity appears to be simply 'wealth' (or 'use-value') devoid of social form because, strangely, its social form appears as a separate thing, money. So we slur the difference between wealth and commodities.[12] At the same time, wealth in the commodity form *has* an exchange-value because it *is* a value, that is, a thing possessed of the power to exchange with all other commodities. Endowed as if by nature with this peculiar social power, wealth in the commodity form is a fetish.

In the case of the second development, again we find the slurring of general and determinate concepts: raw materials with landed property, means of production with capital, and labour with wage labour. By the same token, the division of the wealth created by the capitalist production process into the capitalist forms of revenue (rent, interest and profit of enterprise and wages) is taken as the natural and inevitable outcome of there being three distinguishable factors of the production process. Herein, too, lies the fetishism of the factors of production. Each is taken to be an independent source of value, a conception Marx represents with the image of the three factors as three trees, each bearing its own sort of fruit. The upshot of the parallel developments, then, is (1) that both wealth and the production of wealth in capitalism appear to be devoid of specific social form, hence 'natural' – here is 'the illusion of the economic' – with the result that the specific social forms get slurred with general features of wealth and its production and (2) both the wealth produced and the three distinguishable factors in the production of wealth become fetishes.

Though this second movement of thought in *Capital*, devoted to the 'fetishism of the factors of the capitalist labour process', which is just what the Trinity Formula encapsulates, *follows* the first movement, dedicated to the commodity and money fetishes, the second encompasses the first, while the first presupposes the second.[13] For one result of the

11. In Chapter 51 of Volume III, 'Relations of Distribution and Relations of Production', Marx identifies 'two characteristic traits' of the capitalist mode of production; they correspond to the parallel developments presently under discussion. The two are: (1) the dominant form of the product is the commodity, and (2) the production of surplus-value is the decisive motive of production (Marx, 1894: 1019–20). I take this observation as support for my thesis.
12. This is reinforced in everyday consciousness today through the practice of presenting the Gross Domestic Product as if it were a measure of the 'wealth' created over a year's time.
13. This is to be expected in a work of systematic dialectics; see Arthur, 1997, and Bubner, 1988.

examination of the capitalist production process to which Marx gives special attention (Marx, 1894: 1019–20) is that all its products take the commodity form, just as all its inputs enter as commodities.

This 'two movements–two fetishes' reading adds a facet to a more familiar idea, namely that *Capital* is composed of two 'books', one on commodities and money, and one on capital. Marx divided the *Grundrisse* into the 'chapter on money' and the 'chapter on capital', and the *Contribution to the Critique of Political Economy* was a version of that first 'chapter'. The first movement I identify covers Part One of Volume I, 'Commodities and Money'. Part Two is transitional, covering the genesis of capital, wage labour and surplus-value. And Part Three, which opens with Chapter 7's account of the double character of the labour process under capitalism, begins the treatment of capital proper. That topic absorbs the rest of *Capital*.

What is distinctive in this reading is to see the Trinity Formula as the terminus for a movement of thought that was set up back in Chapter 7 of Volume I, and to recognize the parallel with the movement that begins on *Capital*'s first page with the double character of wealth in the commodity form. The treatment of the general category use-value in the first movement is matched by the treatment of the labour process in general in the second. Likewise the treatment of the value dimension of the commodity in the first is matched by the treatment of the valorization process in the second.[14] A further parallel exists between the role played by the first chapter's section on the fetishism of commodities and the chapter on the Trinity Formula at the close of Volume III; each is basically a commentary on conceptual developments (the systematic dialectic) that have already taken place.

Marx calls attention to the 'two movement–two fetish' structure of *Capital* in summing up the results of his investigation of the Trinity Formula:

> We have already shown in connection with the most simple categories of the capitalist mode of production and commodity production in general, in connection with commodities and money, the mystifying character that transforms the social relations for which the material elements of wealth serve as bearers in the course of production into properties of these things themselves (commodities), still more

14. In adopting this *paired* presentation of general categories (use-value, process of production) with determinate categories (value, valorization process) Marx abandoned an earlier plan, jotted down at the end of the method section of the *Grundrisse*. See Marx, 1939: 108.

> explicitly transforming the relation of production itself into a thing (money) ... In the capitalist mode of production, however, where capital is the dominant category and forms the specific relation of production, this bewitched and distorted world develops much further ... Capital–profit (or better still capital–interest), land–ground rent, labour–wages, this economic trinity as the connection between the components of value and wealth in general and its sources, completes the mystification of the capitalist mode of production, the reification of social relations, and the immediate coalescence of the material relations of production with their historical and social specificity: the bewitched, distorted and upside-down world haunted by Monsieur le Capital and Madame la Terre, who are at the same time social characters and mere things.
>
> Marx, 1894: 965–6, 968–9[15]

Throughout *Capital* Marx sounds the theme of the necessary inversion of capitalism's abstract, Enlightened secularism into a thoroughgoing fetishism that endows both the products and the process of production with uncanny powers; in this passage it reaches its crescendo.

2. The Trinity Formula: a compendium of errors and illusions

For Marx, the Trinity Formula is a compendium of errors and illusions regarding the capitalist mode of production. It epitomizes the misunderstandings endemic to everyday consciousness and language under capitalism and reconfirmed by those boosters of the 'religion of everyday life', the vulgar economists. The less apologetic, more scientific-minded, classical economists made real progress in dispelling some of the necromancy surrounding the Trinity Formula. But they, too, worked under the spell of the most deep-seated illusions operative in the Trinity Formula. To see both where the classical economists advanced and where they bogged down, we need to pick apart the many errors and illusions involved in the several variants of the Trinity Formula. Let us consider them one at a time.

2.1 The first variant of the Trinity Formula

The first versions of the formula (*capital–profit, land–rent and labour–wages* and *capital–interest, land–rent and labour–wages*) absurdly classify capital (a category specific to capitalist societies) with two factors of the labour

15. Further textual support for this reading may be found in Marx, 1894: 963–4, 968–9, 1023–4, and in Marx, 1971: 510.

process in general, land and labour, a mismatch that Marx derides: 'Their mutual relationship is like that of lawyer's fees, beetroot and music' (Marx, 1894: 953). This bumbling is not Marx's prime target, however; he is after the entrenched patterns of misperception and thoughtlessness underneath it.

2.2 The second variant of the Trinity Formula

When that initial match-up is altered (under pressure of trying to make some sense of capital–interest) by substituting 'produced means of production' for 'capital', the absurdity of the original combination is avoided, only to arrive at the 'uniform and symmetrical incongruity' that completes the circuit wired back to Chapter 7 of Volume I, 'The Labour Process and the Valorization Process'. *Produced means of production–interest, land–rent, labour–wages*: this formula expresses the two mystifications that are Marx's two most fundamental targets, 'the illusion of the economic' and 'the fetishism of the factors of the capitalist labour process'.

(i) *Three errors in the phenomenology of the production process.* The assumptions of this consistently incongruous formula include three key phenomenological errors that result from projecting certain perceived or real features of the capitalist production process onto the labour process in general. Foremost of these is to imagine that the labour process *in general* can stand alone, that it can actually exist independently of all determinate social form. This is the 'illusion of the economic'. It is akin to thinking that 'The Fruit' can exist alongside an apple or pear. The mistake here is to believe that there can be an actual labour process devoid of determinate social form and purpose. *There can be no generic economy*. That is why the idea of 'the economic' is an illusion. Furthermore, the assumption in the Trinity Formula is that the capitalist mode of production *is* 'production in general'. This illusion is shared by vulgar and classical economists alike. When Marx wrote of classical economists being prisoners of the 'bourgeois standpoint', he had the 'illusion of the economic' in mind as one of its defining features.[16]

16. We may wonder why evidence of noncapitalist modes of production does not dash this illusion. For one answer see Marx, 1867: 175, n.35 and Marx, 1894: 1017. Marx's conception of 'ideal subsumption' or 'subsumption by analogy', supplies a second answer. 'Ideal subsumption' of noncapitalist social relations under capitalist forms makes the procrustean move of treating noncapitalist phenomenon as if they fit, say, the capitalist forms of revenue. See Marx, 1894: 1015.

One of the peculiarities of the capitalist production process is that it presents itself in ways that facilitate mistaking it for the mirage of an actual production process in general. Marx's several explanations of how capitalist forms propagate this illusion reveal how seriously he takes the whole issue of the ways humans represent their forms of life to themselves. (One important lesson of *Capital* is to treat the ways that participants in a capitalist society represent their life to themselves as a features that belong to a capitalist society and its capacities for reproducing itself.) Marx's explanations count as remarkable contributions to social epistemology and as models for further work.

In Volume I we learn that the specific social form of the product of the capitalist labour process (the commodity) necessarily gets expressed as a separate *thing* – money. It is not surprising that this bit of ventriloquism is not recognized for what it is. Instead, the commodity is thought to have no social form or purpose at all, an idea that conforms well with the conception of the market as a place where consumers with privately determined desires exercise their sovereign choices. Where does social form or purpose figure in that?[17]

In Volume II, Marx points out how a one-sided attention to the circuit of *productive capital* (as opposed to the circuits of money capital and commodity capital), which begins and ends with the *use-values* requisite for the production process, misled the classical political economists into thinking that the capitalist production process was production in general:

> The general form of the movement P ... P' is the form of reproduction, and does not indicate, as does M ... M', that valorization is the purpose of the process. For this reason, classical economics found it all the more easy to ignore the specifically capitalist form of the production process, and to present production as such as the purpose of the process.
>
> Marx, 1885; 1893: 172

17. Left Ricardianism falls into this illusion in its own way when it imagines that, by ending production for the sake of surplus-value, production 'for the sake of use-value' would be left. I call this illusion 'Use-value Romanticism'. *There is no use-value in general.* The specific purpose of the production of use-values in capitalism is to produce and accumulate surplus-value. Only another definite social purpose, with accompanying definite social forms, can replace it. Marxian theory's most profound challenge is to identify those new social forms and that new social purpose.

In other words, isolating the circuit of productive capital from the flow of money capital and attending only to the former allow the classical economists to shear the valorization process from the production process and present the latter as if it were production in general.

In Volume III Marx explains how the mitosis of the profit form into *interest* and *profit of enterprise* serves to make the capitalist production process look like production in general.

> Since the aspect of capital's specific social determination in the capitalist mode of production – capital ownership which possesses the capacity of command over the labour of others – becomes fixed, with interest appearing as the part of surplus-value that capital produces in this connection, so the other part of surplus-value, profit of enterprise, necessarily appears as if it does not derive from capital as capital, but rather from the production process independently of its specific social determination, which indeed has already obtained its particular mode of existence in the form of interest on capital. However, the production process, when separated from capital, is simply the labour process in general. The industrial capitalist, as distinct from the owner of capital, appears therefore not as functioning capital but rather as a functionary independent of capital, as a simple bearer of the labour process in general; as a worker, and a wage-worker at that.
>
> Marx, 1894: 505

Just as the social form of the commodity appears as a separate thing, money, here the social form of the capitalist production process appears as a separate thing, again money, only this time it is money in the role of interest-bearing capital, the most fetishistic of all capitalist forms. There is the pattern: the social form of the product or the production process bizarrely and necessarily expresses itself as a separate thing, whether money *per se*, money capital, or interest-bearing capital, leaving the impression that what remains lacks social form altogether. The 'illusion of the economic', then, is a by-product of the peculiarity of the value forms.

A second root error regarding the phenomenology of the production process is to imagine that each of the three necessary factors in any labour process: produced means of production, the earth's raw materials and living labour can be productive *on their own*. While two of the three factors of the labour process (produced means of production and land) can *exist* independently, what Marx calls '"the" labour' is a mere abstraction. *Within the labour process* none of the three factors can act independently. Yet in *personifying* the three necessary factors of the labour process, the Trinity Formula supposes otherwise:

> In the formula capital–interest, earth–ground-rent, labour–wages, capital, earth and labour appear respectively as sources of interest (instead of profit), ground-rent and wages as their products or fruits – one the basis, the other the result, one the cause, the other the effect – and moreover in such a way that each individual source is related to its product as something extruded from it and produced by it.
>
> Marx, 1894: 955[18]

Marx expands on the image of fruit, saying of the three forms of revenue: 'They appear as fruits of a perennial tree for annual consumption, or rather fruits of three trees' (Marx, 1894: 960).[19] This notion of three independent sources of revenue, the three perennial fruit trees, betrays a false phenomenology of the labour process, one that hypostatizes *distinguishable* factors in the creation of new wealth into three independent sources owned by three different (classes of) persons.[20]

18. Marx introduced this idea of fruits having separate sources back in his discussion of interest and profit of enterprise. See Marx, 1894: 497–8, 501, 516–17. See also Marx, 1971: 511. Though Marx speaks of one tree for capital in the discussion of the Trinity Formula, on page 498 of Volume III he speaks of two, one yielding *interest* and one *profit of enterprise*. Four trees, though, did not suit the rubric of the Trinity Formula.
19. I believe that Marx's use of the image of fruit and the fruit tree is not accidental here but rather a reference to his parody of Hegelian method in the *Holy Family*, according to which the speculative method attributes to the abstraction '"the" Fruit' the remarkable powers of producing actual apples and pears out of its own bosom (Marx and Engels, 1845: 60).

    When Marx takes up the third member of the 'trinity', labour, he writes '*"die" Arbeit*' (Marx, 1894a: 823) to mimic, I believe, '"the" Fruit'. This gets lost in Fernbach's translation of '*"die" Arbeit*' as 'labour' (Marx, 1894: 954). We find this pattern elsewhere in Marx's work. See Marx, 1967a: 234, and Marx, 1879–80: 198.
20. Here David Hume's idea of a 'distinction of reason', is helpful. A distinction of reason identifies an *aspect* of something that is not actually separable from it. (Hegel would call this a 'moment'.) In Hume's example (Hume, 1739–40: 25) we can make a distinction of reason between the whiteness and the spherical shape of a white marble globe, but the two cannot be separated. Determining what is actually separable and what is only conceptually distinguishable is the work of *phenomenology*. Marx's criticism of the Trinity Formula's picture of three separate sources of value, the three fruit trees, is based on his phenomenology of the production process, according to which materials, means and living labour are *inseparable*, though distinguishable, factors of production.

This bewitching idea of interest-bearing capital as an independent source of value captured my imagination as a boy of six, when my parents presented me with my first bank account. I remember being electrified by the thought that the bank intended to pay me three dollars a years for every one hundred dollars of my money that they were keeping safe for me. With a head swelling from my new-found bit of Trinitarian wisdom, I wondered why the government did not just advance every citizen a million dollars so that we could all live comfortably on the returns to the value our banked capital produced each year. As logical and appealing as my plan sounded, it smelled fishy.

The thought that land produces rent, which Marx terms 'the Physiocratic illusion' (Marx, 1867: 176), is a bit more difficult to discharge because of the imaginative association of rent with the fertility of the earth. Writing on revenue forms in the third part of *Theories of Surplus-Value*, Marx observes: 'The *land* or *nature* as the source of *rent* ... is fetishistic enough. But as a result of a convenient confusion of use-value with exchange-value, the common imagination is still able to have recourse to the productive power of nature itself, which, by some kind of hocus-pocus, is personified in the landlord' (Marx, 1971: 454). It is easy enough to grow impatient watching for seeds to sprout; imagine the endurance required to wait till rents shoot forth from the soil!

Marx's criticism of the Trinity Formula is different from, and more fundamental than, the criticism pioneered by Classical Political Economy, that capital and land are not sources of *value*, hence not the sources of interest and rent. For Marx's point here is not that, taken separately, capital and land are not sources of revenue, while labour *is*. The point is not that 'labour' is the sole value-bearing tree. No, '"the" labour' is 'a mere spectre ... nothing but an abstraction and taken by itself cannot exist at all' (Marx, 1894: 954). Taken separately, *none* of the three factors are sources of use-values, and without use-value there is no value. To think otherwise is to adopt the bourgeois standpoint, which ascribes a '*supernatural creative power*' to labour, as Marx charged in his criticism of the Left Ricardianism of the Gotha Programme (Marx, 1891: 3).

A third phenomenological error is to imagine that the 'wealth (or use-value) added' by each of these three necessary components can be discriminated and quantified. One could avoid the previous error and grant that the three factors of the labour process in general do not act *independently*, yet still attempt to gauge their *respective* contributions to the 'use-value added'.[21] John Locke was fond of doing that for land and

21. This is the approach taken in Neoclassical Economics, when it speaks of the 'marginal productivity' of the different factors of production. Geert Reuten

labour (produced means of production revealingly did not figure into his best known examples), on different occasions allotting land one tenth, hundredth, or thousandth of the 'use-value added' (or 'improvement' as Locke liked to call it). In attempting to prove his point, however, Locke fell back on the different *prices* of the yield of uncultivated versus cultivated land, thereby revealing how – and this is quite generally the case with utility theory – the entire thought experiment about the labour process was unwittingly conducted in the shadow of the price form and the valorization process.[22] For Marx, no such apportionment of 'use-value added' is possible, because there is no homogenous measure for use-value, no metric of wealth.[23] Utility is a sham concept, a shadow of price.[24] To think otherwise is to commit a basic phenomenological error.

(ii) *The fetishism of the factors of production.* The second, 'symmetrically incongruous' formulation of the Trinity Formula best fits the description, the 'fetishism of the factors of the capitalist production process', because this variant presents the three factors of the labour process in general as mysteriously invested by nature with the social powers of yielding revenues in the forms of interest, rent and wages. 'Rent, profit and wages thus appear to grow out of the roles that the earth, the produced means of production and labour play in the simple labour process, considering this labour process simply as proceeding between man and nature and ignoring any historical specificity' (Marx, 1894: 964). In terms of the artistic structuring of *Capital* around the two fetishisms, here is where the other shoe falls.

2.3 The third variant of the Trinity Formula

Of course, the three factors of the labour process are far from having any such powers. What is really going on here is that the formula slurs over

---

and Michael Williams reject this Neoclassical doctrine and point out that F.W. Taussig criticized J.B. Clark's Neoclassical doctrine of the marginal productivity of capital (Reuten and Williams, 1989: 72).

22. See Chapter 5 of Locke, 1690.
23. For Marx, the idea of 'purely subjective' utility is a nonstarter based on a false, one-sided phenomenology of desire. He writes in the opening pages of *Capital*, 'The usefulness of a thing makes it a use-value. But this usefulness does not dangle in midair. It is conditioned by the physical properties of the commodity, and has no existence apart from the latter' (Marx, 1867: 126; translation amended). That there is no metric for those physical properties was the premise of Marx's argument that only abstract labour can explain what commodities have in common. This is Marx's answer to all forms of utility theory.
24. See Marx and Engels, 1846: 409.

the distinction between the three factors of the labour process in general and the three chief protagonists of the capitalist production process: means of production with *capitalist*; land with *landed property owner*, and labour with *wage-labourer*. This personification of the three factors of the labour process in general, the 'economic three-in-one' as Marx calls it (Marx, 1894: 953), conflates the defining class structure of capitalism, whereby 'labour' is 'freed' of ownership of land and produced means of production, with the conditions necessary for any labour process. In superimposing the characteristically capitalist class configuration onto the three factors of the labour process, the third variant of the Trinity Formula conveniently bestows the inexorability of the latter on the former. So the Trinity Formula performs the ingenious ideological feat of simultaneously calling attention to what Marx, echoing Ricardo, calls 'the three great classes of modern society' (Marx, 1894: 1025), while doubly neutralizing any suggestion of class conflict: once, by presenting the different revenues as fair compensations for 'value added' from different, naturally occurring sources, and once again by collapsing the three classes into the three naturally occurring factors of the labour process.[25] Perhaps, then, it is no wonder that, when the manuscript to 'Classes', the short final chapter of the book breaks off, Marx is winding up to explain why distinguishing classes on the basis of the different forms of revenue (as opposed to property relations) is a poor idea (Marx, 1894: 1026).[26]

2.4 The fourth variant of the Trinity Formula

If the inconsistency of the original formulas is avoided in the opposite manner to read: *capital–interest, landed property–rent* and *wage labour–wages*, the systematic incongruity is eliminated: now we have three *value* categories paired with three types of revenues in the value

25. How many times have we heard the bromide 'capital and labour need each other', which balls up two truths with two falsehoods? The two truths are: (1) any labour process requires both means of production and living labour; and (2) *capital* and *wage labour* need each other. The two falsehoods, familiar from the Trinity Formula, are: (1) since means of production and living labour are inescapable conditions of the labour process, capital and wage labour are inescapable as well; and (2) that because we can *conceptually distinguish* between the means of production and living labour in the labour process, there must be two distinct economic roles and two types of property owners, the capitalist, who personifies – and owns – the means of production, and the wage-labourer, who personifies labour and owns nothing with which to make a living but his or her own labour-power.
26. For more on this topic see Paul Mattick's chapter in this volume.

form. Something can be said for this formula. Capital does pump out interest, landed property does extract rent; wage labour does pull down a wage – these fetishes work! – but the formula blocks all understanding of *surplus-value* (capital's lifeblood), along with its necessary forms of appearance, profit of enterprise, interest and rent. Instead of recognizing profit of enterprise, interest and rent as portions of surplus-value that was produced originally by wage-labourers, this fourth variant of the Trinity Formula announces that capital and landed property are independent sources of value that simply receive their due in the revenues of interest and rent, respectively, just as profit of enterprise is compensation (wages) for the capitalist's labour.[27]

At least this formula keeps consistently to the realm of value, but within that realm it gets everything twisted up. The falsehood of the Trinity Formula's conception of profits, interest and rent is what Marx had just written almost a thousand complicated pages to prove. I will not attempt here to rehearse that intricate account of the necessary, and necessarily deceptive, forms of appearance of surplus-value. A prima facie case for its falsehood, however, traces back to the beginning of Volume I. Since value is exclusively a matter of the social form of labour in capitalism (Marx, 1859: 35; 1867: 176), capital and landed property cannot be sources of *value*. Labour is the source of all value, consequently, of all surplus-*value*.

What makes this simple refutation hard to swallow, and what likewise can make the Trinity Formula's claim of triple sources of value seem more plausible, is the persistence with which *wealth* (use-value) and *value* keep getting confused with one another. It seems flatly wrong to attribute the production of all *wealth* to labour. And it is! Not only is 'labour' (human labour taken in abstraction from the two other necessary factors in the labour process, produced means of production and raw materials) *not* the source of *all* wealth; it is not the source of *any*. Remember, Marx calls it 'a mere spectre'. '"[T]he" labour' cannot produce anything. Marx states that land is a component in the production of *use-value*: 'The earth, for example, is active as an agent of production in the production of a use-value, a material product, say wheat. But it has nothing to do with producing the *value of the wheat*' (Marx, 1894: 955). Marx immediately reminds us of the lesson from Chapter 1 on the polarity of the value-form and the oddities of the *equivalent form* of value: 'In as much as value is expressed in wheat, the wheat is considered simply as a certain quantum of objectified social labour, this labour

27. See Marx, 1894: 965.

being quite indifferent to the particular material in which it is expressed or to the particular use-value of this material' (Marx, 1894: 955). Nothing that lacks use-value has value; so 'labour' cannot create value on its own. Nevertheless, Marx insists that not one iota of use-value enters into the constitution of value:

> the commodity-form, and the value-relation of the products of labour within which it appears, have absolutely no connection with the physical nature and the material [*dinglich*] relations arising out of this. It is nothing but the definite social relation between men themselves which assumes here, for them, the fantastic form of a relation between things.
>
> Marx, 1867: 165

Remember, *revenues are values.*

It was with regard to this version, consistently formulated on the 'value' plane, that Classical Political Economy made important advances in debunking the Trinity Formula, to which vulgar economists were so attached. The classical doctrine ruled out the notion of either capital or land being sources of value; implicitly at least, it was a theory of surplus-value. And it explicitly theorized interest and rent as deductions from industrial gross profits (the surplus-value pumped out by industrial capital). While it thereby struck a historic blow against the 'fetishism of the factors of the capitalist production process', Classical Political Economy's own shortcomings were many and serious: it failed to recognize what value is (congealed socially necessary abstract labour) and why it necessarily appears as exchange-value (hence it did not understand that or why money is an essential feature of capitalist production); it failed to reconcile its value theory with the needed theory of prices of production; it failed to provide a consistent theory of surplus-value, for it failed to make the distinction between labour and labour-power, an aporia that the Trinity Formula condenses into 'labour–wages'; it failed to discriminate clearly and consistently between surplus-value and its forms of appearance (profit of enterprise, interest, rent); and, consequently, it failed to articulate a theory properly developing the conceptual relationships between surplus-value and its necessary forms of appearance. On more basic levels, such as the level of the 'illusion of the economic', Classical Political Economy entirely lost its advantage over vulgar economics.[28]

28. See Marx, 1971: 500–1.

3. Conclusion: beyond the Left Ricardian interpretation of 'The Trinity Formula'

I have argued that Marx's chapter 'The Trinity Formula' is wrongly understood as a defence of Ricardian (Classical) value theory against vulgar political economy. That ordinary interpretation blocks understanding of Marx's deeper purposes in *Capital*, and more particularly in its concluding part, Part Seven of Volume III. Marx wrote *Capital* as a critique of political economy, and, in the final part of his book, Marx draws together and highlights his fundamental criticisms of both vulgar and Classical Political Economy. I want to close by considering the second to last chapter in Part Seven, 'Relations of Distribution and Relations of Production', for Marx's most fundamental criticism of vulgar and Classical Political Economy alike is that they failed to recognize the capitalist order as a historically specific mode of *production*. In the more complicated cases of John Stuart Mill and the Left Ricardians, both of whom recognized the historical dimension of *distribution*, the mistake lay in not grasping the inseparability of production and distribution. This closing will provide the opportunity to reinforce what I have argued regarding 'the illusion of the economic', which forms the horizon of the secular 'religion of everyday life'. And it gives me the opportunity to gather several of Marx's chief criticisms of Ricardian theory. Since these criticisms apply to Left Ricardian theory, it will also be the occasion for a final effort to dislodge that stubborn obstacle to understanding *Capital*, namely, the mistaken idea that Marx was a Left Ricardian.

I will consider three deep criticisms that Marx makes of Ricardian theory: (1) it fails to understand value and the necessity for value to be expressed as something other than itself, namely, money, consequently, it does not understand money; (2) it fails to grasp either the distinction between *labour-power* and *living labour* or the juridical and moral import of that distinction; consequently, its doctrine of surplus-value is faulty and its political project doomed; and (3) it fails to recognize the point with which Marx intended to begin Part Seven, 'the capitalist process of production is a historically specific form of the social production process in general' (Marx, 1894: 957); in other words, Ricardian theory is trapped in 'the illusion of the economic'. As we will see, Marx holds that this third criticism applies to John Stuart Mill and the Left Ricardians, even though they recognize the historical specificity of different modes of *distribution*.

The first two criticisms of Ricardian theory go back to the early chapters of *Capital* (to Chapter 1 for the first and to Chapters 6 and 7 for the second).

1. Ricardian value theory failed to recognize that what constitutes value is not simply 'embodied labour' (or even 'embodied abstract labour'). If it were, then all human labour, under all historical circumstances, would produce value. That *value* is not a general feature of the human condition, as is labour, constitutes the crux of Marx's profound criticism of Ricardian theory. The point of Chapter 1 of *Capital* is to show that value is a fetish that is the necessary consequence of the peculiarly asocial social form of labour under capitalism. Value is the outcome of commodity-producing labour, which we may call 'practically abstract' labour because it is socially validated only in a roundabout manner, namely, through the exchange of commodities. The point of the analysis of the value-form in the third section of Chapter 1 is to demonstrate that the value of a commodity must appear as something other than itself, namely, as money. Ricardian theory, then, fails to understand that value is a consequence not simply of labour, but of the *specific social form* of labour under capitalism. Consequently, it is in no position to grasp the phenomenological point that *value and money are inseparable* – money is no mere technical aid to exchange; money is necessary to organize production based on value-producing labour.[29] Left Ricardian proposals such as eliminating money in favour of 'time-chits' (certificates of hours worked), which were intended to eliminate the exploitation involved in surplus-value by insuring that the equalitarian rule that equal values be exchanged for equal values be followed, fail to recognize that hours of *actual* commodity-producing labour cannot be *immediately* socially validated. Writing in the *Poverty of Philosophy*, Marx complains that Proudhon fails to see that 'money is not a thing, it is a social relation', and he wonders, 'how can M. Proudhon go on talking about the constitution of a value, since a value is never constituted by itself? It is constituted, not by the time needed to produce it by itself, but in relation to the quota of each and every other product which can be created in the same time' (Marx, 1847: 81, 83). The *nonidentity of value and money*, value's necessary mode of expression, cannot be wished away (Marx, 1939: 138).
2. The second two errors of Ricardian theory are both involved in the Left Ricardian proposal for 'the equalitarian application of the Ricardian theory'. The Left Ricardian idea that wage labourers are being shortchanged is based on a failure to recognize the difference between the value of *labour-power* and the value that labour-power

29. See Martha Campbell, 1998.

produces when it is consumed as *living labour*. Given the fact that the theory of surplus-value lies at the heart of Left Ricardian thinking, this failure is doubly ironic. First, Left Ricardians never penetrated the secret of surplus-value, and, second, they therefore failed to understand how surplus-value can be expropriated without violating the commercial rule of thumb: exchange equal values for equal values. The point of Chapters 6 and 7 of *Capital*, Volume I, is that the proper explanation of surplus-value requires distinguishing between the commodity that wage-labourers sell, their labour-power, and the production of fresh value (including surplus-value) when their labour-power is consumed, as living labour, by capitalists who put them to work in a labour process that is likewise a valorization process. While Marx ridicules the very idea of the value of living labour, comparing it to a yellow logarithm, labour-power is a commodity whose value capitalists can pay in full yet still realize surplus-value, simply by keeping workers at their task long enough. As Marx summarizes his historic solution to the problem of the source of surplus-value, 'Every condition of the problem is satisfied, while the laws governing the exchange of commodities have not been violated in any way. Equivalent has been exchanged for equivalent' (Marx, 1867: 301).

So, not only do Left Ricardians fail to understand the source of surplus-value, if they did, the pipe dream of eliminating surplus-value through an equalitarian application of the law of value would have to be discarded. A critique of the injustice of the capitalist mode of production cannot rely on the bourgeois canons of commutative justice (Marx, 1894: 460–1). Thus, in the *Poverty of Philosophy* Marx concludes his critical treatment of the Left Ricardian John Bray as follows:

> Mr. Bray does not see that this equalitarian relation, this *corrective ideal* that he would like to apply to the world, is itself nothing but the reflection of the actual world; and that therefore it is totally impossible to reconstitute society on the basis of what is merely an embellished shadow of it.
>
> Marx, 1847: 79

If you want to change the world, it is best to understand it.

3. The deep mistake underlying the first error, the one involved in the 'time-chit' proposal, is the third Ricardian misconception and the last that will be considered here. As Marx writes of the Ricardian socialist John Gray, '*goods are supposed to be produced as commodities but not*

> *exchanged as commodities*' (Marx, 1859: 85). The mistake is the phenomenological error of tearing production and distribution asunder (Marx, 1939: 87). This error provides the subject matter of the penultimate chapter of *Capital*, 'Relations of Distribution and Relations of Production'. This chapter is set up by 'The Trinity Formula' inasmuch as *the revenue forms are the forms of distribution*. Marx first observes: 'In the customary view, these relations of distribution appear to be natural relations, relations arising from the nature of all social production, from the laws of human production pure and simple' (Marx, 1894: 1017). Such a conception is, of course, nurtured by the Trinity Formula, according to which the (specifically capitalist) revenue forms sprout from the three factors of the labour process in general. But Marx believes that certain developments in Classical Political Economy undermine this dehistoricizing conception of the forms of distribution. And, in John Stuart Mill, Marx finds 'a more developed and critical awareness' that 'concedes the historically developed character of these relations of distribution'. However, Marx goes on to observe that Mill 'holds all the more firmly to the supposedly constant character of the relations of production themselves, as arising from human nature and hence independent of all historical development' (Marx, 1894: 1018). Mill's advance, the recognition of the historicity of the forms of distribution, is presupposed by the various redistributionist schemes of Left Ricardianism. So too, unfortunately, is Mill's great shortcoming. For the preoccupation of Left Ricardians with the *surplus* in surplus-value, signals their failure to recognize *value* as a historically specific relation of production.

The general truth of the matter, a truth that constitutes one of the primary phenomenological results involved in historical materialism, is this: *relations of production and distribution are inseparable*:

> The so-called relations of distribution, therefore, correspond to and arise from historically particular and specific social forms of the production process and of the relationships which men enter into among themselves in the process of reproducing their human life. The historical character of these relations of distribution is the historical character of the relations of production, and they simply express one side of these.
>
> Marx, 1894: 1023[30]

30. See also Marx, 1847: 79 and Marx, 1939: 87–100.

In *Capital*, Marx demonstrates the inseparability of production and distribution in the specifically *capitalist* mode of production by showing (a) that the purpose of capitalist *production* is valorization, pumping out and accumulating surplus-value, (b) that this is possible only when labour generally takes the specific social form of wage labour, and (c) that profit (interest and profit of enterprise) and rent are the necessary forms of appearance of surplus-value.

So Mill and the Left Ricardians strike a blow against 'the illusion of the economic', but an ineffectual one. Marx comments, 'The view that considers only the relations of distribution to be historical, and not the relations of production, is simply the perspective of a criticism of bourgeois economics that is incipient but still timid and restrained.' Where *production* is concerned, 'the illusion of the economic' lingers, as Marx goes on to say, due to 'a confusion and identification of the social production process with the simple labour process' (Marx, 1894: 1023). Here Marx sends us back to the beginning of the second circuit of thought in *Capital*, Chapter 7 of Volume I, where he insisted that there is no labour process in general – the notion that there is, being 'the illusion of the economic' – and that the capitalist labour process, while it shares features with labour processes throughout history, distinguishes itself from all others by being a valorization process.

Marx concludes Chapter 51 by reminding the reader of the significance of this recognition of the falsehood of 'the illusion of the economic' and the truth of the historical materialist proposition that the production process always has a definite social form with definite historical implications: 'each particular historical form of this process further develops the material foundations and social forms. Once a certain level of maturity is attained, the particular historical form is shed and makes way for a higher form' (Marx, 1894, 1023–4). The reasonable prospect that this is no less true of the capitalist mode of production animated Marx's hopeful critique of political economy and of the 'fiction without fantasy' spread by the 'religion of everyday life'.[31]

Bibliography

Arthur, Christopher (1997), Against the Logical-Historical Method: Dialectical Derivation versus Linear Logic, in F. Moseley and M. Campbell (eds 1997).

Arthur, Christopher and Reuten, Geert (eds) (1998), *The Circulation of Capital: Essays on Volume II of Marx's 'Capital'* (London/New York: Macmillan/St Martin's Press).

31. I want to thank the co-editors of this volume, Geert Reuten and Martha Campbell, along with Chris Arthur, Riccardo Bellofiore, Paul Mattick, Jr, Fred Moseley, Jeanne Schuler and Tony Smith for especially constructive criticisms of previous versions of this chapter.

Bubner, Ruediger (1988), Logic and Capital: On the Method of a 'Critique of Political Economy', in *Essays in Hermeneutics and Critical Theory* (trans. Eric Mathews) (New York: Columbia University Press).

Campbell, Martha (1997), Marx's Theory of Money: A Defense, in F. Moseley and M. Campbell (eds 1997).

Hume, David (1739–40), *A Treatise of Human Nature*, ed. by P.H. Nidditch (Oxford: Clarendon Press, 1989).

Lebowitz, Michael (1992), *Beyond Capital: Marx's Political Economy of the Working Class* (London: Macmillan).

Locke, John (1690), *Second Treatise of Government*, ed. by C.B. Macpherson (Indianapolis: Hackett, 1980).

Marx, Karl, (1939), *Grundrisse* (trans. Martin Nicolaus) (Harmondsworth: Penguin/NLB, 1973).

— (1843), Contribution to the Critique of Hegel's Philosophy of Law: Introduction (trans. Martin Milligan and Barbara Ruhemann), in *Karl Marx and Frederick Engels, Collected Works, Volume III* (New York: International Publishers, 1975).

— (1844), *Economic and Philosophic Manuscripts of 1844* (trans. Martin Milligan and Dirk J. Struik), in *Works, III.*

— (1844a), On the Jewish Question (trans. Clemens Dutt), in *Works, III.*

— (1847), *The Poverty of Philosophy* (New York: International Publishers, 1963).

— (1859), *A Contribution to the Critique of Political Economy* (trans. S.W. Ryazanskaya), ed. Maurice Dobb (New York: International Publishers, 1970).

— (1867), *Capital, Volume I* (trans. Ben Fowkes) (New York: Vintage, 1977).

— (1867a), Ware und Geld, from the first edition of *Das Kapital, Band I*, in *Karl Marx, Friedrich Engels: Studienausgabe in 4 Baenden*, Vol. 2: *Politische Oekonomie*, ed. Irving Fetscher (Frankfurt am Main: Fischer Taschenbuch Verlag, 1966).

— *Results of the Immediate Production Process*, in *Capital, Volume I, translation by Fowkes.*

— (1879–80), Notes on Wagner (trans. Terrell Carver), in *Texts on Method*, ed. Terrell Carver (Oxford: Basil Blackwell, 1975).

— (1885, 1893), *Capital, Volume II* (trans. David Fernbach) (Harmondsworth: Penguin, 1978).

— (1891), *Critique of the Gotha Programme*, ed. C.P. Dutt (New York: International Publishers, 1938, 1966).

— (1894), *Capital, Volume III* (1st German edn 1894, 1st English edn 1909) (trans. David Fernbach) (Harmondsworth: Penguin/NLB, 1981).

— (1894a), *Das Kapital: Kritik der Politischen Oekonomie, Band III, Der Gesamtprozess der kapitalistischen Produktion*, ed. Friedrich Engels, MEW 25 (Berlin: Dietz Verlag, 1972).

— (1971), *Theories of Surplus-Value*, Part III (trans. J. Cohen and S.W. Ryazanskaya) ed. S.W. Ryazanskaya and R. Dixon (London: Lawrence & Wishart, 1972).

Marx, Karl, and Engels, Friedrich (1845), *The Holy Family* (trans. Richard Dixon and Clemens Dutt), in *Karl Marx and Frederick Engels, Collected Works, Volume IV* (New York: International Publishers, 1975).

— (1846), *The German Ideology* (trans. Clemens Dutt, W. Lough and C.P. Magill), in *Karl Marx and Frederick Engels, Collected Works, Volume V* (New York: International Publishers, 1976).

Moseley, Fred (1998), Marx's Reproduction Schemes and Smith's Dogma, in C.J. Arthur and G. Reuten (eds 1998).

Moseley, Fred and Campbell, Martha (eds) (1997), *New Investigations of Marx's Method* (Atlantic Highlands, NJ: Humanities Press).
Murray, Patrick (1988), *Marx's Theory of Scientific Knowledge* (Atlantic Highlands, NJ: Humanities Press).
— (1998), Beyond the 'Commerce and Industry' Picture of Capital, in C.J. Arthur and G. Reuten (eds 1998).
Reuten, Geert (1998), The Status of Marx's Reproduction Schemes: Conventional or Dialectical Logic?, in C.J. Arthur and G. Reuten (eds 1998).
Reuten, Geert and Williams, Michael (1989), *Value-Form and the State: the tendencies of accumulation and the determination of economic policy in capitalist society* (London/New York: Routledge).
Rosdolsky, Roman (1968), *The Making of Marx's 'Capital'* (London: Pluto Press, 1977).
Rubel, Maximilien (1981), *Rubel on Karl Marx: Five Essays*, ed. Joseph O'Malley and Keith Algozin (Cambridge: Cambridge University Press).
Shortall, Felton (1994), *The Incomplete Marx* (Aldershot: Avebury).

Subject Index

Author Index